Social Anthropology
An Alternative Introduction

by
Angela P. Cheater

£2
Tyen
16/31

 MAMBO PRESS

MAMBO PRESS
Gweru, P.O. Box 779
Harare, P.O. Box 66002, Kopje
Gokomere, P. Bag 9213, Masvingo

SOCIAL ANTHROPOLOGY: AN ALTERNATIVE INTRODUCTION

First published 1986

ISBN   0 86922 415 8

Printed and published in Zimbabwe
by Mambo Press, Senga Road, Gweru
1986

Table of Contents

PREFACE

I am often asked by my first-year students: `How applicable is what you've just said to present-day Zimbabwe? How might we apply what we have learned here in the jobs we hope to have later?´ My standard answer in the past has emphasised how important it is to overcome ethnocentricity, to realise that rural folk are neither stupid nor irrational, but have good reasons for rejecting efforts to change them, and so on. But for some years I have been nagged by the feeling that this answer is inadequate. Not only do the students find it somewhat abstract and unconvincing, increasingly I find myself unconvinced! The reasons, I think, have to do with the widening gap between the standard content of introductory anthropology courses, designed for western students and focussing on the `primitive´ exotic, and the personal experiences of those who are born, reared and who work in the developing world. If anthropology is to be relevant to our experience, it must be updated and refocussed. That is what this text seeks to do, with respect both to the theoretical approaches to the discipline and to the ethnographic material incorporated. It seeks to be more directly `applicable´ to the life-worlds of underdevelopment. As such, it suffers from the usual difficulty of deciding what to include in limited space. My policy has been to include material if the answers to the questions `is this relevant to us?´ and `is this relevant to today?´ are positive. To any accusations of ethnocentricity on this score, I must emphasise my own teaching needs!

Looking firstly at theoretical issues, Thomas Kuhn (1970: 136ff) has noted that textbooks communicate the accepted state of knowledge in a scientific discipline, and therefore require extensive rewriting whenever this state of knowledge is changed by revolutionary advances in theoretical understanding. So one of my excuses for writing yet another introductory text in the field of social anthropology, is that none yet has attempted to incorporate into our basic introductions to the discipline the implications of marxist insights which have been current in anthropology for the past two decades. The very layout of this text reflects my concern to `domesticate´ marxist perspectives, working as it does through `base´ and `superstructural´ issues in a rather orthodox format. I agree with Lewis (1976:10) that the decision about where to break into anthropology is essentially arbitrary, because wherever one starts will lead elsewhere, but everyone recognises that food is fundamental, that without production to meet basic needs, there will be no institutions, no culture, no society. And indeed, much contemporary marxist anthropology is precisely about the production, distribution and consumption of food.

Turning to issues of ethnography, from the viewpoint of students in the third world in the late twentieth century, it seems useful to abandon the image of anthropology as concerned with foreign exotica, rather than with our own contemporary, mundane reality. Social anthropology has much to offer those concerned with change and development, but only, I think, if we are prepared to abandon our traditional commitment to what one television series aptly described as the `disappearing world´, and our own past propensity to treat `social change´ as a dichotomous afterthought.

We cannot expect anyone to conceptualise their own life as `social change´. Change must become integral to our analysis. In place of our traditional distinction between society and social change, then, we need to concentrate on those issues of ongoing change that affect contemporary society, such as land tenure, class formation, the roles of women, and the complex processes of peasantisation, proletarianisation, industrialisation and urbanisation. One irony of this perspective is that it takes us back at least fifty years, to the expectations that early colonial administrators had of social anthropology! In this way, however, we may start to close the gap, based partly on the colonial experience, between the western home of academic anthropology, and the descendants of those cultures and societies which the discipline has customarily depicted as exotically different, and who now comprise an increasing proportion of its students.

This text, then, treats as history what is history. It does not attempt to mystify the past by using the formerly ubiquitous `ethnographic present´, but tries to give students encountering social anthropology for the first time a sense both of historical time and of the conceptual development of the discipline within historical time. It does not, however, dwell on the history of anthropology, which has been recounted in other introductory texts, except when disciplinary history is integrally connected to modes of analysis and interpretation. Nor does it focus on the area of `culture´ so important to American anthropology.

Instead, this text uses a range of material that speaks to contemporary problems of both policy and administration in the third world, even where this material belongs to the past. It pays relatively scant and analytically divergent attention to the `traditional´ interests of anthropologists in kinship and symbolism, while emphasising both the `material´ and `ideological´ nature of these areas of disciplinary expertise. It seeks to use ethnographic data explicitly to evaluate the usefulness of new (especially marxist) analytical interpretations, and to demonstrate their areas of inadequacy. To this end, on occasion, it borrows material from the field researches of non-anthropologists. It tries to raise questions of significance for contemporary investigation and analysis, as pointers to a future for anthropology. On all these counts, reflecting what I interpret as paradigmatic change (in the Kuhnian sense) in social anthropology, this text may be regarded as radical, if not heretical, in its attempt to be useful.

In the end, however, I fear that I have been able to do no more than incorporate some of the effects of the colonial experience into our disciplinary perceptions, which represents a small move forward. Time continues to move on, widening the gap between research and the publication of its distilled results. By its very nature, an introductory text which presents research findings of lasting conceptual value, must remain behind the times. But I should like to think that this one is at least slightly less dated than others! I hope it may also prove stimulating, at least to those for whom it is primarily intended.

In producing this text, I have incurred certain debts, the major one to my Memotech RS128 and its word processing software, Newword. Without their collaboration, it would not have been possible to fit six months' work by one author and four typists into my three-month summer vacation! For assistance in keeping the overworked system going under such stress, in a technologically remote corner of the globe, I thank Memotech's technical advisory service and Bill Kinsey. For solving the problem of printing camera-ready copy, I am most grateful to Richard Harlen and Joe King, and for allowing me the use of their printer, the Department of Psychology at the University of Zimbabwe. Finally, Mrs. Juliana Nkrumah, who had earlier suffered the trauma of coming into our teaching programme midway through her own degree, was good enough to read and criticise the manuscript with her own student experiences in mind. I am most grateful to her for undertaking this scrutiny, on behalf of future students, at a time when she herself was doing two other jobs!

Angela Cheater
Harare
June 1986

CHAPTER ONE

THEORETICAL UNDERPINNINGS

The Birth of a Discipline

Anthropology was born in the nineteenth century. In France and the U.K. its original designation was `ethnology´, as in the Societe Ethnologique de Paris (founded in 1839) and the Ethnological Society of London (dating from 1843). `Anthropology´, until the 1870s, referred more narrowly to what is today called physical anthropology, but with the formation of the (Royal) Anthropological Institute of Great Britain and Ireland in 1871, this name replaced the older `ethnology´. It was under the name `anthropology´ that the first formal teaching in this discipline began at Oxford University in 1884, with the first (honorary) British chair of anthropology being created at the University of Liverpool in 1908, to which Sir James George Frazer was appointed.

The Greek roots of anthropology (`anthropos´ and `logos´) suggest that it is `the study of man´. However, this transliteration is too broad to be useful as an academic definition: many university disciplines study man in one way or another. We might therefore go back to its eighteenth-century precursors to pin down more carefully what anthropology is and does. During this period of the European `enlightenment´, there was a widespread concern to explain, as Europe learned more about the rest of the world, why other people and other societies were not the same as those of Europe. Europeans were of course aware of their own internal differences from one another, but these were minor compared to the descriptions of, say, China emanating from Marco Polo and the Jesuits, or of the South Seas coming from Captain Cook, of Africa as experienced by Portuguese missionaries, or of the Americas seen through the eyes of the Spanish explorers and conquistadors. These large cultural differences were seen, by European intellectuals, as problematic, to be explained rather than merely accepted.

Eighteenth-century European explanations for these cultural differences ranged very widely between the romantic view associated especially with Rousseau that `the noble savage´ could be equated in Christian theology with man before Adam´s fall from grace, and the Hobbesian characterisation of savage life as `solitary, poor, nasty, brutish, and short´ by comparison with that of Europe. The romantics lost the fight to those who believed that Europe had experienced `progress´ through the changes that had built on the early Greek and

1

Roman social foundations. These changes were seen to be cumulative and beneficial in many different spheres - technological, economic, legal, political. It is in this eighteenth-century notion of `progess´, then, that we find the origin of European ethnocentrism, which became reflected later, in the nineteenth century, in schemas of societal evolution which always placed contemporary European practice at the most advanced level. Although Darwin´s views on biological evolution undoubtedly influenced social thinkers in the nineteenth century, it is important to note that evolutionary schemas pertaining to society (such as Comte´s (1853) view that all knowledge advanced from theological to metaphysical assumptions before becoming `positivist´ in its search for causal regularity) were floated long before The Origin of Species was published in 1859.

Evolutionary Perspectives

In reality, then, evolutionary perspectives in anthropology perhaps date back to the eighteenth-century French social philosophers such as Montesquieu, Condorcet and Rousseau, rather than to Darwin´s ideas which were contemporaneous with the emergence of anthropology under that name. Evolutionary ideas have changed considerably in the intervening years, but still inform other approaches, even when they are not - as they sometimes are - espoused as theories in their own right. No anthropologist today attempts to reconstruct social history with reference either to items of material culture such as pottery, or to social institutions such as marriage. However, the notion of stages of development, ordered in an evolutionary sequence, is still important to marxism, while Radcliffe-Brown (1957, 1958), the founder of `structural-functionalism´, was at his death still trying to construct a model of social change within an evolutionary framework. Malinowski (1944), who is normally remembered as the arch-functionalist who publicly demolished the `diffusionist´ thinking which, for a while, succeeded evolutionism in anthropology, was nonetheless in sympathy with many of the basic evolutionist ideas of Frazer. And in the twentieth century, there have also been Americans, such as Leslie White and Julian Steward, who have tried to construct `neo-evolutionist´ models of societal development on the basis of more sophisticated indicators, such as energy usage. The idea of evolution, based on the older notion of `progress´, remains a powerful influence on anthropological theory generally.

Evolution, as a technical concept, comprises two fundamental aspects: the ideas that a common form becomes differentiated, and that a simple form becomes more complex. These

twin notions of differentiation and increasing complexity
underlie all anthropological applications of evolutionary
reasoning, including those of the nineteenth century. Technological differentiation and complexity, for example, were the
criteria used to distinguish `savage´ from `barbarous´ culture
(and both from `civilisation´), `barbarians´ having discovered
the techniques of pottery and metallurgy while remaining
illiterate. Lewis Henry Morgan (1871), the `father´ of
American cultural anthropology, who influenced Frederick
Engels´ views on the family, traced the increasing complexity
of sexual and family relationships from promiscuity, through
15 stages of group marriage and polygamy, to monogamy.
Patriliny (the system of tracing relationships through men)
was thought, by McLennan (1865), to have developed, via
polyandry (the marriage of one woman to a number of men), from
matriliny (where descent is traced through women), which in
turn had emerged from pristine promiscuity via female infanticide and exogamy (which caused men to seek women from groups
other than their own). Maine (1861) argued that legal systems
based on contracts between individuals reflected greater
social variety and complexity than systems which fixed the
individual´s rights in law on the basis of his or her prior
status in respect of age, sex or kinship. Enhanced knowledge,
leading to better control of the environment, was used by
Frazer (1890) to explain why, having failed to manipulate the
physical world through magical means, people turned to the
religious postulate that unseen suprahuman forces controlled
this physical world; and also why, when their knowledge of the
physical world increased still further through the development
of science, religion lost at least some of its attraction.

The difficulty with many if not all of these arguments,
is that they arguably tell us more about the thought processes
of their proponents than about the evolution of society.
Particularly where such arguments were based on logical
thought from the comfort of an armchair in an intellectual´s
study, rather than on direct observation of what happened in
other societies, we should be suspicious of their relevance to
real life. These and other evolutionary schemas have been
characterised as `intellectualist´ rather than `empiricist´ in
their orientation. A prominent twentieth-century anthropologist, Radcliffe-Brown (as reported in Gluckman (1965:2)),
alleged that their authors should be compared to the American
farmer who, having found his paddock empty, ambled to the
gate, chewing grass, and asked himself `Now, if I were that
horse, where would I have gone´? Yet there is a problem with
this criticism, for anthropologists do in fact try, along with
some other social scientists, to place themselves in the
position of those they study, in order to understand empirically as well as intellectually what life is like from a

different perspective. That is what `participant observation´ is all about. That is why anthropologists do fieldwork in the Malinowskian tradition. But the current mix of logic and empiricism in anthropology was achieved only slowly and with difficulty.

The evolutionary schemas of nineteen-century anthropology were speculative attempts to reconstruct the lost past of society´s origins. Yet they were based on some substantive evidence, such as the pottery fragments recovered by archaeologists, and the reports of missionaries, traders and travellers about contemporary behaviour in foreign places. They were also complicated by the interests of other intellectual disciplines (notably biology and medicine) and politically liberal, philanthropic organisations (such as the Aboriginals´ Protection Society), in the emerging field of anthropology. The emotive issues of race and the extermination of indigenous populations became inextricably part of the intellectual problem of how to explain social and cultural differences. In particular, the question of whether man had a single biological origin (the thesis of `monogenesis´) or whether different races of homo sapiens had separate origins (`polygenesis´), plagued the related issue of cultural differences. Although polygenesis faded from the debate by the end of the nineteenth century, the general confusion was resolved only much later, in the twentieth century, through the separation of physical from social and cultural anthropology, with archaeology and palaeontology distancing themselves from all of the anthropological sub-disciplines and addressing themselves specifically to the past. Social anthropology came to focus on the contemporary organisation of society, while cultural anthropology concerned itself with the differences among human cultures. The tangled interrelationships of these different disciplines, and others such as linguistics, serology and genetics, are still reflected in the coverage of MAN, the prestigious journal of the Royal Anthropological Institute.

The Development of Empiricism

In part, it was the collection of more and more empirical data in these different fields that made their separation possible. In the area of social and cultural anthropology, this information was generated first by the systematisation of questions. Nineteenth-century anthropologists such as Morgan and Frazer, and later the Royal Anthropological Institute itself, circulated lists of questions to those in a position to collect the answers to them, in an attempt to draw (rather superficial) comparisons between different societies. Later, toward the close of the nineteenth century, anthropologists

4

themselves went out to seek the answers to their own questions. For a while, the expedition in 1898-9 of Cambridge academics to the Torres Straits (separating Australia from Papua-New Guinea) became the model for such investigations. Later, following the example of Boas in North America, Seligmann, Rivers and Radcliffe-Brown undertook individual research respectively in Africa, India and the Andaman Islands (off the Burmese coast). But these early field trips were generally short, a few weeks or months at the most. Perhaps for this reason, they did not revolutionise anthropology in the way that Malinowski´s later `internment´ on the Trobriand Islands was to do. Instead, they reinforced the `comparative method´ of the evolutionists.

By the turn of the twentieth century, as more and more factual information piled up, the older monogenetic arguments in favour of a single origin for all races and all cultures, as opposed to a number of distinct origins, were being rein-forced by the `diffusionists´, who demonstrated that items of material culture found in widely-dispersed localities could indeed have travelled outwards from a central source. Some, such as Elliot-Smith in the U.K., identified this original source as Egypt. Anthropology for a short while become en-tangled in the fad of Egyptology which was popularised by archaeological discoveries. However, while pyramidal edifices and mummification may indeed have been transported to Central America by the type of papyrus boat in which Thor Heyerdahl crossed the Atlantic in the 1970s, anthropologists were beginning to realise, from their own personal investigations into foreign life-styles, that such uses of the comparative method were relatively unrewarding. Much more can be known by looking at a custom in its normal social context than by ripping it out of that context and comparing it with another custom similarly isolated from some other society. The mere fact that pyramidal structures are found in both Mayan and Egyptian cultures, tells us nothing of what they are used for in these different societies, their relative aesthetic appeal, or indeed how they are constructed. The answers to these questions are likely to yield a greater understanding of cultural differences than is the speculation about common origins. This revolutionary theoretical insight was a direct result of the experiences of an `enemy alien´ during the first world war.

Early Functionalism

Bronislaw Malinowski (1884-1942) was born and studied physics, mathematics and philosophy in Poland before going to England in 1910 to read anthropology. His doctoral thesis in

5

anthropology, presented to the London School of Economics, concerned aboriginal family organisation in Australia and was based on limited fieldwork. At the outbreak of the first world war, he was again in Australia. As an Austrian subject he was technically at war with the British Empire, but the imperial and dominion bureaucracies permitted him to proceed with his research plans in the Trobriand Islands off the south-east coast of New Guinea. He was <u>not</u> interned on the Trobriands: during the war years he made a number of trips to the Australian mainland. But he did spend two and a half years living in island villages, about ten times the duration of any previous anthropological field trip, and came to know Trobriand society and culture much more intimately than any previous anthropologists had been able to know other systems. During the 1920s, back at the London School of Economics, Malinowski demolished the diffusionists´ arguments in public polemics and popularised through his postgraduate anthropology seminar his own new `functionalist´ approach. As a charismatic teacher with students from China, Europe and the British Empire, including Africa, and access to Rockerfeller funding for field research, Malinowski´s intellectual influence spread very rapidly.

Malinowski´s functionalism started from the premiss that human beings must do certain fundamental things in order to survive. Their `basic´ or `biological´ needs include eating, drinking, excreting, and reproducing. If any of these activities is not done, humankind will not survive. But it is possible to meet these basic needs in many different ways, and that is what culture is all about. Different cultures lay down different rules concerning approved ways of meeting these fundamental requirements, thus creating a secondary level of `cultural´ or `derived´ needs in society. The individual, in meeting his basic needs, conforms to his society´s cultural expectations of his behaviour. Indeed, he has a vested interest in co-operating with and conforming to the expectations of others, because many of his objectives (including at least reproduction from the list of basic needs), he cannot achieve alone.

Such co-operation with others creates `institutions´ in society, which are concerned with organising the activities for which they are responsible. Malinowski (1944) identified seven principles by which activities are integrated in many specific types of institution: reproductive; territorial; physiological; voluntarily associated; those based on occupation or profession; on rank and status; and on what he called the `comprehensive´ principle. He noted, too, that there is no simple one-to-one relationship between a social institution and either the basic or the derived needs which it functions

6

to satisfy, because any given institution may be responsible for meeting a number of different needs, at least in part. For example, the family may be geared mainly toward the need to reproduce, but it is also involved in meeting other physiological needs and has territorial and economic implications. Institutions are, therefore, interconnected: what happens in one affects others, either directly or indirectly, and this can be shown visually on charts, such as those Malinowski used to order his own data from the Trobriands, which cross-tabulate institutions and needs.

Finally, Malinowski noted that a culture is welded together not merely by the interconnections between the institutions which are instrumental in meeting individual needs in society, but also by additional `integrative´ devices such as language (in which all of life is conceptualised), knowledge itself, and religion. To be understood fully, therefore, any culture must be analysed at the three different levels of the individual, the institutions, and the culture as an integrated whole.

Malinowski described his new approach as `functionalist´, analysing the needs satisfied by customs in a living society. All customs, he argued, had contemporary functions, even if these were only vaguely concerned with reinforcing the importance of traditional ways of behaving. Culture was not an historical thing of `shreds and patches´, but an integrated, working, contemporary whole. There were no `survivals´ of the kind Tylor (1871) had identified as cultural hangovers from the past, lacking contemporary relevance. If behaviour ceased to have contemporary relevance, it would die out. Therefore, present customs cannot be used as indicators of past conditions. They must be seen in their existing social context to be understood.

This argument undermined very fundamentally evolutionist and diffusionist approaches which sought to draw comparisons between different societies, in different historical periods, on the basis of isolated customs or artefacts that were apparently common to both. Malinowski´s functionalism concentrated attention on the present, arguing that in preliterate societies the past was essentially unknowable, and speculation about the unknowable was academically unprofitable. History was fine, but conjectural history was unacceptable. Into the category of conjectural history he placed verbal accounts of the past, which then had to be treated as mythical. However, the functions of myths (for example, of origin, or of governance) were clearly contemporary, designed to explain and justify the existence and distribution of political power in the present. So oral history was not discounted, but it was treated as having merely contemporary relevance, not as being an accurate record of the past. In this approach lies the criticism of functionalism that it is `ahistorical´, lacking a sense of history.

Of greater importance, perhaps, is the criticism that functionalist theory is incapable of explaining change. This criticism arose from Malinowski´s eagerness to demonstrate the contemporary relevance of all components of an existing society, on the one hand, and on the other, his argument that each component is essential to the smooth operation of that society. In Malinowski´s (1944:40, 142) own words: `...no invention, no revolution, no social or intellectual change, ever occurs except when new needs are created ... no crucial system of activities can persist without being connected, directly or indirectly, with human needs and their satisfaction´

The criticism that functionalism is incapable of explaining change, also indicts Durkheim´s (1895) view that dissent from `collective representations´ and societal norms is dysfunctional. However, Malinowski´s own view of individual eccentricity was much more flexible than that of Durkheim. Malinowski (1926) saw the constraint on the individual to conform to society´s expectations, as lying primarily in his own long-term self-interest, rather than in the normative force of institutionalised arrangements. But although Malinowski´s ideas concerning the individual proved inspiring to a later generation of `transactionalist´ anthropologists trying to explain change, he himself did not pursue them in this way. His own attempts to analyse South Africa as a society in change were adjudged a failure by his contemporaries. His dialectical model of `traditional´ society interacting with its `modern´ (colonial) competitor to produce a `synthesis´ that contained elements of both but was recognisably neither, was rejected by Radcliffe-Brown (1952:3-4, 202) as reifying `culture´ in its failure to recognise that culture-bearing individuals interact, but not the cultures themselves.

Structural-Functionalism

Malinowski´s functionalist analysis of society was a rather simple one, reflecting his own view that `to identify is the same as to understand´ (1944:71). In anthropology it was soon challenged by the more sophisticated analytical capabilities of Radcliffe-Brown (1881-1955), with whom we associate `structural-functionalism´. In the 1920s, Radcliffe-Brown supported Malinowski´s new functionalist approach against its speculative evolutionist and diffusionist rivals.

By 1935, however, he had become dissatisfied with its intellectual range and argued that the concept of `function´ should be subsumed under that of `structure´.

Radcliffe-Brown (1952/1940:190) finally defined social structure as `a complex network of ... actually existing ... social relations´ among actors in institutionalised roles. His model of structure, as a set of invisible relationships which produce a visible outcome on the surface of society, in the form of institutionalised behaviour, was borrowed from the natural sciences, especially physics, where the relationships between sub-atomic particles structure each atom and give it its specific elemental identity. So in dyadic social relationships, for example between a mother and her child, the invisible relationship produces social behaviour which will be recognisably similar between each mother-child pair in that particular society, and recognisably different from the behaviour arising from a different relationship linking, say, brother and sister, or father and child.

Every society has a cultural model of each of the relationships which it regards as important. Socialisation into these models produces the similarity in behaviour patterns among numerous individuals, all of whom find themselves in the same structural position in these relationships. Hence Radcliffe-Brown, following Durkheim, distinguished the human being, who is individually unique, from the social person, who acts out society´s specified roles. But in fact, among adult actors who have `internalised´ their society´s expectations in the course of their upbringing or `socialisation´, there is no real difference between the individual and the social person. The one becomes the other. So Radcliffe-Brown, like Durkheim but unlike Malinowski, was not interested in the variation in performance among different individual actors playing their social roles. Instead, he was concerned to establish, from a wide range of specific examples, the `standard´ or average performance as an index of that society´s model of the relationship in question, in order to understand how the total social structure is built up from many such models.

Radcliffe-Brown argued that `structure´, as a network of relationships, comprises three interrelated aspects. Firstly there is structure itself (what Durkheim (1895/1938) called `social morphology´), which is seen concretely in social roles as the nodes in that lattice of relationships which constitutes society. This visible aspect of social structure can be compared with the anatomy of living creatures, but we must remember that the real structure comprises the invisible relationships, not their behavioural manifestations. This real or invisible structure is essentially static. In the natural

9

sciences, structural relationships can often be expressed in formulae, as when, for example, the difference in number and position of the protons within the nucleus defines the difference between hydrogen and helium. Social scientists also tend to assume that structural relationships in society are invariant, but these relationships cannot be expressed with such precision.

However, societies are not static, and Radcliffe-Brown used the concept of `function´ (Durkheim´s `social physiology´) to describe the structure `in action´. Each part of a structure contributes both to the specific identity and to the operation of that structure, in the same way that each organ of the body contributes to the life of a specific individual. Radcliffe-Brown regarded this activity as `functioning´ to maintain the structure. In what many have viewed as an unsuccessful attempt to avoid the circularity of Malinowski´s view that `function´ was concerned with the satisfaction of needs, Radcliffe-Brown (1952/1940:200) defined the `function´ of a `socially standardised mode of activity, or mode of thought, as its relation to the social structure to the existence and continuity of which it makes some contribution´. He insisted that the concept of function should be used only in this technical sense, not as a synonym for `use´ or `purpose´ or `meaning´ (1952/1940:200).

Finally, change or `social evolution´ is the third component of Radcliffe-Brown´s view of social structure and, like `social morphology´ and `social physiology´, was borrowed from Durkheim. But we must distinguish Radcliffe-Brown, as a structuralist, from Durkheim as the sociological ancestor of `functionalism´. Radcliffe-Brown subsumed both function and change under his concept of structure. Both are integral to structure in his view. Durkheim had no such concept of structure. His concern was with the reciprocal link between social order and social behaviour, and his view of social evolution was a purely historical one, concerned with explaining past variations among societies rather than envisaging structural alterations in the future. For Durkheim, deviation from the social norms could be functional in the sense of re-emphasising the importance of those norms in the ensuing punishment. But Durkheim never contemplated Radcliffe-Brown´s later view that `a society that is thrown into a condition of functional disunity or inconsistency (for this we now provisionally identify with [Durkheim´s] dysnomia) will not die, except in such comparatively rare instances as an Australian tribe overwhelmed by the white man´s destructive force, but will continue to struggle toward some sort of eunomia, some kind of social health, and may, in the course of this, change its structural type´ (1952/1935:183; my emphasis).

Radcliffe-Brown was the first anthropologist to recognise that a society's capacity to change itself may be the mechanism which enables it to survive a structural revolution that may result from an operational breakdown or functional failure. His distinction between `radical´ change (of the structure itself) and the ongoing change of personnel which every society experiences through the demographic processes of birth and death, is useful, but he did not complete his work on social change before his death in 1955. Furthermore, the thrust of his unfinished work on change was within an evolutionary framework which owed much to Durkheim but which did little to allay the marxist criticism that `functionalism´ of whatever kind is incapable of explaining radical change satisfactorily.

Neither Radcliffe-Brown nor Malinowski bequeathed to social anthropology a theory of change, being more concerned to understand how non-western societies fitted into their own present than to predict the future. However, one should note that - contrary to some views - neither was an apologist for colonialism. Alvin Gouldner (1972:132) displays his ignorance of both Malinowski and his functionalist approach when he alleges that anthropological functionalism, in its concern to serve the British Empire, was emphatically not interested in tutoring revolutionaries. Not only did Malinowski teach anti-colonial radicals such as Jomo Kenyatta, he also identified in print the military, political and legal as well as economic reasons for the assymetrical domination of western colonial regimes over subordinated cultures. His views, expressed in The Dynamics of Culture Change (1945) and shared by his research students, were part reason for the vilification of anthropologists as having `gone native´ in the eyes of conservative whites in both Europe and its colonies.

In similar fashion, though much less flamboyantly, Radcliffe-Brown was instrumental in establishing social anthropology as a teaching discipline in universities throughout the Commonwealth, in countries where the reality of political and cultural domination by `more advanced societies´ he conceptualised as structural change and incorporation. Presumably borrowing this term from Furnivall's (1939) economic analysis of Indonesia, Radcliffe-Brown (1952/1940:202) suggested that `plural´ or `composite´ be used to describe `the interaction of individuals and groups [of different cultural backgrounds] within an established social structure which is itself in the process of change´. Citing South Africa as an example, Radcliffe-Brown argued that such a composite social structure was nonetheless characterised by a single economic and political system, an argument that few marxists would dispute. Both Malinowski and Radcliffe-Brown, then, were in their own ways involved in changing the world of anthropology by understanding it differently, but neither fully satisfied the marxist criterion that political activism directed towards change should follow such a new understanding.

The Marxist `Revolution´ in Anthropology

The efflorescence of social anthropology in Britain after the first world war occurred within the context of research opportunities available in colonised countries. Not only did anthropologists take advantage of such research opportunities. Some of them were actually employed by colonial administrations as research officers, and others offerred advice on administration which they sincerely felt to be in the best interests of those people they had studied. There was a degree of collaboration between anthropologists and colonial authorities, even while this relationship was simultaneously marked by conflicts of varying kinds (see Asad 1973). With the advent of political independence in erstwhile colonies after the second world war, then, anthropology was stigmatised as the exploitative `hand-maiden [sometimes `bastard´] of colonialism´, especially in formerly British parts of Africa.

Somewhat paradoxically, at roughly the same time, anthropology in France was only just beginning to enter the phase of concentrating on empirical fieldwork, which had been so much the hallmark of British anthropology for the three decades since Malinowski´s impact in the 1920s. Partly as a result of their philosophical tradition, French researchers, such as Claude Meillassoux, who began their African fieldwork in the late 1950s when the independence of the former French colonies was imminent, carried with them marxist rather than functionalist analytical tools. At a time of crisis for social anthropology, then, which took another decade to develop fully, French marxist anthropology was making its earliest debut. The later popularity of marxist inspiration was perhaps not unrelated to the international political context in which it emerged in anthropology. Radical intellectuals at this time indeed experienced the possibility of changing the world as well as understanding it.

Anthropological marxism was somewhat hampered, however, by the poverty of the material which Marx had used to construct his evolutionary sequencing in the mid-nineteenth century, in which `modes of production´ inexorably succeeded one another. (A mode of production combines specific technologies and ways of organising labour in particular societies at given historical times. It is not the same as a particular type of economic activity.) `Primitive communalism´ of the pre-class,

prehistoric era gave way to the `ancient´ mode of the Mediter-
ranean city-states, which in turn became the `feudal´ mode,
which was then displaced by industrial capitalism. The difficulty of incorporating Asian history, economics, politics and
society into what was fundamentally an analysis of European
history, led Marx to haver between placing the `Asiatic mode
of production´ at the beginning of this sequence or totally
outside it.

Much of the earliest marxist literature in anthropology
was, therefore, completely remote from the structural-functionalist concerns of the 1950s and 1960s, agonising as it did
over whether African societies of the mid-twentieth century
fitted best into the prehistoric phase of `primitive communal-
ism´, or whether they belonged under the heading of the `Asia-
tic mode of production´. Subsequently an ever-burgeoning list
of modes of production was invented to accommodate problem
cases from the third world which simply would not fit into
Marx´s original scheme. In Africa, these new possibilities
included an African mode, a lineage mode, a slave mode, a
colonial capitalist mode and, among many others, a domestic
mode that was identified by a non-marxist (Sahlins 1974) and
extended to practically all non-industrial societies. In the
eyes of empiricists, even those who were politically on the
left, marxists earned themselves considerable disrepute during
this phase. Later, however, the less orthodox and more empiri-
cist among them began to argue that Marx´s own ideas could not
provide more than a general guide to analysis and that radical
modifications to Marx´s own views on pre-industrial societies
would be necessary to accommodate twentieth-century African
reality. While we may argue over whether these imaginative
`neo-marxist´ approaches actually owe very much to Marx, they
certainly revitalised social anthropology in the 1970s.

The basic problem with orthodox marxism, when applied to
non-industrial societies, is its assumption that economic
relationships (the `relations of production´) have an in-
fluencing or conditioning effect on all other relations in
society. In societies where pre-industrial production out-
strips consumption requirements by only small margins, and
where currencies and markets are poorly developed and affect
only a small part of people´s total lives, this assumption
often cannot be sustained. Many societies, especially but not
exclusively in Africa, were and sometimes still are organised
not around economic relationships, but on the basis of kinship
and marriage. House, family, lineage and clan groupings
provide the framework within which co-operation occurs in
economic, social, legal, political and even religious matters.
In still other pre-industrial societies, as Godelier (1978)
has indicated, religion or politics may provide the primary

The differences between orthodox and neo-marxist analytical frameworks with respect to anthropological data.

ORTHODOX MARXIST ANALYTICAL FRAME WORK		ONE NEO-MARXIST ANALYTICAL FRAMEWORK (following Meillassoux)
S U P E R S T R U C T U R E		**K I N S H I P**
ideology		ancestral cults
politics and law (state/ruling class as executive of bourgeoisie)		family/lineage dispute settlement; hereditary succession to office
	+	
social relations (kinship, marriage, neighbourhood)		neighbourhood: kin-based settlement patterns
B A S E	**A F F I N I T Y**	
instruments, forces, means, and relations of production		access to means of production, labour and labour co-operation, consumption groupings all based on kinship and marriage
mode of production		

ideological assumptions around which society was or is organised. In such situations, the orthodox marxist distinction between conditioning economic base and conditioned societal superstructure, divided into different levels at different distances from the base, had little option but to give way to a different conception, emphasising mutual rather than causative interrelationships and sitting somewhat closer to functionalist views (see diagram 1).

Instead of postulating a causal relationship between economic and other relations in society, these neo-marxist approaches emphasised reciprocal interdependencies between institutions and relationships in society. These approaches were willing to accept, for example, that labour may be organised within kinship groups, without insisting that such labour co-operation must define kinship. Economic determinism, the `vulgar marxism´ from which Marx dissociated himself shortly before his death, was thus replaced by the notion of mutual influence between economic and other variables. Such bi-directional conditioning is not dissimilar to the functionalist notion of interconnectedness. Indeed, Marx´s best known work, Capital, can be regarded as a model for this kind of approach, for in it he was concerned to understand precisely how capitalism was structured and how it perpetuated (in marxist jargon, `reproduced´) itself, in order to identify and exploit its weak points in the process of revolutionary change. Far from being mutually antagonistic, then, marxist and structural-functionalist approaches may be entirely compatible and even complementary, for functionalism especially is holistic. That is, it stresses the significance, for its functional integrity, of each and every component of a society or culture. Anthropological functionalists, therefore, have regarded as somewhat surprising marxist pleas for an `integrated´ social science, to demolish the artificial boundaries between politics, economics, history, law and so on, for they have always tried to achieve such coverage themselves.

Nonetheless, the marxist influence did focus attention on production in non-industrial societies, where functionalists had tended to concentrate on issues of distribution, in systems of exchange and trade. The (evolutionist) idea of a technological continuum stretching from hunting and gathering to post-industrial systems was perhaps enhanced by the marxist distinction between land as `subject´ of labour and land as `object´ of labour. This distinction is not the same as the modern western classification into extractive production (including mining) as opposed to agriculture, but it does help us to understand some of the differences between hunting, gathering, fishing and pastoral nomadism on the one hand, and both shifting and settled agriculture on the other. We readily

15

understand the greater ideological significance of land that incorporates labour (land as object or instrument of labour), as opposed to land or sea (as subject of labour) that merely provides natural products which are there for the taking.

Marxists have distinguished in specific ways between the `instruments´ or tools of production; the `forces´ of production (including the natural resource base, the scientific and technological knowledge used to manufacture the instruments of production, and human labour); and the `means´ of production (including all of these plus capital). These distinctions, which branch from means to forces to instruments of production, have helped anthropologists to systematise both the collection and the analysis of information on small-scale production of all kinds, not merely agricultural production.

Finally, marxists postulate that labour, or its product, may be `appropriated´ by others through relations of production that differentiate social categories with reference to their control over the means of production. This concept has provided anthropology with a powerful alternative to the functionalist notion that inequality is necessary in order that society be integrated on the basis of complementarity. In particular, the notion that social and political inequalities arise from differential control over the means of production, has proved extremely fruitful in analysing the `gender relations´ between men and women in society. In this instance, the `orthodox´ marxist postulate of economic causation has yielded important insights, even though it has been queried and modified in other contexts.

So, although the marxist concept of a `mode of production´, based on a specific combination of means and relations of production in a particular society at a given time period, has run into trouble in anthropology, individual components of this concept have proved their worth as new analytical tools. Whether these concepts have been extended to the limits of their usefulness is an issue of current interest. They have certainly been pushed far beyond their original formulation by French anthropologists such as Meillassoux, Godelier, Terray, Copans and others. These neo-marxist approaches have proved a valuable foil to functionalist analyses of non-industrial economies, helping us to understand such economic behaviour in new ways.

At least in anthropology, these neo-marxist endeavours have also argued with and modified orthodox marxist assumptions. In particular, Godelier´s (1978) contribution to the debate about the relationship between ideology and relations of production is worth noting. Godelier argues that it is

16

impossible to make a distinction, even for heuristic or analytical purposes, between language as the vehicle of conceptualisation, and social, including productive, action. It is all very well to isolate knowledge (of soils, climate, and so forth) as part of the `forces´ of production, but in fact there would never be any production at all without the prior and wider conceptualisation in the human mind of that type of productive activity. Like the architect who plans a building before its construction (which, as Marx (1867/1976: 284) pointed out, distinguishes the worst architect from the best bee), the agricultural producer has a knowledge of the biophysical environment which, while it is constructed from experience, is in a sense prior to the experiment of production. Knowledge indeed forms part of the economic base, and it is reinforced and supplemented by productive behaviour, but it is also and more importantly a variable which is independent of this base, on which economic activities themselves crucially depend. Furthermore, for Godelier language is not the only `ideel reality´ which helps structure human behaviour. So do all other ideological assumptions (such as patriliny, patriarchy, hagiarchy and others) which penetrate and structure the relations of production themselves. In this view, to identify the structuring ideological principle(s) in any given society, is to understand its organisation, which is very different from the orthodox marxist perspective that considers the organisation of society as a whole to be structured by the relations of production in the economic base.

Theory in the Nineteen-Eighties

The demise of orthodox marxism is related mainly to its limited ability to explain societal data from non-western systems, notwithstanding the fast-spreading influence of the west. However, Godelier´s view (expressed at a conference in 1983) that even neo-marxist approaches have reached the limit of their usefulness in social anthropology, does not appear to be shared by others who have also invested their academic reputations in this area, although `modes of production´ are now distinctly passe. `Relations of production´, in contrast, are still actively pursued by those investigating society from feminist perspectives. Their similarity of focus on `gender relations´, incidentally, has done much to blur the disciplinary boundaries between social anthropologists, sociologists, economists and political scientists concentrating on such issues.

Orthodox structural-functionalism, like orthodox marxism, today suffers from a most unfashionable image, except, perhaps in the cybernetic models of that particular brand of ecological anthropology which has been associated with the universities of Michigan and Columbia in the USA. Gluckman (1968) has defended what he calls `equilibrium models´ with some cogency, but ultimately their general demise is related to the difficulty of drawing even arbitrary research boundaries around local societies that are being tied more and more firmly into larger economic, political and bureaucratic structures.

As anthropology has found itself investigating more complex, especially urban, societies, so the functionalist assumptions of holism have become more and more difficult to sustain. Instead, anthropological research has focussed on `part-societies´ and has become more individual- and problem-oriented in heterogeneous, multi-cultural neighbourhoods and workplaces. `Society´ is constructed from the perspectives of different individual actors within it, for example through mapping ego-centred social networks and tracing the ways in which they are constructed on the basis of friendship, employment, common membership of associations and so forth. It is almost impossible to regard a city neighbourhood, or a factory, as an independent whole around which boundaries may be drawn to isolate it from external influences in order to analyse it purely as an entity in itself. Increasingly, of course, the same is true of rural villages, where we ·see a contemporary emphasis on understanding how farmers make decisions about production, or what work women do, or how children´s labour fits into the relations of production, or how local politics work.

This switch of anthropological focus, from `culture´ or `society´ to individual behaviour, has not altered the inductive and empirical nature of the discipline. However, this approach does regard the individual from a Malinowskian rather than a Durkheimian perspective. The individual is no longer seen merely as the average bearer of a particular culture, or the structurally determined and properly socialised role incumbent. He or she is the rebel, innovator, deviant, above all the <u>thinking</u> manipulator of people and customs, always with an eye to his or her advantage. This advantage may be long- or short-term, economic, social, political or even religious. Neo-functionalist approaches are wrongly accused of assuming that `man the manipulator´ fits the simple mould of <u>homo oeconomicus</u> or <u>homo politicus</u>. But this change of emphasis is important theoretically, for it allows that individuals interact with social organisation in such a way as to change this organisation, rather than simply being moulded by it. This view is the result of investigative techniques (including social drama and network analysis) which enjoin an extended familiarity with the individuals, as well as the

18

society, being studied.

Arguably the most important outcome of this change of focus has been transactional theory. `Transactionalism´ is a rather fancy term for the basically simple principle that `you scratch my back and I´ll scratch your´s´. It owes much to Malinowski and somewhat less to Marx. In the hands of Frederik Barth (1959, 1966, 1967), simple propositions about exchange and reciprocity have yielded an understanding of how individual decisions, about the deployment of time and socio-political as well as productive resources, simultaneously generate different patterns of behaviour, some of which `reproduce´ custom, while others institute change. This type of approach has a particular appeal to anthropologists working in societies that are undergoing rapid and visible change, for it has proved immeasurably more useful than any of the evolutionary alternatives in explaining how and why such change occurs, whether in the economy or in political organisation. Its `instrumental´ and individualistic approach, however, has been somewhat less satisfactory when applied to `ideological´ areas of social life, such as law or religion.

While it is possible, then, to view structural-function-alist and marxist approaches as different and opposed theoret-ical `paradigms´ in the Kuhnian sense, it seems more profit-able to acknowledge the theoretical eclecticism of social anthropology, and to examine those theoretical approaches which, like transactionalism, have borrowed from both of these (and other) sources. While the parental perspectives have collapsed, such offspring still survive despite opposition. For example, Levi-Strauss´s version of structuralism, which is a love or hate affair for most anthropologists, persists notwithstanding the opposition of those who hate it.

Some years after Radcliffe-Brown´s death in 1955, Levi-Strauss (1962/1964) commended his forays into a mode of ana-lysis not substantially different from the Hegelian dialectic which underpins marxism. In seeking to explain `totemism´ as a ritual relationship between man and nature, Radcliffe-Brown (1929, 1951/1958) had rested his argument, at first implicitly and later explicitly, on the ancient Chinese concept of the `unity of opposites´. Levi-Strauss took up this Hegelian theme and used it together with elements of marxism to construct a fundamentally simple but superficially most complex method of analysis.

Levi-Strauss (1962/1964, 1978) superimposed the base-superstructure model of orthodox marxism on the distinction (borrowed incompletely from Freud) between the unconscious and conscious aspects of the human mind. In equating the human unconscious with the collectivity, and conscious behaviour with the individual, Levi-Strauss echoed Durkheim's (1895/1938) distinction between `collective representations' and `individual consciousness'. In this view, conscious behaviour, including `custom', is thus derived from the unconscious, which Levi-Strauss regarded as reflecting the universally-invariant structure, or `wiring', of the human brain. Physiologically, information is transmitted along neural pathways, and particularly at the nerve synapses, by a combination of electrical and chemical `firings'. This is an all or nothing phenomenon: either the synapse `fires' or it does not, in what is known as a `digital' or binary pattern of response on which computers are constructed: yes OR no, positive OR negative. If the synapse fires, information is transmitted; if it fails to fire, no information is passed on. This normal pattern can of course be broken by physical injury, for example by severing the nerve pathway; and - a factor which Levi-Strauss did not allow for - a synapse can also be stimulated into firing repeatedly and very rapidly in what resembles a continuous, or analogic, rather than a digital pattern. Levi-Strauss ignored this latter possibility, and argued that human thought is structured by the digital pattern of transmission.

Culture and custom, therefore, in Levi-Strauss' view, appear as the surface refractions of what goes on in the human mind. Because the mind is `wired' identically in all humans, their conscious, cultural behaviour can be analysed by disentangling its constituent binary oppositions. All cultures, in Levi-Strauss' view, are constructed from these binary oppositions. The binary discrimination is made unconsciously, but is externalised as conscious behaviour, and therefore reflects the dialectical synthesis of unconscious and conscious, collective and individual, natural and cultural. All one needs, to understand this synthesis, is the master key which decodes the pattern, and Levi-Strauss has provided a form of decoding matrix for this purpose. However sceptically one may approach such a claim, the fact remains that numerous anthropologists have used this formula, in particular to analyse myths and legends in many different cultures, and have found that it does, indeed, work!

Finally, then, it would seem that we can explain rather simply, if indeed an explanation is required at all, why so many different theoretical approaches continue to exist in social anthropology? Each one addresses itself with more success than the others to a specific area of societal organisation. Transactionalism explains the process of social, political and economic change. `Relations of production' help us to understand how exploitation works. Levi-Straussian structuralism has no competitor when it comes to analysing myth; and so on. Social anthropology has no 'grand theory' that works equally well for all sectors of society, merely a set of relatively discrete, 'sectional' theories which address different micro-problems. Whether an over-arching theory in such a discipline is possible, is perhaps a question for the philosophers of knowledge rather than mere social anthropologists, most of whom since Malinowski have lived their professional lives closer to practice than to theory, in a form of inductive praxis disapproved by more theoretically-inclined and deductive disciplines.

Methodology and Fieldwork Methods

In most sciences there is a close relationship between the theory governing an investigation and the methods of investigation that are used. Social anthropology is no exception. The comparative method, deductive and generalising as it is, was a logical outcome of armchair theorising about social evolution. Modified slightly at the turn of this century by the fieldworkers' direct observation of their subjects, the comparative method today remains the favoured tool of anthropologists seeking to establish structural regularities across a wide range of cultures and societies. Goody (1976), for example, has attempted to isolate Eurasia from Africa with reference to their different technologies of production, marriage preferences, inheritance rules and kinship terminologies. In the last two decades, such attempts have regularly drawn their material from the computerised Ethnographic Atlas compiled by Murdock for precisely this kind of investigation.

For some fifteen years before Malinowski entered the discipline, anthropologists had been collecting their own information from exotic places. But it is with Malinowski that we associate the technique of 'participant' (as opposed to 'direct') observation, based on personal fluency in the language of the society concerned. It is not accidental that Malinowski's 'functionalist' theorising accompanied his change of fieldwork method. To demonstrate the interconnections among social institutions in a functionalist analysis, requires deep and lengthy immersion in a working culture. So undertaking fieldwork successfully in a foreign culture was for many decades an essential 'rite of passage' to recognition as a professional anthropologist. Those who were able to 'swim' when thrown into the 'deep end' of fieldwork, survived in the profession. Many more, however, failed this acid test. In the past two decades an increasing number of doctoral theses have been based on library research rather than fieldwork.

Participant observation is often romanticised and misunderstood. A stranger very rarely becomes fully part of the society he or she studies. More often, the anthropologist is in but not fully of that society, a privileged outsider even when partaking in its social activity. The `social distance' based on differences of race, class, education, culture, language and power, is never fully closed. Nor, indeed, can men participate fully in women's activities (though the reverse is often easier), nor the young in the affairs of the elderly (and vice versa). If the anthropologist does become identified with a particular political faction in the field, as is quite easy, this identification is likely to prejudice the collection of information from rival factions. The romanticised idea of participant observation naively denies the differences which exist in all societies. This social differentiation makes total participation impossible, given the anthropologist's ultimate objective of understanding that society comprehensively, as a whole. The wise anthropologist, therefore, tries to retain and use the advantages of being a (relatively) neutral outsider. Outsiders can ask questions which would be inappropriate among locals; they can associate (if the minimum protocol is observed) with almost anyone; they are expected to behave incomprehensibly to some degree.

Furthermore, participation by itself does not yield much usable information. To elicit why people do what they do, it is necessary to ask questions in addition to observing and imitating the behaviour of others. Some mode of interviewing is, therefore, an essential complement to action. This `opportunistic' interviewing is informal and unstructured. There is, of course, also the perennial problem of trying to close the gap between what people say should be done and why, and what they actually do (what Firth (1951/1971) conceptualised as the difference between the ideal social structure and the empirical social organisation respectively). This is a problem for analysis rather than investigation, but it is essential, knowing that this gap exists, to record both what is said and what is done, whether on film, tape, or in old-fashioned notebooks. Immediate recording is not always possible. People object. The anthropologist doesn't have an unlimited budget for tapes or film. But one's notebook should never be left behind! So the anthropologist needs, in addition to a finely-tuned social sensitivity, a good memory based on the ability to concentrate selectively on what is going on around him or her, for later recall when immediate recording is not possible.

Given the gap between ideal and behaviour, and the fact of political competition, it is frequently desirable if not essential to record systematically the same information from different people, without using formal, structured questionnaires. In anthropology, questionnaire schedules are often inappropriate because the exact questions are unknown. Especially in competitive situations, people may also respond to them very negatively. A brief and unobstrusive list of points or questions, in the form of an aide memoire, is useful under such circumstances. However, anthropologists do use formal questionnaires on occasion. Production and population census schedules are quite common. Quantitative information is increasingly important to anthropologists who are harried by other disciplines to provide precise answers to questions such as `how much?´ and `how many?´ which arise from qualitative data. Malinowski´s exhortation to `measure, weigh and count everything´ therefore remains excellent advice to the fieldworker, and this requires the cartographic skills to map accurately the layout of fields and villages among farmers, as well as migratory routes among hunters and nomadic herders.

For the anthropologist working in an urban setting, or investigating work in a factory, there will exist many more written sources of information than are normally found in rural societies. Sometimes the techniques of verification used by historians must be applied to this type of information. Very often the statistical analysis of such data is not only possible but necessary. Individualising techniques of investigation, such as the recording of life and work histories, and the construction and analysis of ego-centric social networks, are common in urban fieldwork, but are also useful in rural contexts. Tracing the ongoing saga of disputes and conflict through the `extended case method´ and `social drama´ analysis is also important in both settings.

At the end of this list of the techniques which every anthropologist should expect to use during fieldwork, there are two methods of collecting information which are virtually unique to anthropology among the social sciences. The first is the recording of genealogies, or `family trees´. Rivers first used this technique nearly a century ago, and it is still used to collect systematic data on kinship, marriage, divorce and parentage, in order to show how kin-based societies are structured. Inevitably, genealogies will reveal deviations from the rules, which are often useful in showing how exceptional cases are handled. They will also change over time, more in response to the exigencies of contemporary political legitimation than to a simple failure of memory on the part of respondants. And occasionally, the fortunate fieldworker (such as Lipuma 1983) will stumble into the process whereby deviations are being reconstructed to suit the rules, which is exceptionally useful for understanding how the system really works in practice!

The second technique unique to anthropology is also Victorian in its origin, but has a specific purpose in anthropo-

logy. Fieldworkers are advised to keep a personal diary to act
as a private record of their own psychological reactions to
their work situations, a safety valve to defuse the tensions
and strains associated with always being a pleasant, friendly,
equable and good-natured participant in a strange. culture,
whatever the circumstances. Anthropologists do suffer what the
Americans have popularised as `culture shock´ and they are
removed from the support of their own friends and kin. Throwing temper tantrums and sulking militate against collecting
any useful data, but anthropologists are no more saintly than
other humans, while their work situation is more difficult
than most. American anthropologists often recommend psycho-
analysis to help cope with the work strains, but anthropologists from cultures which regard such practices as abnormal,
tend instead to weed out (usually at the post-graduate level)
those who are thought to be unsuited to the fieldwork
requirements of the profession.

Fieldwork is a uniquely subjective and personalised experience, which explains in part why different fieldworkers
give different accounts of the same society. But even those
anthropologists who have returned a generation after their
initial fieldwork to the `same´ society, have tended to exper-
ience it differently. Societies do change. People convert to
different religions, change their educational and political
systems, and even their values. They also grow older, and in
so doing participate in society from a different set of roles
and positions. Anthropologists grow old too, even though their
professional role is not supposed to change, and they also
participate differently. So `replication´ studies have proved
virtually impossible in anthopology and, in emphasising the
subjectivity and self-reflexivity of our methodology, have
raised important questions about the status of anthropology as
a `science´. This debate still continues and is unlikely to be
resolved as simply as Malinowski and Radcliffe-Brown envisaged. Social anthropology or `comparative sociology´ as
`the natural science of society´ today seems a somewhat naive
and uncomplicated perspective.

In concluding this brief resume of methods and methodology, it is necessary to make specific mention of the differences between anthropologists as `strangers´ and anthropolo-
gists working in their own societies. Working at home is
becoming more and more frequent, despite the traditional view
of anthropology as concerned only with the foreign and exotic.
The anthropologist as stranger, even as a long-term visitor,
can never know the society he or she is studying as intimately, or from the same perspective, as the anthropologist whose
society it is. On the other hand, familiarity does very often
breed contempt of what is to be known as knowledge, as opposed

to what is accepted as social practice. In many ways, these
issues are bringing social anthropology philosophically closer
to its cognate sociological specialisations of phenomenology
and ethnomethodology, than was formerly recognised to be the
case. At the same time, as anthropology `comes home´, the
wider economic, political, legal and historical context of
anthropological research is also becoming more important.
Whether social anthropologists like it or not, then, in the
process of its own change, their discipline is increasingly
being drawn into closer relationships with its sister social
sciences.

CHAPTER TWO

MARGINALISED ECONOMIC ACTIVITIES IN THE WORLD SYSTEM

One place to start in introducing students to the data used by social anthropology is with people who invest no labour in making the land produce but merely use its natural products. Here we are talking of productive activities that, although they still exist today in some places, are associated in technologically advanced societies with man´s prehistory. Hunting and gathering, as a means of making a living, are associated with the `old stone age´ or palaeolithic era, while the domestication of animals began, contemporaneously with the growth of agriculture in the neolithic or `new stone age´, some 12,000 years ago.

The Land as `Subject of Labour´

In relying exclusively on natural products, herdsmen and hunters have been regarded as enslaved by their environment. Montesquieu (1748/1949) was perhaps the first to popularise deterministic explanations of economic activity. He regarded production as depending on the climate, the fertility of the soil and topography, and population density as being affected by the labour requirements of the different productive activities so determined. Environmental determinism has found its way into school geography textbooks, with their emphasis on the way Eskimo and Bedouin lifestyles are constrained by and adapted to the exigencies of the Arctic tundra and the Arabian desert.

But productive activities are themselves cultural, and in the same environments we find very different economies. While the Eskimo of the North American taiga and tundra were hunters, gatherers and fishermen, drawing a very clear distinction between their summer and winter activities, today in Alaska they are the recipients of windfall oil revenues that have drawn some of them into industrial employment and others into the alcoholism of boredom. The Lapps of the Russian and Scandinavian taiga-tundra, in contrast, used to follow and live off reindeer herds. Today, in the USSR herding has been collectivised, while in Scandinavian countries a substantial proportion of former herders have been reduced to living off welfare rather than animals. The Bedouin of Saudi Arabia today drive cadillacs as well as keeping camels and practising falconry, thanks to their oil revenues. As yet the Somali of the Ogaden desert have not been affected by the energy industry. They continue to herd their camels, sheep and goats in quite different units to those of their immediate Ogaden neighbours, the Boran Galla, even though their physical environments are practically identical. So even under the same environmental circumstances, different societies produce and organise their production differently. Culture counts even in the exploitation of nature: the adaptation of men to their environments is not passive, even where land is merely the subject of labour.

The inventions that have enabled men progressively to shape and control, rather than merely respond to, their environments, Bronowski (1973:20) calls a `brilliant sequence of cultural peaks´, or The Ascent of Man. This model of ascent, of movement upward toward a `better´ system, summarises and informs the evolutionists´ attitude to those who have been left behind by progress, those whom Sahlins (1974:8) described as the `palaeolithic disenfranchised´. Even fishermen, with their factory ships that enable modern fleets to remain at sea for up to six months without putting into port, have retained something of the stigma that attaches to nomadic herdsmen and hunters. Those who hunt, follow or herd animal species are relegated to the margins of production, as well as to the margins of society, by their sedentary fellow-humans. `Developing´ the mobile is usually envisaged as finding them an alternative, settled occupation.

There are a number of reasons for this attitude. Nomadic lifestyles require vast tracts of land or sea to support small human populations on their natural products and may, therefore, be seen to be ecologically wasteful. In fact the reverse is often the case. As Sahlins (1974:33) noted, constant movement permits environmental resources to be used but not exhausted, where settlement would strain a fragile resource base. Moreover, the lands to which contemporary hunters and herdsmen have been forced to retreat - the deserts and semi-arid regions, the arctic tundra and the mountains, the jungle and the forest - are not readily exploited in any other way. Though some deserts and seas conceal oil and minerals below their surfaces, the recovery of such resources requires the use of only small parts of the total surface area, which remains available for exploitation in other ways. And while the Amazonian jungle may be cleared for sugarcane cultivation, that clearing is far more likely than hunting and gathering to destroy the existing ecosystem.

While nomadic people do not in reality pose an ecological threat, then, we may regard the slander that they do as part of the justification for wishing to settle them in a lifestyle more amenable to central political and administrative control. The social marginalisation of the mobile is reflected in stereotypes of the criminal and anti-social activities of those who are `here today and gone tomorrow´. Such stereotypes attach as much, if not more, to gypsies in Europe as they do to itinerant Pygmies on the margins of the Ituri forest in Zaire, Central Africa, while Tanka boat-dwellers in Hong Kong have been described as six-toed non-Chinese, as well as `exemplars of loose sexual morality´ (Ward 1965).

In turn, the stereotyping of the mobile perhaps relates to their disdain of property. Those who travel, travel light, unencumbered by the ideology of property ownership. Indeed, when the elderly or injured can no longer move, they stay behind: Scott´s `sacrifice´ in the Antarctic is commonplace among those whose lives as well as livelihood depend on their mobility. Their equipment and tools are simple, easily replaced when worn out or broken, by the small labour of any adult. Particularly what hunters carry must be light enough not to weigh them down, whereas the property of boat-dwelling fishermen and nomadic pastoralists is slightly less restricted, to what their boats or their pack animals can carry. The material lifestyle of nomads, then, is usually less comfortable than that of sedentary people. However, their material deprivation is relative, for, as Sahlins (1974) points out, their environment contains most of what <u>they</u> want in abundance. Such `original affluence´, of course, rests on what Sahlins (1974:11) calls `an objectively low standard of living´, in combination with an ethos of sharing rather than laying exclusive claim to whatever is available.

Hunter-Gatherers of Desert and Forest

In contrast to the outsider´s view of hunter-gatherers as struggling to find enough to eat, Sahlins´ (1974) corrective emphasises their `pristine affluence´. Firstly, their environment yields a wide range of nutritious foods (allowing a daily intake of over 2000 Calories), which require an average adult working day of some 3-5 hours to collect, prepare and eat. This work is not continuous, but is punctuated by frequent interruptions, and the collector´s yield generally supports one and a half consumers. Hunting bands can therefore support producer-consumer ratios not dissimilar to those of sedentary societies and also allow for a certain amount of sheer idleness. As Sahlins (1974:34) puts it: `Hunters keep banker´s hours, notably less than modern industrial workers (unionised), who would surely settle for a 21-35 hour week´. Hence it is not surprising that, although the material possessions of hunter-gatherers are few and simple, their non-material culture is often very complex, as may be demonstrated by the Pygmy hunters of the Ituri tropical rain forest, Zaire, who call themselves Mbuti.

Turnbull (1961) studied the Mbuti in the 1950s, and by 1956 they were already being drawn into wage labour at new settlements and encouraged to clear plantations in the forest for agricultural purposes. In areas more accessible than the one Turnbull studied, the Mbuti had earlier been incorporated into the tourist economy. The co-operative hunting groups of half a dozen or more families, each with their own net, were thus already under threat as some families began to withdraw from the hunting economy.

The Mbuti had traditionally spent some of their time in Negro villages fringing the forest, for purposes of ritual and trade, the adult women shifting household possessions and dried meat in the baskets carried on their backs but supported from their foreheads, and the men carrying their hunting bows and arrows, nets and spears. On the trail, the women took advantage of their loads to walk slowly, visually scouring the ground for foodstuffs such as mushrooms, wild fruits, edible roots, termites, nuts, berries and, prized above all else, honey. The men on the trail sought small game such as birds and monkeys, for organising a hunt with nets and beaters took much more time. They set up semi-permanent camp in both village and forest, building shelters of saplings and leaves that lasted a few months. And yet, even in the forest, foodstuffs such as rice and plantains, beans and groundnuts, which were trade goods, gifts, or straight extortions from the Negro villagers, were enjoyed during the time of Turnbull's research.

Although the Mbuti lived in two worlds and had done so for generations, they identified themselves with the forest, as its `children´. From the forest came all of their material needs for food, clothing, shelter, hunting equipment and ornamentation, to which it was normally responsive. But occasionally, in the same way as disaster could befall the sleeping human, the forest fell asleep without care for its children. Then it was, in Mbuti belief, that death and illness befell themselves, signalling that it was time to return to and awaken the forest through the extended ritual of the molimo and its music, which lasted some months. The molimo was, until its final rites, a nocturnal affair of the men, after the women and children had withdrawn into their shelters. In the climax of this ritual, however, the women played a leading role and the children participated too. But even this most serious aspect of Mbuti life had been penetrated by their `other world´. To Turnbull's shock and horror, the molimo instruments which amplified the beautiful singing of the men turned out to be fifteen-foot lengths of

29

metal drainpipe, carefully kept in secluded parts of the forest just like their wooden and bamboo predecessors had been!

In amplifying their essentially monotheistic religion, the Mbuti differed from the San, or `Bushmen´, of the Kalahari desert in Botswana and Namibia. Although authors such as Lewis-Williams (1980) have regarded the rock paintings of the ancient San as evidence of their past religious elaboration, in more recent times the San seem to have had no rituals comparable to the molimo of the Mbuti. They had a similar social organisation based on small bands of mobile hunters, but perhaps because their open, arid terrain entailed shifting camp more frequently, as well as a different technique of hunting based on spears rather than nets, the San bands tended to be considerably smaller than those of the Mbuti. Like the Mbuti, the San tradition of hunting had been jeopardised by their involvement in wage labour, in this case on ranches as cattle-herders for Tswana, Herero and white employers.

The San differed not only from hunter-gatherers of the African forests, but also from those of other deserts. For example, the San had a naming system based on less than 50 names each for men and women, which by their allocation linked, among others, grandparents and the grandchildren named after them. However, this system was not nearly as complex as the systems of sections and sub-sections (according to the `skin´) which classified groups and regulated marriage among Australian Aboriginal hunter-gatherers. It has taken the skills of mathematical statistics to unravel, for anthropological understanding, the intricacies of systems which used up to 64 different marital categories according to very strict rules of who was marriageable and who not. The more intricate these systems, the larger was the minimum size of the population necessary to allow the rules to operate. And as more and more Aborigines in the past fifty years have been drawn into wage labour and urban settlement, fewer and fewer of these marriage systems have been able to continue to work. Somewhat strangely, the most intricate of these systems were found in the most arid areas of Australia.

Godelier (1975) has suggested that both the naming system of the San and the marriage sections of Aboriginal societies, functioned to enable hunting bands to exploit territories that were normally associated with other bands. Bands did not `own´ hunting territories, but had some association with the area they normally exploited. However, when times were bad, access to other hunting grounds was mediated through marriage links, and to a lesser extent kinship, based on names among the San and marriage sections among the Aborigines. The more complex

the section system, the wider was the area available for
potential exploitation, which is perhaps why the most complex
systems were found in the most arid regions. In contrast, the
exchange of `sisters´ in Mbuti marriages widened the range of
exploitation very little, for in the abundance of the forest
it was rarely necessary for one band to use the territory of
another, although for personal reasons individuals and families did sometimes move from one band to another.

Notwithstanding their differences, most hunter-gatherer
societies have shared with `advanced capitalist´ (and social-
ist) societies an emphasis on monogamous marriage (often, in
both cases, serially). (The Mbuti, who from Turnbull´s (1961)
description seemed to have a significant proportion of polygamous marriages, were rather unusual in this respect.)
Furthermore, anthropologists such as Draper (1975) have argued
that these `originally affluent societies´ displayed a greater
equality between men and women than any other society has ever
managed to achieve. Although as a general rule men hunted and
women gathered, this division of labour was not rigid. As
Turnbull (1961) and others have described, men also collected
foodstuffs and women participated in the hunt, though generally not as killers or butchers of the game. Men also undertook
domestic tasks and cared for, nursed and entertained their
children. Draper showed, however, that as soon as the San
moved out of their desert environment, into an economy and
lifestyle which assumed the dependence of women on men, this
equality was lost. Men earned wages and women became subordinated within the domestic sphere in a way they had not been in
the desert when they had collected perhaps a majority proportion of the family food supply.

Pastoralism

Wage labour and welfare payments represent possible exits
from a hunting economy, but so too does the transformation
from hunting animals to herding them. This change involves a
more complex division of labour between the sexes than is
characteristic of hunting economies, but is not necessarily
identical with the domestication of animals, which can be
`herded´ in a rather loose fashion even when wild, as Ingold
(1976) points out. Pastoralism and ranching, in Ingold´s view,
also differ from hunting by dividing rights in living animals
among private owners, where hunters appropriate only dead
animals in their systems of dividing the product of their
hunting activities.

Sandford (1983:1) offers a usefully vague definition of
pastoralists as `people who derive most of their income or

31

sustenance from keeping domestic livestock in conditions where most of the feed that their livestock eat is natural forage rather than cultivated fodders and pastures´. In a more precise manner, Ingold (1980) has distinguished `protective´ pastoralism from `predatory´ ranching, on the grounds that pastoralists divide their animals, but not the land they roam, into individualised units; whereas ranching is based on the division of both land and animals.

Within Ingold´s `pastoral´ category, we may also identify a continuum stretching from sedentary, through transhumant, to nomadic possibilities. Pastoralists who are settled in one place may be involved, usually through their womenfolk, in annual cultivation. Transhumant or semi-nomadic people often manage to cultivate in the summer or in the wet season, as do those who divide their animals into different herding units which migrate over different but standard routes at varying distances from the home base. Fully nomadic pastoralists, however, who are continuously on the move, undertake no cultivation at all. They rely on trading animal products (dairy products, hides, wool, hair, blood, meat) for grains and other vegetable foodstuffs, either with the farmers whose lands they pass through or at established markets.

Although marginalised, in absolute terms pastoralists may today number as many as 30 million people, over half of whom are thought to live in Africa and a quarter in Asia (Sandford 1983:2). Their numbers are affected not only by natural population growth, but also by unsuccessful herders `dropping out´ (usually temporarily), and by farmers in certain regions, whose only mode of long-term investment is in livestock, opting to become herders rather than entrusting their accumulated capital to the care of others. Ten countries, including the USA, each have a million or more pastoralists.

Many pastoralists remain nomadic, despite the tendencies among expanding communities of cultivators to intrude upon their traditional pastures, and governments to settle them. Their mobility is one part of their strategy for spreading and thereby diminishing their specific risks of production in arid and semi-arid lands, by using natural resources briefly (but sometimes heavily, to undermine insect breeding conditions), before allowing them time to regenerate. Pastoralists spread their risks in other ways, too. They keep different species of animals and fragment their total livestock holdings among different herders in different localities, to avoid disease wiping out a full herd and to maximise the access of different animals with different needs to the grazing and water resources that are available in different ecological niches. Hence the Northern Somali, for example, allocate long-range camel-herding in the Ogaden desert to young, unmarried men, while their sheep, goats and cattle are herded in shorter migratory cycles by family units in the wetter areas. Pastoralists also aim to maximise their herd numbers, as an insurance against the inevitable losses of the bad years which may endanger their survival as pastoralists. Perhaps inevitably, these strategies cause the unthinking to regard them as ecological menaces.

Although most pastoralists inhabit Africa, for none of these people do we have reliable historical information on precolonial herding and, as Sandford (1983:14) has indicated, their known history has in many cases been distorted by the impact of rinderpest and other diseases at the beginning of the colonial period, as well as by the impact of colonial administration itself. To take a longer view of herding, then, it is necessary first to look at Europe and Asia.

The Lapps of Northern Scandinavia were plagued by social scientists after the second world war, Ingold (1976) having been the most recent anthropological visitor to the Skolt Lapps of Northern Finland in the early 1970s. By then, a minority of the Skolt community was still involved in `herding´ reindeer, using the new technology of motorcycles in summer, snowmobiles (introduced in 1963) in autumn and winter, and light aircraft when necessary. In fact the reindeer generally ran wild and were only mustered in spring and in autumn for slaughter and sale.

Their increasing wildness was partly attributable to the noise of the new herding technology, but Ingold (1976) has argued that it rested more basically on the earlier deterioration of the winter lichen pastures and the growth of the commercial market for reindeer meat, which together made this technology viable. The engine noise caused the reindeer to scatter in search of increasingly remote and inaccessible pastures; to panic and run so that they lost condition generally and in particular calf mortality increased and the females´ calving ratios fell from 60 to 20 per cent; and generally to avoid contact with humans. On top of the deterioration in their lichen pastures which tided the reindeer through the snow-bound winters, the new herding technology undoubtedly contributed to a decline in their numbers.

However, the reindeer were only semi-domesticated prior to the introduction of motorcycles, snowmobiles and aircraft. Individual reindeer had been tamed for milking and transport and as hunting decoys as early as the sixteenth century. However, only during the nineteenth century, after the virtual disappearance of the wild herds, did the Lapps switch from

33

hunting to following reindeer and privatising their ownership, in what Ingold (1976:24) has called `expansive pastoralism´. At first small herds of tame deer were enclosed in summer pastures, but these perimeter fences were abandoned as the tame herds grew. The free-grazing deer were then mustered in autumn by herdsmen on foot and skis and, from the mustering points, sorted and returned to their owners to see out the winter on lichen pastures close to the villages. They were moved to spring settlements before the calving began.

This system of gentle handling had effectively been destroyed in the late nineteenth century by the introduction of round-up fences and corrals for the autumn `separations´. The new, noisy machines of the mid-twentieth century merely exacerbated the problem. The tallying of animals at the separations was necessitated by the bounding of pastures to control their use, and the consequent payment (to the controlling reindeer owners´ associations) of membership subscriptions and levies per head of reindeer. Each reindeer had to be accounted for in autumn and if necessary returned home after its owner had been `fined´ by the association whose resources it had used illegally. Herders were hired by the associations to round up the deer. With snowmobiles, they were paid at twice the rate for a man on foot and skis, on the assumption that they could work twice as fast. Herders therefore had no option but to mechanise, and in so doing, reduce the number of men employed and undermine further the already precarious relationship between men and reindeer. By the early 1970s, only between one-fifth and one-third of all able-bodied Skolt men were still actively involved in herding (Ingold 1976:74). The rest were seasonal workers in agriculture and forestry, unemployed, or had migrated to the towns and cities of Southern Finland.

Pelto (1973) has argued that the `snowmobile revolution´ not only caused the decline in the reindeer herds and its associated unemployment, but also led to the dependence of the formerly autonomous Lappish economy on external forces and energy sources. As we have already seen, in Ingold´s view the decline of the herds was caused by a number of factors, the snowmobile being only one of them, though he has not disputed the problem of external dependency. Ingold´s sharpest disagreement with Pelto concerned the question of what caused the emerging class differentiation that both of them noted within the Skolt Lapp community. Pelto argued that the mechanisation of herding caused poor families to drop out of herding altogether because they could not afford the costs, thereby redistributing the ownership of reindeer from older men to the young and energetic. Ingold (1976:67, 71) has, however, shown that `the general picture [was] ... of a proliferation of

34

small ownership, a reversal of fortunes for previous large owners, and the rise to prominence of a few leading invest- ors´, youngish `big-men´ who were `boastful, extravagant, generous and sociable´, who drank heavily, and whose rise to prominence had relied on claiming as many unmarked deer as possible at the autumn musterings. Perhaps part of the dis- agreement between Pelto and Ingold on the issue of class formation relates to their obviously different evaluations of the entrepreneurial behaviour of these younger reindeer owners.

Lappish herding communities in Scandinavia have seen their traditional relations of production altered by a new technology of herding, their sons and especially their daugh- ters leave the home communities for good, and have enjoyed the benefits of unemployment and other welfare payments to cushion them against these changes. In contrast, pastoralists in socialist economies, such as the Mongolian People´s Republic, have experienced collectivisation of their herds.

Humphrey (1978) has described the Mongolian economy, both past and present, as essentially pastoral, notwithstanding its contemporary industrialisation. Cattle, horses, sheep, goats and camels ate and still eat different grasses, being herded separately (except for sheep and goats in winter, when in mixed flocks sheep keep the goats warm) and using the pastures sequentially. Within these different animal units, further distinctions were based on age, sex and reproductive status. These distinctions have formed the basis for a highly special- ised division of labour within contemporary herding collec- tives.

Traditionally the Mongols ranged over territorial divi- sions called khoshun (`banners´). Although khoshun land was in theory communally owned, the migratory routes were set by feudal officials and herdsmen could be punished for leaving this territory without permission. After the 1921 revolution, but before the first attempt at collectivisation in the late 1920s, the `banner´ lands were sub-divided into sum, each of which accommodated roughly 150 households grouped into the traditional herding units (xot-ail) of two or three families within a patrilineage. Herders remained, as before, fully migratory in both summer and winter, moving their felt-covered yurts or willow-frame tents, as well as their household equip- ment, on their pack-animals.

Collectivisation was first attempted at roughly the same time as Stalin was collectivising Soviet agriculture, and was characterised by physical harrassment as well as crippling taxes, particularly on private caravan transport. After having

35

to suppress insurrections in the west, the Mongolian government abandoned its policy of compulsory collectivisation in
favour of voluntary co-operation in hay-making, building
cattle byres and other herding activities. In 1960, following
a decade of massive assistance to these co-operatives, membership once again became compulsory. However, by this time the
richer stock-owners found themselves short of labour because
all of their poorer counterparts had joined the co-operatives
earlier, and had little option but to participate. By the
1970s, virtually all herdsmen belonged to the new negdel
(collective) organisation, although more than one-fifth of all
animals were still privately owned. (It is unclear from Humphrey's account whether these privately-owned animals were
herded with the others, or separately.) In 1975, there were
259 negdels, each occupying a sum (the smallest territorial
division of the Mongolian People's Republic).

Each negdel comprised four or five brigades, including an
`auxiliary brigade' which sent relief workers to smaller units
experiencing temporary labour shortages as well as providing
services to the collective as a whole. In turn, each brigade
had its own territory and was sub-divided into surrs, a number
of which were grouped into the intermediate khesags in `neigh-
bourhood' units. Roughly equivalent in size to the old xot-ail
herding units, the surrs were more thoroughly specialised in
particular types of animal. The brigade council allocated
pastures among its surrs, not least to ensure that lands
closest to the negdel community centre were not overused by
herdsmen preferring to remain close to social amenities.
Pasture use was scientifically planned to avoid ecological
degradation, but not surprisingly bore a close resemblance to
traditional usage. Humphrey (1978:149) noted explicitly that
`[i]t is probable that the migration routes of the surrs are
based on pre-collectivisation routes which contained built-in
features of traditional herding practices, such as adequate
year-round pasture without hay or fodder, and natural shelter
in winter rather than byres'.

The reason for this congruence between traditional and
collectivised herding techiques concerned attempts to sedentarise the Mongolian pastoralists as far as possible. By
specialising the work, the government was able to sedentarise
all but a few necessarily mobile herders. Even the migratory
range of surr units had, where possible, been cut by the
development of regular watering points and the provision of
winter fodder and hay from sedentarised workers. Hence, by the
1970s, the constraints on production appeared to revolve
around inadequate water supplies and winter fodder supple-
ments, not summer pastures.

In Humphrey's opinion, the collectivisation of Mongolian herding had been beneficial, even though the efficiency of Mongolian pastoralism had always been able to support large numbers of unproductive lamas, aristocrats and state officials. The survival rates for young animals were higher among privately-owned than collectively-owned animals, but these rates had risen generally for all animals, except camels. Animal husbandry, including processed products, accounted for 80 per cent of Mongolian exports. Mongolians were among the best-fed on the Asian continent, not least because private stock and their products surplus to selling quotas were generally slaughtered and shared among related families. Educational levels had risen dramatically, easing the process of industrialisation as well as modernising the herding technology. Health and social amenities had been greatly improved.

Yet there was still unused potential in the herding system. Although the national herd had expanded from less than 10 million animals prior to the 1921 revolution to some 24 million in 1975, experts estimated the carrying capacity of the summer pastures at double the latter figure. The constraints lay in the provision of water and winter fodder, where greater efficiencies were possible. In a very real sense, and in contrast to the situation among Lapp herders, Mongolian collectivisation in its later form had systematically exploited the potential of the traditional herding system, rather than altering either its techniques or its relations of production. Therein lay its success.

The Mongolian system also contrasted with what happened to African pastoralists during the same time period. The nomadic Fulbe (or, as the Hausa call them and as they have come to be known in the English literature, Fulani or Bororo), are perhaps the best-known of the Sahelian herders. From the coast of West Africa to Chad, these patrilineal Muslims herd their zebu cattle in the savannah zone, between the fringes of the Sahara desert at 15 degrees north latitude and the forest belt stretching south from 7 degrees north. Although this area is tsetse country, the Fulani used to avoid the fly by migrating north during the summer rains (from April to November) and south during the dry season. In the dry season they dispersed into small herding units of a few families, but aggregated into larger units of 50 to 60 households during the wet season, which was `a time of concentrated ritual and ceremonial activity´ (Stenning 1957:66).

The Fulani migration routes averaged up to 120 miles between turn-around points. Every four days they moved on. They passed through the lands of settled cultivators, like the Hausa of Northern Nigeria, and on their southward migrations grazed their cattle on the grain stover as well as natural grass. Sometimes, as by the Gwari of Northern Nigeria, they were paid for manuring the fields. The Fulani women traded dairy products for grain. The men sometimes sold their cattle to the Hausa long distance traders described by Cohen (1969), who supplied meat to most West African cities from Senegal to the Central African Republic.

Although the Fulani used the land, they had no ownership rights over pasture, water supplies or migration routes. They depended completely on the goodwill of those cultivators through whose territory they passed for access to the means of pastoral production. As Stenning (1957) has described, sometimes they came into armed conflict with `pagans´ and could not use their resources until colonial `pacification´ opened up, for example, the highland pastures of the Jos Plateau in Nigeria. Fulani relations with the Muslim states of the Sahel were, in contrast, those of political subordination, marked by their payment of taxes, alms and tribute. It was from what they regarded as the excessive exactions of these centralised states that the Fulani `fled´ into new migratory routes when necessary.

The Fulani also shifted their migratory routes in response to environmental changes. Usually they explored new areas by minor extensions to their known tracks, rather than by moving rapidly to an entirely new area. But as the cultivating populations of the Sahel have expanded into formerly pastoral areas, this strategy of `migratory drift´, as Stenning (1957) has called it, has proved less and less viable in finding adequate pasturage. Conflicts between nomads and the sedentary communities (as well as with central governments attempting to sedentarise them) have increased. In the 1970s, the Sahel gained international notoriety for its famine deaths and the temporary wiping out of its pastoral adaptations as the majority of nomads lost their entire herds in a series of bad droughts. One strategy for rebuilding the herds, used by aid agencies, was adapted from traditional relations of pastoral production. It involved lending `animals of friendship´ to pastoralists for a number of years, to rebuild their herds, against the collateral only of customary obligation.

African pastoralists in particular have been stigmatised as irrational in economic terms, as preferring to build up herds of inferior animals rather than to breed good beef for the market. In part this stigma derives from what Herskovits (1926) called the `cattle complex´, an unfortunate term used to encapsulate the social and religious significance, as well as productive importance, that cattle have to pastoralists. In Kenya, white settlers gave the concept of the `cattle complex´

a Freudian slant; and we may wonder whether the stigmatisation of African herders was not racial in its intent, for other pastoralists had and probably still have similar attachments to their animals, without having had a similar `complex´ attributed to them.

As many authors have pointed out, it is unnecessary to invoke such a `complex´ to explain the entirely rational behaviour of African pastoralists. Exotic breeds fare badly in the African savannah, much worse than locally-adapted breeds whose resistance to disease is more important to herdsmen than their milk or meat yield for the market. The Fulani, for example, deliberately cross-bred their zebu with the locally-adapted Red Longhorn of the Sudan Savannah, and the White Longhorn of the Guinea Savannah. Large numbers are necessary for subsistence if milk yields are low and herds are fragmented into smaller units to avoid total loss through epidemic disease. Pastoral lifestyles are materially austere, having little use for monetary gain except to reinvest in livestock. Therefore pastoralists sell only what is necessary to buy in imported subsistence goods. Their response to the market, to withdraw some animals if prices rise, does not mean that they are irrational.

The notion of the `cattle complex´ has been partly responsible for causing both colonial and independent African governments to try to settle their nomadic pastoralists in a ranching mode. But in countries such as Botswana, providing borehole water caused immeasurably more ecological damage than did traditional `range management´, as large numbers of cattle trampled out the grazing for a 15-kilometre radius from permanent water supplies. The fencing of traditional pastures to create ranches has had similar effects in Kenya by cutting out important parts of traditional migratory routes on which Maasai cattle depended. On the whole, then, Africa has not built on its traditional techniques of pastoral management, but has instead tried to use models of animal husbandry imported from developed countries, with very negative effects on pastoral economy and society.

The Sea as `Subject of Labour´: Fishing

If equality between the sexes is characteristic of those who hunt on land, this pattern does not extend to those who hunt at sea or in inland waters. As Firth (1984) has recalled of earlier fieldwork, women may be involved in the simpler techniques of fishing on beach, reef and river bank, and may trade in fish, but neither in Tikopia nor in Malaya were women generally employed in traditional deep-water fishing, even

39

when female deities were significant to fishing success. Nor are crew-women often found on factory trawlers in the industrial fishing sector.

Fishing is big business, yielding in the 1980s an international total of some 75 million tonnes annually (compared to 140 million tonnes of meat). Of this catch, some 13 per cent was wasted one way or another, by industrial producers throwing back into the sea unsaleable species and by artisanal fishermen's inadequate processing techniques; and over one-quarter was turned into animal foodstuffs rather than going to increase the intake of protein among undernourished human consumers.

Relative to sea-fishing, inland lake-fishing, river-fishing and aquaculture or fish farming remain unimportant, producing only some 12 per cent of the world's total catch (slightly less than the proportion wasted). However, in the 1980s, inland fisheries were expanding faster than sea-fishing, and were obviously important to landlocked countries which did not have a 200-mile offshore zone of the sea for their exclusive exploitation. The building of Lake Kariba, for example, has enabled Zimbabwe to produce over 10,000 tonnes of pelagic fish annually, using capital-intensive techniques to do so.

By the 1980s, however, capitalising and industrialising fisheries were beginning to be seen as a less efficient development strategy (in terms of yields, returns to investment, and the creation of jobs) than the upgrading of traditional artisanal fishing techniques. The only surprise about this change of attitude was that it had taken so long to occur, for in his study of the offshore fishery in the east coast state of Kelantan, Malaya, at the beginning of the second world war, Firth (1946) had arrived at a similar conclusion and made precisely such recommendations.

Malayan fishermen, Muslims who for centuries had been linked into larger political entities and regional fish-trading networks stretching over a thousand miles, were part of a fully-monetised peasant economy. Few were involved in agriculture: most sold their fish in order to buy in other household necessities. Like fishermen everywhere, they invested capital in a high-risk occupation, but one which yielded immediate returns for consumption, unlike rice cultivation. Sea-fishing was virtually impossible during the monsoon months of December and January, and when the fishing was good, there were immediate problems of processing, storage and disposal in a market very sensitive to supply factors. Given this uncertainty in their production, full-time fishermen emphasised short-term planning and the marginal use of part-time (and less skilled) fishermen when extra labour was required. Their individual output was low, averaging less than 2 tons annually, as compared with the contemporary figures for Japanese fishermen of 8.3 tons and the Pangkor Chinese of the Malayan west coast of 10 tons. In part, this low output reflected their inefficient use of time. Firth calculated that only one-third of the available fishing time was actually used for that purpose, though much time was lost to weather unfavourable for fishing in their shallow-draught, undecked, 40-foot sailing boats.

Although individuals and small groups co-operated in beach fishing, the use of large seine and gill nets (and boat lines) in the open sea required quite large fishing units, of at least half a dozen boats and some 40-odd crew to handle the nets. Leaders of such units were themselves skilled and wealthy fishermen, who recruited young, fit men, including those of their kin, affines and friends who were suitable. Their work association was based on an agreed distribution of the fish caught, and the financing of his crew by the leader during the monsoon, when fishing was impossible. The fish caught were generally sent in for sale, before the `fleet´ returned to shore, with the carrier boat captained by the sales negotiator accompanied by the unit´s debt collector (who worked hardest on Fridays, when the fishermen stayed home to attend mosque). Sales were usually on credit until the end of that week, and the system was financed by the leader with or without the help of a Chinese fish-trader.

Malay fishermen were linked not only into wider trade networks, but also to those who supplied their fishing equipment. While the smaller nets, like the lures, traps, baskets and lines, were manufactured within the fishermen´s households, boat-building and making the very large seine and drift nets were specialist activities. The more valuable equipment was often bought on credit, advanced by its maker, a Chinese fish-trader, or a wealthy local fishing expert (known as juru selam). The life-span of this equipment made from local materials was not long. A net might be made to last for six years, but after one year the costs of repairing it were high. Boats endured for perhaps twice this time, lures and lines perhaps half. Maintenance costs were ongoing, and repairs fairly frequent. Some of the labour, especially for net maintenance and repairs, came from the members of each fishing unit as part of their full-time employment, without additional remuneration, but the twine and dye and caulking materials for net and boat maintenance still had to be bought.

Linked to the rapid ageing of fishing equipment was a

thriving market in second-hand gear, whereby battered and depreciated capital goods left the hands of relatively wealthy owners, in exchange for full cash payment, and ended up with the young, hard-working and enthusiastic - but relatively poor - fishermen who could not afford new equipment. Firth noted a very gradual capitalisation of the fishery through this strategy of capitalising labour, but remarked too that it was inadequate to lift the fishery out of its existing low-level equilibrium, and improve output dramatically and quickly, without external assistance.

Class differentiation was marked in this peasant fishing economy, which Firth did not regard as `precapitalist´ even though he emphasised that it had few proper `capitalists´. Only one-third of all fishermen owned their boats or had shares in a boat. Two-fifths owned no shares at all in nets, another two-fifths owned shares only, and only 20 per cent owned a full net or more. The majority of fishermen owned only hand-equipment (baskets, nets and lines). As Firth (1946:294) noted, this was not `a community in which wealth [was] fairly evenly distributed´. There was also a wide range in average weekly incomes, from M$1.50 to M$20.00. The top 5 per cent of fishermen took 20 per cent of the total fishing income, while the bottom 85 per cent absorbed only 65 per cent of this income. One-fifth of all households barely managed to subsist, and one-third found it impossible to accumulate any capital at all. The reason for this stratification lay in the method of dividing the catch and remunerating the fishermen.

As appears to be near-universal fishing practice, the catch was divided into `shares´, in this case accruing to the equipment (lures, nets and boats) as well as to labour. In the large fishing units, the share of the total catch that was divided among the equipment employed, varied from 30 to 60 per cent. Of the 70 to 40 per cent divided among the 40-odd crewmen, the lion´s share went to the juru selam as leader of the group for his fish-finding and managerial skills. Smaller shares went to the captains of the co-operating boats, including the carrier boat and the `catcher´ or debt-collector, and the net-boss. Roughly one-third of the total remained to be shared among the ordinary crewmen, each of whose earnings, after the free daily fish ration for household consumption had been distributed, came to roughly 1.5 per cent of the total catch. In contrast, the juru selam could expect to take home one-third of the catch from his shares in the boats and nets plus his rewards for his labour skills.

Although it was possible to hire boats and nets on a long-term basis, the hire charges ran between half and two-thirds of the total catch, or required that the catch be sold

42

to the lessor at below-market prices. Trying to break into the
slow spiral of accumulation through hiring equipment, then,
worked only if catches were consistently excellent. No-one
would sell equipment on credit to poor fishermen. Mobilising
capital by throwing a feast, to which others contributed both
food and cash, was likewise closed to those who were deemed
unlikely to meet the long-term obligations so incurred.

The system therefore reproduced itself, even though there
were no hereditary or skill-based `classes´. Indeed, the rules
of Islamic inheritance militated against the transmission of
wealth between the generations, instead sharing a man´s wealth
in equal portions among all of his sons and giving half-shares
to each of his daughters. Notwithstanding such redistributive
mechanisms, a clear distinction existed between owners and
non-owners of capital goods in this fishery. This `class´
distinction overlapped the ethnic distinction between Chinese
and Malays, for even where the Chinese were not fishermen
themselves, it was their capital that underpinned production
as well as the regional fish trade.

In assessing the Kelantan fishery, Firth suggested that
some fairly simple improvements would help to increase productivity, though they might also reinforce these class distinctions. Nylon nets to replace those made from natural fibres;
outboard motors instead of sail and paddles; refrigeration and
icing facilities would all help to catch more, preserve the
fish and get them to the market faster and in better condition. Over the next two decades, all of these improvements
were rapidly adopted, with financial assistance from the
government for their purchase. While they indeed helped to
raise output, they also had the inevitable effects of increasing both the costs of fishing and the dependence of the
local fishermen on outside resources in the form of fuel and
imported equipment. By upgrading their fishing techniques,
Malay fishermen became even more closely tied into external
economies than they had been before, even though their fishery
was not `industrialised´ in the way that North Atlantic fish-
eries were at roughly the same time.

Cod-fishing in the Norwegian fjords, for example, traditionally used 20-foot boats, about half the length of those of
the Malayan offshore fishermen, and until some fifty years ago
none was motorised. But cod-fishing on the offshore banks,
like fishing for herring and other pelagic species, required
much larger boats with more powerful engines and mechanised
winches for hauling in the seine nets, as well as on-board
refrigeration to preserve large quantities of fish, and suitable offloading facilities in deep harbours. Deep-sea fishing
thus became extremely capital-intensive, relying on fleets

rather than individual boats, and often co-ordinated from the accompanying factory ship or from a shore base which processed incoming and constantly changing information on fish localities. Both fish finding (using sonar) and the co-ordination of information is today often computerised, and individual boat owners are under unavoidable pressure either to form co-operatives or to be bought out by larger fishing companies. Given the traditions of independence among fishermen of the North Atlantic countries and islands, this pressure is often greatly resented, for the bureaucratisation of `industrial´ fishing changes the relationships among the fishermen themselves. Under these circumstances, fishing co-operatives have become very important in Scandinavia, Iceland and the Faroe Islands, because they have enabled individual boat ownership and older productive relationships to be combined with economies of scale. There has been a steady demand for medium-sized fishing boats, even though governments have subsidised larger ones, and the fisheries in these countries have generally been healthy. (We will examine the contrasting situation of fishing in Newfoundland, Eastern Canada, later.)

As Barth (1966) has described, the relationships between skipper and crew on individual Norwegian herring boats were very complex. The skipper, who hired his crewmen individually for the two-month herring season in winter, in theory exercised absolute control over the enterprise, having sole responsibility for directing the large (100- to 150-foot) `mother ship´ to a herring shoal. Once a shoal had been located, the net-boss assumed individual responsibility for netting as many of the herring as possible, directing the `throw´ of the purse-seine net from his two smaller casting boats. At all times, the labour of the 20 or so fishermen was under the complete control either of the skipper or of the net-boss. Notwithstanding this hierarchy of command, however, the crew were to be found at all hours of the day and night on the ship´s bridge, normally the exclusive preserve of a ship´s captain or his deputy, collecting, sifting and discussing the incoming information on the hunt as if they were all skippers!

Barth explains this unusual shipboard behaviour as the outcome of the `bargaining relation´ between herring skippers and their hand-picked crew who were rewarded with a share in the catch. Their interdependence in a physically and financially risky hunt on board a privately-owned boat militated against formal relations of command, in favour of relations of trust, without which the whole enterprise could founder on interpersonal antagonisms. It is precisely such relations of trust that are undermined in the way production is organised in fully industrialised fishing enterprises, by the permanent employment of crews within a bureaucratically-organised fleet.

Deep-sea trawling by securely-capitalised companies was the Newfoundland government's preferred solution to the plight of its `outport´ communities after its confederation with Canada in 1949. These numerous small, isolated hamlets had been founded by the British sailors who `jumped ship´ from the sixteenth century onwards and who settled in the most inaccessible places they could find in order to evade recapture. Their economy was based on summer cod fishing and subsistence cultivation. The cod was salted and marketed through companies which ensured the ongoing indebtedness of the fishermen whose families processed their catches. The decline of the salt-fish trade in the twentieth century was related to the growth of the market for frozen and tinned fish from 8 to 40 per cent of the world total between 1950 and 1980. Internationally, the proportion of cured fish declined from 34 to 11 per cent in the same period, and Newfoundland salt-fish suffered from this change in consumer tastes.

Cod and other fish species were caught using small boats (`dories´ and trapskiffs), gillnets and traps in the inshore fishery. In the 1960s, few fishermen upgraded their boats to `longliners´ or used electronic aids to navigation or fish-finding, despite government subsidies to certain types of fishing capital (larger boats, nylon gillnets and seine- or ring-nets, and longlines). Co-operatives made no headway in the outports, and the trawling companies had considerable difficulty in recruiting fishermen to their deep-sea vacancies, despite high rates of unemployment. The fishermen themselves suffered the public image of hide-bound traditionalists sponging off the welfare state by `fishing for stamps´ (that is, producing enough - and no more - in summer to qualify for unemployment payments during the winter, when no inshore fishing was possible).

Brox (1972) has argued that all of these problems revolved around the inadequate prices paid for fish landed by whatever means. In the 1960s, Newfoundland prices were a little over one-quarter of those paid to Norwegian fishermen, and were set primarily with the US mass market in mind. The returns to the fishermen were fundamentally inadequate to allow capitalisation of their production, even with external subsidies. Hence the Newfoundland fishery remained, in contrast to its other North Atlantic competitors, essentially unviable, repeating its old problem of the salt-fish trade whose transport costs were so high that the product was uncompetitive on the much more profitable European markets.

*   *   *   *

In these examples of hunting, pastoral and fishing economies, the theme of the negative effects of external dependency is almost a litany. In entering into relationships with the outside world and the international economy, these systems of production have been undermined in many ways. They have lost labour to alternative jobs, endangering the viability of traditional production units. They have modernised their technologies and become dependent on external sources of energy and external markets. In becoming subject to international pricing, the returns to labour expended have often been eroded so far as to threaten the continued viability of production based on the new technology. Those who have remained within the traditional relations of production have been stigmatised as backward, conservative, dying species. Even those who have adapted their traditional technology and productive organisation reasonably successfully to the demands of external markets and authorities, have not been fully incorporated into the mainstream of their national societies. Both the economies and the societies of these people have been increasingly relegated to the margins of the international system. As previously independent systems, they have been undermined more radically than sedentary agricultural economies which have also been drawn into new relationships with the outside world over the past one and a half centuries.

CHAPTER THREE

RELATIONS OF PRODUCTION IN PEASANT AND COMMERCIAL AGRICULTURE

Most evolutionary perspectives on social and technical change regard settled or sedentary agriculture as the turning point in the cultural history of man. Settled agriculture generates a surplus which may be invested in aesthetic pursuits, in the support of socio-political stratification and `leisured´ and administrative classes, in the growth of knowledge through philosophy and science. All three patterns increase socio-cultural complexity through their differentiation of activity. The labour theory of value and marxist approaches based on it characterise this turning point as the planned investment of human labour on the land in order to reap a relatively assured future return, in which land becomes the object or instrument of labour.

Land as `Object of Labour´

Neo-marxists such as Meillassoux (1981) as well as cultural ecologists such as Rappaport (1968) have pushed this idea beyond simple preparation of the land and retention of seed for the next crop, to examine the issues of the total energy required for population growth, including the support of non-workers (children, the elderly and disabled and so on) in a system of production, distribution and consumption that must extend over generations rather than merely years. In economies based on an unsophisticated technology, this process of growth, resting as it does on the capacity to guarantee the caloric energy requirements of an expanding population, is constrained by low-yielding seed varieties that on planting generally do not treble their own mass, and by storage facilities that waste 30 per cent or more of the total harvest, through losses to insects, rodents, fungi and general deterioration.

The extent to which labour may be required to achieve an equilibrium between resource base and population has been graphically described by Netting (1981) for a Swiss alpine village in a remote valley. The production system in Torbel has always been constrained by its altitude (1500 metres), the climate (winter snow and short summers), and its mountainous topography. Over some 800 years of its recorded history, Torbel´s production rested on manual labour and local self-reliance. Only recently has some mechanised equipment (hay-cutters and motorised carts) eased the burden of human labour. People constructed and still maintain the irrigation canals,

47

cleaning and repairing them every spring, diverting the irrigation water to the hay meadows, patrolling on foot 10 kilometres of waterway every day. People guarded their soil against loss by erosion, building and repairing stone terraces and transporting washed-out dirt from the bottom to the top of the field by shovel and mule each spring. People collected conifer needles, moss, leaves and humus from the forest to supplement the inadequate supply of grain straw for animal bedding in winter, in order to maximise manure applications to the soil. Both men and women repaired the meadows every year, raking up fallen twigs, draining and filling in soil cavities, and repairing pathways, fencing and terracing. And these were merely the preparatory activities. Tilling the grain and potato fields, the gardens and the vines came later, as did herding the livestock between pastures in summer and mucking out their quarters in winter, making hay for the wintering of the livestock, milking, making cheese, preserving meat, and keeping the home going. By the 1970s, only mowing, hay baling, milking and transport had benefitted from mechanisation, thus enabling a decreasing number of full-time farmers in a declining population to continue farming the products best suited to this environment.

Under such circumstances, redistribution either of labour from those households with a surplus to those deficient in labour, or of part of the product from its producers to those consumers who produce less than they themselves need, assumes great importance. The mechanisms by which this redistribution is effected are many and varied. They range from standard ways of dividing the trophy of the hunt to feasting at the expense of `big men´. The exchange of gifts is basic to most of these mechanisms, while exchanges of labour tend to be more specific: both are considered in detail in chapter 5 of this text.

Fundamental to any understanding of how such redistribution works, however, are the issues of who is permitted to exploit what resources under which conditions: the issues of ownership of, control over and access to the means of production. While these issues might appear fairly straightforward if we assume that `the history of all hitherto existing society is the history of class struggles´ (Marx and Engels 1848/1972:335), a problem arises for those societies that marxists classify as `prehistoric´ or `preclass´. By marxist definition (based largely on the work of the nineteenth-century American anthropologist, Lewis Henry Morgan), preclass or `gentile´ societies are characterised by communal ownership of the means of production and collectivised responsibility for consumption. But this evolutionist assumption is in fact an oversimplification of empirical reality, at least in the twentieth century, as a review of African systems of

48

land tenure readily reveals. Furthermore, the ownership and control of relatively `high-tech´ equipment, such as draught animals and tractors, and of storage, processing and marketing facilities, may be quite as important as access to land in the contemporary process of rural class formation, whereby some grow wealthier than others, in part by exploiting the labour of others for their own production, and in part by appropriating a share of the value of others´ products.

Land Tenure and Land Rights

It is necessary to distinguish the different rights which individuals or groups may hold in land, from the descriptions of tenurial systems as a whole. In Africa, tenurial systems have often been glossed as `communal´ or community-based, whereas in fact they have individualised rights of use, or usufruct. It is also important to note that tenurial systems are not static: they change over time. For example, fully individualised control of virgin land by the person who cleared it for the first time, may change into a system of joint ownership and lineage control in two or three generations´ time. Or an ostensibly `communal´ system may be individualised by the growth of a land market in that society, under the impact of land scarcity and/or new economic opportunities.

Furthermore, both ecology and investment also seem to influence land tenure. There are some alluvial areas of natural fertility in the great African river basins, such as the Zambezi, where for example the Tonga river gardens were individually owned and inherited. In other areas, as among the Kofyar of the Jos plateau in Nigeria, or the MaTengo of Tanzania, labour and/or capital have been invested in terracing and deep manuring hill slopes to make infertile lands productive, often under circumstances of external aggression. Such lands have tended to be individualised in perpetuity in their patterns of ownership and control.

In certain parts of Africa, then, concepts of rights to land approached quite closely those of western countries, where `ownership´ implies full rights of control, use and disposal (including by sale, lease or mortgage) of property, mitigated only by the residual over-rights of the state to claim land for public use in return for market-based compensation. But generally the concept of `ownership´ in precolonial African societies had much more limited connotations of specific usufructuary control, which is why tenurial systems were so frequently misperceived as `communal´. At least three very different tenurial systems have fallen under this rubric, so I shall start by distinguishing between tenurial control based on political authority, kinship, and spatial contiguity, which generated `feudal´, `lineage´, and `village´ systems of tenure respectively.

Ethiopia before the 1974 revolution had a very complex system of land tenure and has been regarded as an example of `feudal´ tenure with reference to its <u>gult</u> system, though I am ignoring here the many other interconnected systems by which kin groups, villages, individuals, the church and the state also held rights to land. It was the <u>gult</u> system that led to the 1975 land reform in which all land was taken into state ownership, but control of agricultural land was devolved upon the peasant associations. In the <u>gult</u> system, tributary rights to land were devolved upon individual or corporate administrators (the Orthodox church was an example of the latter) by the monarch. In return for collecting taxes on behalf of the state, these <u>gult</u>-holders were supported by part of this revenue derived from peasants working `their´ land. <u>Gult</u> fiefs could be withdrawn by the monarch, and could not be disposed of by their holders, although they often became hereditary, as <u>rist gult</u> holdings, within the families of aristocrats and influential clerics. Whether or not the Ethiopian <u>gult</u> system and similar systems in the interlacustrine monarchies of East Africa (Buganda, Bunyoro, Toro and others), are identical to mediaeval European fiefdoms, they have been described as examples of `feudal´ land ownership, since they depended on politico-administrative endowment from the monarch, while others held rights of usufruct to the land concerned.

`Lineage´-based tenurial systems are most common in West Africa, but their ambiguity is perhaps best revealed by the Gikuyu of Kenya. Kenyatta (1938:21) argued very strongly that `every inch of land within [Gikuyu territory] had its owner´, but not everyone would accept his characterisation of <u>mbari</u> (or `family´) land as individualised. Kenyatta begins with the territorial expansion of the Gikuyu in the mythical past, which involved their individual purchases of land from the neighbouring Ndorobo (who as hunters had little use for agricultural land), as well as the clearing of virgin bush for cultivation. Both purchase and clearing established full individual control over that land. The problem started with the death of the original owner and the inheritance of the land by all of his sons jointly and equally. When this happened, the eldest son became <u>moramati</u>, or trustee of the interests of the whole sibling group, although his own portion of the inherited land was no bigger than those of his brothers, he could not dispose of it without consulting them and offering them first option on it, and he could do nothing concerning the land as a whole without their knowledge and consent. Inherited land could be sold, by individual heirs

50

with the consent of their joint owners, or by the sibling group as a unit, but Kenyatta notes that the elders brought moral pressure to bear on any owner who jeopardised the rights of future generations by so doing. Although the local kiama (council of elders) had no authority to prevent land transfers, this moral pressure suggests some community involvement, however informal, in the land rights of individuals.

By the time the second division by inheritance occurred, control of the Gikuyu mbari land had become very complex, for Kenyatta's description suggests that there would, at that point, have been a plurality of moramatis deriving from each of the original inheriting sons, not merely one. Perhaps it was at this point that the elders were called in to divide the land formally, to re-individualise rights to it among the numerous heirs, in a boundary-marking ritual. The descriptions by non-Gikuyu, in contrast to Kenyatta's, emphasise that mbari land was lineage land, to which all male patrikin had rights, but they do not speak to this matter of re-individualising `family´ land.

Even if we examine subordinate methods of acquiring land in an attempt to sort out whether or not the Gikuyu system was `communal´ in the way the white Kenyan settlers assumed, the pattern is unclear. Land-owners could certainly lease portions of their land to tenants, as ahoi, who obtained cultivation rights in exchange for payment in kind (notably alcohol); or as athami, who gained both cultivation and residence rights. Affines (athoni) and adoptees (aciarwa) could also be allocated portions of land by individual holders, though all of these allocations had to be approved collectively by the owners of the mbari land. So the Gikuyu illustrate rather well the problem of determining the precise status of African systems of land tenure, as do the Ibo of Eastern Nigeria, whose landholding system, unlike that of the Gikuyu, was not materially affected by the intrusion of white agricultural settlers.

The patrilineal Ibo illustrate village-based systems of land tenure. They live in villages which are aggregated into village groups, each of which was formerly autonomous under the political control of a village council, composed of all adult men but dominated by those holding the most important village titles. At the spatial centre of the village group is the public meeting place, where the council met to make its decisions about village affairs, including land use.

Jones (1949) has described Ibo landholding as it was some two generations ago, but the basic principles are unlikely to have changed in the intervening forty years. Ibo villages

51

tended to grow in three phases, though it is probable that today all villages have reached the third and last phase and are hampered in their tendency to repeat the cycle by the acute land shortage. Outmigration to other, less densely populated parts of Nigeria predated the civil war of the 1960s, the casualties of which could have eased the position only marginally.

In the phase of colonisation, when the population density at less than 250 people per square mile was relatively low and land was relatively freely available, new land could still be brought under cultivation. As the population increased four-fold and all usable land came under cultivation, the village passed through its consolidation period, before disintegrating through emigration caused by agricultural population densities of up to 2,000 per square mile. In this final phase, land parcels were fragmented by inheritance to miniscule proportions, as small as 10 x 8 yards. As the Ibo village went through these three phases, the rights of individual men to residential and arable land changed. (In general, Ibo women did not hold land in their own right, though daughters occasionally inherited land if a family had no sons.)

In the colonisation phase, the residential `houseland´ formed the centre of the village land, and was used to plant permanent tree-crops (mainly palms for wine and oil) as well as for building houses. In this phase, the houseland was under the complete control of individual household heads. As in many other parts of West Africa, the `owners´ of such land could pledge, mortgage or sell it outright, even to strangers, without so much as consulting the village council. To all intents and purposes, then, within the traditional framework of Ibo land tenure, the houseland during the colonisation phase was `owned´ in the western sense.

In contrast, during the same phase, the arable `farmland´ surrounding the houseland was completely controlled by the village council. All households within the village had a right to use part of the farmland to produce seasonal crops, but the village council determined from one season to the next exactly which land would be used by which household, what portion of the total farmland would be fallowed, and what crops would be grown where. This system retained absolute control of cropping as well as the cropland in the hands of the village council, and prevented individual households from developing any long-term identification with a particular portion of the village farmland. In this phase, the council was quite happy to allow strangers the same rights as villagers to cultivate farmland, even if they lived elsewhere.

In the colonisation phase of Ibo village growth, then, we might be tempted to typify houseland tenure as `individual´ and farmland tenure as `communal´, within one total system. But these systems of access changed, as land became less available as the population increased. Firstly, as more people required housing, the houseland ate into the arable farmland in the typical pattern of urban development everywhere, and by the final stage of disintegration, there was no farmland left. We might then be tempted to think that this example merely supports capitalist notions of the individualisation of ownership under circumstances of increasing competition, as the `communal´ system of the first phase disappeared and was replaced by expanding individualised ownership.

But such thinking would be contradicted by the fact that, as the population increased, the village council took more and more control over the conditions of tenure of houseland. The first step was to bar new strangers from access to both farmland and houseland, without necessarily ejecting those already within the system. Then the village council restricted the previously unfettered rights of individuals to dispose of their houseland, requiring all proposed transfers of ownership to be approved by the council. Finally, in the disintegration phase, the only method of disposal that the council permitted was the devolution of houseland by inheritance equally to all sons of the family. Not even brothers could transfer the ownership of houseland among themselves. While `communally´ owned farmland disappeared, then, `individually´ owned houseland became subject to community control.

We can understand this pattern of development only by comprehending the Ibo principles on which all land use rested. Each of these three principles was stressed differently in the different phases of village growth. In the colonising phase, the basic principle that ultimately all land belonged to the village group was stressed with respect to the farmland, but ignored for the houseland in favour of the second principle, that each member of the village as a political community, whether resident or not, should have personal security of access to and holding of land for residential and productive purposes. This second principle was overridden at a later stage by the first principle, in order to satisfy the third injunction, that no village resident might be denied land for subsistence when required.

Before assuming that the Ibo example has a specifically African cultural flavour, let us compare it with the Swiss alpine village of Torbel, mentioned earlier, in which there was a similar co-existence of individually- and communally-owned land. (Netting (1981:63) has indeed argued that this

53

situation is characteristic of all food-producing economies.)
Although in Torbel practically all the land that was used
intensively was owned by individuals in multiply-fragmented
parcels, Torbel had regarded itself as a __bauernzunft__ or
`peasant corporation´ as early as the thirteenth century,
buying both tithes and land as a community and ruling on the
conditions under which its inhabitants could use its cor-
porately-owned alpine grazing, forests and waste lands. Like
the Ibo village council, the Torbel `peasant corporation´
reserved to itself the right to grant to strangers usufructuary rights to its commonly-owned property. It also restricted
the use of alpine grazing in summer to the number of cattle
that a household could feed through the subsequent winter,
thus, like the Ibo control of cropping, ensuring that commonly-owned resources would not be overused by individuals
seeking private gain, in this case by overgrazing summer
pastures with livestock to be sold in the autumn. Breaches of
these regulations were punishable by the community. As Netting
(1981:62) noted:

> The people of Torbel had both the will and the power to
> institute their own binding regulations... The fact that
> their rules met practical needs and were tailored to the
> characteristics of the community´s own environment and
> population accounts for the long-continued observance of
> many of the code´s provisions.´

In seeking to understand any system of land tenure, then,
a useful place to start is with the political community which,
in the widest sense, `owns´ the land falling within its
boundaries. Where in precolonial African societies the polity
was centralised, in a monarchy or equivalent, the king or
chief was conceptualised as the ultimate `owner of the land´
(and often livestock as well), as in Ethiopia, among the Lozi
of Western Zambia, the Tutsi of Rwanda, the Swazi, and many
others. This ultimate __political__ right to the land, as representative of the nation, was never exercised as a __usufructuary__
right. Monarchs and chiefs never (voluntarily) worked the land
themselves, not even the fields designated as their individual
holdings. These were tilled by the monarch´s wives and his
subjects, as a form of labour tax.

Instead, the political `owners´ of the land delegated
authority over it to those whom Gluckman (1965:40), with
specific reference to the Lozi, has called `primary´ right-
holders, those administrative subordinates (usually village
heads) who actually allocated the land for the purposes of
cultivation. In turn, these primary right-holders devolved
responsibility for particular portions of land to `secondary´
right-holders, usually household heads. They often disaggre-
gated the land still further, and allocated specific plots to

`tertiary´ holders, including their wives, married sons and other adult dependants, who actually worked the land.

I personally find Gluckman´s three-tier system, of primary and secondary rights based on `estates of administration´ and tertiary rights vesting in the `estate of production´, rather confusing. As pressure on the land increased during the colonial period, as a result of enforced sedentarisation and increased populations, so the village headman´s `primary´ rights in his `estate of administration´ tended to lapse. Scarce land in overpopulated villages in sub-Saharan Africa is often no longer under the <u>de facto</u> control of the headman, even where his office continues to exist and gives him <u>de jure</u> control. Instead, heads of household have come to exercise rights over their land in perpetuity, often in exchange for a material consideration paid to the headman when their rights in that land were first confirmed. These rights are then inherited, even when that culture gives the headman the normative right to reallocate to others the usufruct of this land on the holder´s death. In many African countries, including Tanzania and Zimbabwe, these `primary´ rights to land of the headman´s `estate of administration´, where they existed, have formally been destroyed by legal and administrative changes, and land allocation has become the responsibility of village committees, which are responsible to the state rather than to the local community. (To what extent these new allocating authorities have actually displaced traditional ones is a moot point.)

In contrast to Gluckman, therefore, today I find it more useful to regard those who receive usufructuary rights formally from an allocating authority, as primary rightholders with primary responsibilities (for land conservation, for example); and those to whom they in turn make essentially temporary allocations, as holding `secondary´ or informal rights to that land. Whatever terminology is adopted, however, it should be quite clear that individual rights of cultivation are located at the end of a chain of rights: they nest within other rights. The wife´s garden is part of her husband´s allocation from the headman or village committee, representing the broadest rights of the traditional monarch or the contemporary state to that land.

Furthermore, these vertically-related rights of cultivation are complicated by other claims to use the land which come from within the local community. In Shona society, for example, everyone had the right to use public pathways, springs and wild fruit trees, whether or not they were located on land to which individuals had cultivation rights. Among the Gikuyu, salt licks may be added to this list of public

facilities or `rights of avail´. Rights to depasture live-
stock, to build homes, to mine the land for minerals, to hunt,
to gather wild products, to fish, and to bury the dead, also
involved the use of land, often in confict with but sometimes
complementary to its use for growing crops. All of these
different usufructuary rights must be considered in relation
to one another if the tenurial system is to be fully
understood.

Land Sales and the Commercialisation of Agriculture

`Communal´ patterns of tenure have generally protected
individual rights of usufruct through membership of a wider
community, whether this was based on kinship or territory.
This very protection of access to the means of subsistence was
seen by white settlers and colonial authorities in Africa as
detracting from agricultural `modernisation´ and `development´
by protecting the idle, incompetent and conservative elements
of local society. New systems of individualised tenure were
introduced, ostensibly to motivate the `progressive´ farmers
and encourage production for international markets. The myth
of `communal´ tenure was also used to justify the transfer of
land to people who were expected `to use it properly´. Yet
this move was perhaps misplaced, because all over this
continent, for at least a century, chiefs as the custodians of
community-based systems of tenure, have been selling land to
outsiders, whether to the trekking Afrikaners moving north
from the Southern Cape, or to the indigenous cocoa entrepreneurs of West Africa. Retrospectively, these cases have
been characterised as non-sales, as cross-cultural misunder-
standings. In this view, chiefs were supposed merely to have
allocated usufructuary rights in return for tokens of esteem
and appreciation, while purchasers thought - quite wrongly -
that they were getting the equivalent of freehold title.
Certainly in some areas, such as Akim Abuakwa, strangers
obtained land from Ghanaian chiefs in return for two-thirds of
the cocoa crop when their trees came into full bearing. This
arrangement does suggest that chiefs wished to retain a long-
term interest in the product of, if not control of, the land,
through sharecropping, but does not necessarily imply that
they were not prepared to dispose of it. The argument of
`invalid´ alienation, of course, has provided a legal as well
as a moral justification for claiming back that land on behalf
of its original `owners´.

However, an alternative view, which is supported by at
least some nineteenth- and twentieth-century examples, might
see such sales as confirming the extent to which `estates of
administration´ had the right to control the land itself as

56

opposed to its usufruct. Kenyatta (1938) has depicted the Gikuyu acquisition of Ndorobo land in the mythical past as a result of individual purchase, while Feldman (1974) described a mid-twentieth century example of immigrants acquiring large tracts of land in the traditional manner from Tanzanian Hehe headmen, and then selling and leasing parts of it to later immigrants. Since Tanzania at that time did not permit a market in land as the basic means of agricultural production, such sales and leases were disguised as `compensation´ payments for labour invested on the land, for example in stumping it of tree roots in order to permit ploughing, notwithstanding the fact that its initial fertility had been eroded by some years of cultivation and had not been replenished by fertilisation. Such contemporary examples may be dismissed as the evil influence of colonial capitalism, but they do not contradict the historical information on land transactions in Africa.

If we look, for example, at the commercial cocoa farmers of Southern Ghana, Hill (1963) has identified two distinct patterns of purchase in the late nineteenth and early twentieth centuries, which are even today reflected in different patterns of landholding. On the one hand, migrant entrepreneurs from mainly patrilineal societies formed `companies´ of kinsmen and friends to buy land for commercial cocoa production. This land was then divided among the members in proportion to their contributions in cash to the company´s buying fund. This division was based on the measurement of outstretched arms (`ropes´) along the narrowest boundary. When these `strip´ farms were sub-divided by inheritance, they were again divided by `ropes´ along the narrowest boundary, thus creating on maps a very distinctive pattern of long, thin farms. (The colonial government mapped the cocoa areas in the 1950s, in order to compensate farmers for cocoa-trees suffering from swollen shoot disease, which had to be uprooted and burnt. In addition to the differences in the configuration of farms, this mapping also revealed roads and bridges which had been planned and constructed by the cocoa farmers themselves, who had hired Swiss engineers to provide the technical expertise which they themselves lacked.)

In contrast to the individualised `strip´ farms which resulted from company purchase, the `mosaic´ farms or `family lands´ were associated with matrilineal landholding. Here farmers had also bought the land to produce cocoa for the market, but on behalf of their matrilineages, not for themselves as individuals. However, although this land was owned corporately, farming was an individual affair. Lineage allocations of usufruct tended to work outwards from the centre of the land, at which community educational, health and marketing facilities were later located. Within the framework of lineage control, devolution by inheritance transmitted the individual portions of land intact to the heir (usually a younger brother or sister´s son of the deceased usufruct-holder), as trustee for the larger family unit. Some farmers from matrilineal systems owned ´strip´ farms as well as having usufructuary rights in lineage cocoa farms. They bought land individually in order to transfer it to their own children, which their customary rules of matrilineal inheritance did not permit.

These cocoa entrepreneurs of both types migrated into the forest belt from the coastal region of Ghana and bought unused land on a speculative basis from the chiefs of ethnic groups different from their own. Some of them, mainly the patrilineal Krobo, were seeking to move into a more lucrative crop than the palm-oil they had earlier sold to ´the soap-boilers of Africa´ (Lever Brothers), because the price of palm-oil had fallen in the 1880s. It was the traditional Krobo huza, incidentally, that provided the model for the cocoa ´company´, which disintegrated after it had bought the land. Cocoa had first been introduced to Ghana early in the nineteenth century. Experimental production was started by the Basel missionaries in 1843, and the first companies bought land in 1892, the year before Ghana first began to export cocoa. By 1914, exports exceeded 50,000 tons, which Hill attributes mainly to the commercial growers. For forty-odd years, from 1911, Ghana was the world´s leading cocoa producer. By the 1950s, however, Hill estimated that only a quarter of all the cocoa came from the commercial producers described above, while the remainder came from small peasants producing it as a sideline cash-crop. The commercial growers reinvested their profits first in expanding their landholdings and in the development of a transport infrastructure to get the crop to the coastal ports. Only later did they construct community facilities in the ´family lands´ and invest in housing in their home towns.

Hill regarded the cocoa entrepreneurs as ´creative capitalists´, very rapidly taking advantage of changing opportunities on international commodity markets, within organisational frameworks based on tradition but permitting individual enterprise and profit. The price of land rose with cocoa production, as people experienced cocoa farming as a new route to wealth; and unlike the Ibo example discussed earlier, no community control protected the less successful from losing their land by sale to the expanding entrepreneurs. The market for land was long-established in the customs of Southern Ghana, and was not distorted by white immigration as happened in East, Central and Southern Africa. In any terms, then, it is difficult to classify these cocoa farmers as ´precapital-

ist´, but one should also ask whether their ownership of land
and involvement with the international market in cocoa, or
even their hiring of labour to produce it, made them `capital-
ists´ in Marx´s sense?

The question of whether the ownership of land, as the
most important means of agricultural production, in itself
creates classes, is one to which Marx in fact gave no clear
answer. However, his treatment of land ownership in the
ancient Mediterranean city-states and in barbaric Europe,
suggests not, since he constructed the relations of production
in these systems on different foundations (notably on
citizenship and political rights). Even in feudal Europe the
relations of production differentiated politico-legal ownership of the land by the aristocracy, from the customary rights
of virtually inalienable usufruct held by both free peasants
and serfs, which in Marx´s (1867/1976) view were finally
destroyed by the state (in the UK, through the enclosure acts
and conversion to individual ownership of the Scottish clan
lands), rather than by direct class predation by existing
feudal landowners.

In twentieth-century Africa, the gap between the ownership and use of land producing cash crops may be substantially
less than in feudal Britain, as the Ghanaian example suggests.
However, this gap still exists to some extent. In the black
freehold areas of Zimbabwe, which originated in 1930 in
legislation seeking to control the growth of landownership by
blacks, only one owner was permitted in law and the fragmenta-
tion of land parcels through inheritance was strictly controlled during the colonial period. Nonetheless, by the mid-1970s
more than half of the farms in one freehold area, Msengezi,
accommodated people who were tilling portions of the owner´s
land for subsistance and very small crop sales. As a result of
refugee migration during the liberation war, by 1981 this
figure had risen to three-quarters (Cheater 1982, 1984). In
absolute terms, 652 people other than the 329 farm owners had
acquired informal, and strictly speaking illegal, usufructuary
rights to arable land on these farms, while 157 cattle-owners
enjoyed grazing usufruct for their livestock (Cheater 1983).

There was a clear gap in output between the land-owners
producing commercially, and those who tilled small portions of
their land for subsistance; but at the same time, these
allocations meant that even the legally landless actually had
access to the use of the land. `Relations of production´
constructed purely on the basis of land ownership, then, would
be very misleading in this freehold area as in many other
parts of Africa where customary tenures still prevail, for
these rights cannot be fully comprehended within the framework

of either leasehold or sharecropping. A small minority of those who acquired such informal usufructuary rights were hired workers, while the vast majority were relatives and in-laws of the owners. With a handful of exceptions, none paid any form of rent for this land. The colonial government regarded them all as `squatters´, while not all of the farm owners themselves were enthusiastic about acting charitably towards kin in need. Allocating land to these cultivators, after all, had an opportunity cost in the sense that those who actually owned the land could not use it themselves. In commercial production, such opportunities foregone may be substantial, but where no rent is charged, they may also be at least partly counter-balanced by labour contributions to the land-owner´s own production, and by the social merit which results from meeting (however reluctantly) the obligations of kinship or affinity. One might, of course, regard this as a system of labour-rent, except that it enjoined no <u>specific</u> labour obligation. One might, perhaps, regard it as a form of sharecropping, except that the land-owner received nothing of the land-user´s output.

Sharecropping is normally defined as the combination of factors of production (usually land, implements, inputs and labour) from different individuals for the purpose of specific production. The output is shared among the contributing parties in mutually agreed proportions, which usually return to the provider of labour between one-third and two-thirds of the total. Such `sharecropping´ is also found among fishermen (as we have seen in Malaya and Norway) and pastoralists (where stockless herders receive some of the offspring of the animals they tend), as well as cultivators. Sharecropping is extremely widespread in precapitalist economies.

As Robertson (1980) has indicated, sharecropping often links kin and affines in productive relationships, and may be defended most vigorously by those who supply labour. Robertson (1980:420) has also noted that `to be labourless is as much a disadvantage in [agricultural] production, and just as stig-matic, as to be landless´. On Ghanaian cocoa farms, for example, the bargaining power of labour was seen in the ability of the sharecropper or <u>abusa</u> worker to negotiate his share up from one-third to one-half on old farms with declining yields and elderly owners bereft of other labour. In such relatively egalitarian contexts, the flexibility and `social efficiency´ of share contracts makes it particularly inappropriate to regard sharecropping as a method of appro-priating surplus which bridges the transition between feudal and capitalist relations of production.

For example, in Ghana there has been a progressive

sequence of hiring labour on cocoa farms. On new cocoa farms established for less than five years, on which the trees have not started bearing, owners have tended to hire casual labour on a daily basis. When bearing starts, to supplement the annual contract workers, seasonal workers may be hired for weeding or picking, with their remuneration sometimes calculated on a share per bag varying between one-fifth and one-third of the total and regarded as greatly inferior to abusa proper. But in the 1960s, on mature cocoa farms of twelve years or older, most permanent workers were abusa sharecroppers taking one-third of the crop. Hill noted in the 1950s that two-thirds of all owners of cocoa land were involved in the abusa system, which they tended to see as a form of hiring labour, in contrast to the workers´ interpretation of it as a form of leasing land. Half (abunu) and quarter (abunan) shares were much less common than ´thirds´, the former being found on low-yielding young or old farms, the latter on mature farms.

Robertson (1982) noted that sharecropping on the cocoa farms had important social as well as economic implications, which helped to explain its popularity. While some sharecroppers were strangers from Northern Ghana, many were young southerners, related to the owner as sister´s son and matrilineal heir; or as son. In such cases the sharecropping arrangement often preceded and in a sense validated the transfer of ownership of the land to the son before the father died, in order to sidestep the normal pattern of matrilineal inheritance. Under such circumstances, to define sharecropping as detrimental to the interests of those who contribute labour, and favouring the landowners, is to miss some of the most important long-term aspects of the total relationship.

Which brings us back to issues of interpretation that are of particular significance when it is proposed to change the relations of production by altering the patterns of ownership of the land.

Land Reform and Resettlement

If, indeed, the landless are exploited by those who own land, it makes sense in welfare terms to guarantee them access to land under less-exploitative conditions. That is what numerous examples of land reform have tried to do, with varying degrees of success. On the whole, the greatest successes have been scored by the more radical reforms, though these have not been without their costs in terms of low productivity. If we look at China, for example, where landlessness in the pre-liberation era caused enormous rural suffering, we can readily understand why Mao´s government moved very quickly from the simple redistribution of land under the existing conditions of its ownership and control by the chia (what Fei (1939:28) calls the `expanded family´, but which corresponds better empirically to the independent household), to a form of collectivisation that destroyed the identification of particular households with particular portions of land. Unlike the Union of Soviet Socialist Republics, the People´s Republic of China did not nationalise village land. Instead it confirmed collective ownership at the xiang or `administrative´ village level of all land falling within the village boundaries. To this extent, the collectivisation of land in China resembled that of the traditional Ibo system described earlier, and achieved much the same objectives. The post-1978 structural reforms have not changed this pattern of ownership, but they have contracted usufructuary control of the land to individual households, the constituent units of the traditional chia, in order to boost agricultural output. (Output was depressed, during the two decades of fully collectivised production, by state policies on the procurement of `commodity grain´, as well as by the impaired motivation of individual peasants which resulted from the actual organisation of labour in production.)

The impact of land reform in China is best seen at the level of a specific case study, the village of Kaixian´gong, which has been the focus of anthropological interest since Fei Xiao-Dong´s original fieldwork there in 1936. Kaixian´gong lies in the `heartland´ of China, 100 kilometres west of Shanghai as the crow flies. By the 1980s, it produced four silk-cocoon crops and grew three grain crops each year. Since the `responsibility system´ handed production decisions back to the household level, around 1981, Kaixian´gong has been able to feed its own population and meet its state procurement quotas, and to sell its surplus grain and fish on the more distant free markets in Wujiang county and the city of Suzhou.

Kaixian´gong in the mid-1980s was a not untypical Han Chinese village. Its per capita income from collectively-distributed sources was some 30 per cent higher than the rural average, but it did not show the grossly polarising extremes of wealth that some other villages have produced since 1979. Like many other villages, the focus of its development in the 1980s was industry rather than agriculture, as the `responsibility system´ had greatly increased the productivity of agricultural labour and revealed the extent of under-employment in the collectivised system. By 1984, less than 40 per cent of all households were employed full-time in agricultural production. But although it tried in the strategy of vertical integration to build silk weaving onto its fifty-year-old history of silk production and spinning, the state monopoly

62

over silk weaving and the economic interests of the inter-
nationally-famous, state-owned Suzhou silk factories had by
then permitted the village to weave only synthetic fabrics.

In nearly 50 years, Kaixian´gong had increased its
population 1,6 times (to nearly 2,400) and its grain output
4,3 times, mainly by treble-cropping its 170-odd hectares of
land. In doubling its yields compared to its population,
Kaixian´gong´s performance was twice as good as the national
average. (However, one-third of this improvement had occurred
since 1981, when the `responsibility system´ was introduced.)
Undoubtedly its favourable location contributed substantially
to this improvement, but the impact of land reform was also
important.

In the village, as the population grew, the average
landholding per chia or household fell from 8.5 mu in 1936 to
5.5 mu in 1984 (6 mu = 1 acre). In 1936, however, Fei
(1939:192) recorded the official estimate that 75.8 per cent
of the 360 households owned less than 4 mu apiece, while a
mere 2.2 per cent owned 15 mu (= 1 hectare) or more. In the
context of this unequal distribution, it is not surprising
that a quarter of all value produced then went to external
appropriations, notably rent and tax. Yet while the land
reform of 1949-52 evened out landholding, thus providing an
improvement in household subsistance, state appropriations
after 1949 actually rose above 25 per cent, to a peak of 40
per cent in the late 1950s (when a generation disappeared from
this village) but falling off to 33 per cent in 1984. After
the `responsibility system´ was implemented, external appro-
priations increasingly took the form of taxes and levies,
rather than grain procurement, but statutory procurement of
all silk yarn still occurred at non-negotiable prices set by
the state.

In the Chinese case, then, although the land reform
itself, in conjunction with agricultural intensification, was
fairly successful in raising and redistributing output, it was
to some extent offset by state appropriations. Much the same
could be said of similar changes in land tenure in the USSR.
In both of these countries, the collectivised sector of agriculture has generally been more successful than the national-
sed sector (the state farms). However, yields have compared
unfavourably with individual smallholdings in other countries,
and indeed with those from the `private plots´ allocated to
individual households in both nationalised and collectivised
farming sectors of these countries themselves. In the past, a
substantial part of household income was derived from these
plots. The contemporary structural reforms in China and the
USSR may well alter this situation in the future.

If problems of productivity and appropriation have plagued socialist land reforms, quite different problems have been characteristic of land reforms in other developing economies. In Africa, attempts have been made to change customary patterns of tenure mainly through the resettlement of people on state-owned land to which customary tenure has been legislated not to apply. Classically irrigation schemes have fallen into this category. Less frequently, as in colonial Kenya and Zimbabwe, direct assaults have been made on customary forms of tenure. In Kenya, under the Swynnerton plan and the ideological domination of Gikuyu cultural precepts, since the mid-1950s individual land parcels have been surveyed and registered, not least in an attempt to regularise the land market. In Southern Rhodesia, the Native Land Husbandry Act of 1951 tried to register arable and grazing `rights´ in what were known as the `native reserves´, largely in order that the state might be able to hold individuals accountable for their husbandry practices and ecological conservation. One of the most important effects of such changes has been to destroy secondary or informal usufructuary rights, together with the latent rights of temporary absentees, and occasionally even to encroach on existing formal or primary rights, as a Tanzanian example demonstrates.

In much the same way as states dislike nomadic pastoralists because they are so difficult to control, states also dislike dispersed patterns of settlement on agricultural land, preferring the aggregation of people in villages in the pattern described as `nucleated´. For the state seeking to develop its countryside, it is administratively and financially more convenient to provide roads, clean water supplies, electricity, schools and clinics to a single centre, than it is to service a widely-dispersed population. `Villagisation´ has therefore been a prominent policy in those countries in which farmers have traditionally preferred to live on their lands so as to avoid lengthy walks to their fields.

In Tanzania, as Kjekshus (1977) noted, this policy of concentrating the rural population dates back to the British colonial administration in the late 1940s, and was first crystallised in the 1955 Report of the Royal Commission on Land and Population in East Africa. Following independence in 1962, the Village Settlement Scheme was officially launched by President Nyerere in December of that year. It cost £2 million to settle 3,500 families on 15,000 acres in 23 separate settlements, and ran until 1966, at which point its inadequacies were recognised. However, in the 1967 Arusha Declaration, the process of nucleation provided the one element of continuity with former policies, as the government orientation changed to the ujamaa policy of self-reliance and collectivisation. In 1973, when only 14 per cent of rural Tanzanians had voluntarily moved into ujamaa villages, the ruling party (TANU) decided to enforce compliance by using the army, and to turn these villages legally into multi-purpose co-operatives. Within two years, 65 per cent of the people had been moved and, against known peasant resistance, the decision was taken to complete resettlement by the end of 1976. By 1977, the president had frankly admitted the problems of the ujamaa programme, which was finally abandoned as a policy in 1982. However, `villagisation´ (without ujamaa) has subsequently persisted as a fundamental tenet of Tanzanian policy on rural development, notwithstanding the ecological problems it has caused by aggregating people and livestock in small areas.

The local implications of villagisation have been articulated very clearly by Brain (1976), in his study of one resettlement scheme in Eastern Tanzania in 1965-6, just before the Village Settlement Scheme was abandoned. The Kutu and Luguru are neighbouring matrilineal peoples, the Luguru from the hilly region and the Kutu from the adjoining plain. Among the Kutu, clearing readily-available virgin land established individual rights to it, among men and women equally, which were not transmitted by inheritance because the land was abundant. In the Luguru hills, however, land was scarce (in part because of white settlement) and was held tenaciously by the individual men and women who had inherited it from matrikin or parents. Women had full primary rights over their land in both societies, and used it to maintain their economic independence of their menfolk. As in most matrilineal systems, divorce rates were high and were both cause and effect of the women´s economic independence.

Into this situation was introduced a dryland resettlement scheme, planned and administered by Tanzanians from patrilineal systems, who assumed that male heads of households should control productive resources. Despite the land shortage among the Luguru, little interest was generated in this scheme among either of the local societies, because of the conditions of settlement. Only married men were accepted as settlers; and when they died, their widows were expected to disappear from the scheme, since only a son might inherit the lease and no kin beyond the elementary family were permitted. Not unexpectedly, no Luguru or Kutu women who owned their lands were prepared to accompany their husbands to such a proposition and endanger their own land rights at home by their absence. Nor were the Luguru men keen to endanger their individual holdings in the hills. They much preferred to leave their wives behind to look after these and `pick up´ a Kutu divorcee in order to satisfy the scheme requirements! While such a union lasted, the woman was entitled to be paid half of the proceeds from

65

the man's holding, on the assumption that both worked an eight-hour day on the land (no account was taken of the woman's domestic labour as a contribution to the household). However, should such a `settlement marriage´ break up, the scheme administrators were not prepared to pay even that amount to the woman. Even the Kutu and Luguru men regarded the conditions of settlement as unjust, in terms of their own customs.

Although this scheme provides one of the more extreme examples of African resettlement, most such schemes have expected settlers to exchange quite good security of tenure for relative insecurity, have made no provision for the informal allocation of usufructuary rights to persons other than the nominated settler, nor absorbed people who have lost such rights, sometimes as a result of the scheme itself. It is hardly surprising, therefore, that settlement schemes have enjoyed limited popularity with those whom they were ostensibly intended to benefit and generally have not produced as much as their planners intended.

Strategies for Increasing Agricultural Production

Land, as the basic means of production in third world countries, is generally underproductive. Netting (1981:42) has identified three strategies which may be used to increase output: the intensification of existing land use, through irrigation, more efficient tillage, improved hybrid seeds and fertilisation, in what has come to be known as the `green revolution´; expansion into new lands; and socio-cultural regulation of the local ecosystem, to prevent environmental degradation and the consequent collapse of the productive system. Here I shall examine two of the possibilities for intensifying land use.

Irrigation: Enabling the Land to Yield

Because the lack of water in rainfed agriculture is one of the most obvious constraints on output, irrigation, like villagisation, has become a cornerstone of development policy in many states. Irrigation is of course indigenous to the Middle East and much of South, South-East and East Asia, with a history based on the qanats of some three millenia. Asian societies generally use the relatively inexpensive technique of canal or furrow irrigation based on gravitational flow of the water. Although most irrigation is small in scale, in aggregate the irrigated area may be enormous, like China's 45 million hectares concentrated in the east and south-east of the country. Although Africa too has its traditional, small-scale types of irrigation, based on swamp or _vlei_ cultivation (_bas-fonds_ in French) and canals fed from perennial mountain streams, it is on this continent that the world´s massive irrigation schemes (like the 750,000 hectare Gezira project in Sudan) have been sited. And although most of these schemes are canal-based, some use the `high-tech´ methods of overhead and drip irrigation. Perhaps the majority, especially of Africa´s smaller schemes, concentrate on locally-consumed food crops (particularly grains), but many of the larger ones are oriented to industrial crops: cotton on the Gezira, sugar, tea, coffee, citrus. Although they often fail in this respect, one intention of these schemes is to raise rural incomes by making agriculture more intensive, so that even those with very small holdings can improve their lives.

Irrigation, then, unlike land reform, is not intended to alter existing relations of production. Indeed, it may have the effect of reinforcing and intensifying these, rather than changing them, as Epstein´s (1962) study of two villages in Mysore state, South India, showed. In Wangala, the village fully incorporated into a newly-irrigated area, irrigation enabled growth to occur on the existing base of caste relations, partible inheritance, and domination of the main organ of local government, the village council or _panchayat_, by lineage elders whose position was hereditary. However, wives (whose work here as elsewhere in Eurasia was primarily domestic rather than productive) exploited the new marketing opportunities to earn money of their own.

In contrast, in the village located on the periphery of the irrigated area, practically everything else changed except the position of women, as Dalena men migrated out of their village to seek employment in irrigated farming as well as in the nearby town administratively responsible for this area. Their wives remained at home guarding village tradition in much the same way as happened all over Africa during the past century. But the traditions of caste and other social relations, which stood in the way of Dalena´s economic diversification, were rapidly abandoned by the men whose new opportunities they hampered.

For those directly involved in farming, irrigation imposes a new set of constraints on their production. The rules, especially on large, state-owned schemes, not only lay down procedures and schedules for planting, watering, pesticide applications, harvesting, marketing and payouts, but may even stipulate the crops to be grown. However, farmers are very adept at bending, if not breaking, such rules to meet their own objectives. Barnett (1977), for example, described how Gezira farmers managed to ensure that `our daily bread´ (their staple crop of <u>dura</u>), which could be grown on only one-ninth of a holding, never went short of water, even if `the government´s cotton´ was withering on the other eight-ninths.

Some Gezira farmers had special arrangements with the gatekeepers whereby they acquired extra allocations of water: they tended to be the wealthy and the politically- and religiously-influential. Those whose cotton yields suffered as a consequence of their arrangements tended to be the poor and powerless, of much lower socio-ethnic status in the Gezira system, as well as the always-disadvantaged `tail-enders´ at the end of the watering line. But no-one complained so long as their <u>dura</u> received its fill of water, even if the poor had to purchase extra food in the `short´ seasons from these wealthier producers, who had bought up their <u>dura</u> immediately after harvest to enable them to pay their most pressing private debts; and then raised the price of <u>dura</u> when its supply was short.

In a fully monetised system, then, in which irrigated holdings were equivalent, a slightly uneven distribution of water both between holdings and between crops, together with the cycle of private indebtedness among poor farmers, created substantial differences of wealth among Gezira producers as a whole, even when their farming effectiveness was supposedly guaranteed by the irrigation authority in the automatic provision of and deductions for necessary inputs. Clearly, this type of class differentiation (if it is indeed that) cannot be attributed to differences in access to any of the means of production (except, possibly, marginal quantities of water). It arose mainly through the debt cycle that was linked to production through the minor crop, <u>dura</u>, although better cotton yields among the poor would have helped to alleviate this problem. Yet in Barnett´s assessment of the Gezira scheme, such internal differentiation was critical to his `bottom-up´ view that the scheme had not been as successful as the `top-down´ perspective liked to believe. In contrast to the regularity with which such differentiation occurs on `public´ irrigation schemes, equality of water use, policed by the community, is more characteristic of schemes built by small village communities themselves.

Mechanisation: <u>Producing</u> <u>More</u> <u>Efficiently</u>

In the last section we have seen that small differences in inputs may cause large differences in output from equal landholdings, and reinforce existing if not actually generate new differentials of wealth. Much the same holds regarding the degrees of efficiency with which farmers actually use their land, which are critically affected by the amount of energy

68

which they can direct to production. Draught power is more efficient than manual labour; and mechanisation increases dramatically the investment of energy in production. Agriculture itself is a process of transforming energy from one form to another. Clearly, then, the more energy a farmer can invest in his production, the greater his output will be. The mechanised farmer has a considerable advantage over his counterpart who relies to a greater extent, or even completely, on human energy, even when there is no difference in their landholdings. Indeed, in the super-mechanised farms of the USA, where a handful of people can work up to a couple of thousand hectares, it is debatable whether the energy output (in the form of the caloric value of crops and/or livestock) actually balances the energy (in the form of fuel and fertilisers) which is consumed to achieve this output, even though the system may be cost-effective. (It does not appear to be cost-effective on the medium-sized holdings which, since the mid-1970s, have been bankrupted more frequently than large and small American farms.)

It is in this context that we must see Leslie White's (1959) attempt to use energy consumption as a measure of social evolution, for on average each American consumes, directly or indirectly, ten times the amount of energy of the average person in the underdeveloped world. Most of this energy is consumed in the process of production.

However, mechanisation is rarely achieved overnight. For most farmers in developing countries with balance of payments problems, importation is difficult and machinery is generally not produced locally, so mechanisation is a long, slow, piecemeal process. Usually the first farming operation to be mechanised is land preparation. Tractors plough, plant and cultivate, enabling a larger area to be brought under cultivation in Netting's strategy of expansion and, in Africa, doing much of the traditional work of <u>men</u> in agriculture. Such partial mechanisation then creates a bottleneck of insufficient human labour to complete operations later in the growing cycle, notably manual weeding and harvesting. Such labour deficits may be made up by hiring casual or seasonal workers, but often the core of the labour force among commercial producers is expanded by marrying additional wives. Hill (1963) first noted this strategy among the Ghanaian cocoa farmers. It is also common in Uganda (Richards et al 1973) and Zimbabwe (Cheater 1981, 1984).

Against this background we can understand why underdeveloped socialist countries tried to modernise their peasant farming through collectivisation and the simultaneous provision of machine centres, machine tractor stations, tractor

stations and similar institutions to service these collectives. In Israel, too, the moshavim ovdim in the past provided
machinery from their co-operatively-owned resources and
frowned upon the acquisition of privately-owned capital equipment, seeing such investment as the thin end of the wedge of
unacceptable distinctions of wealth within a co-operative of
equals. Baldwin (1972) and Abarbanel (1974) have shown this
fear to be justified. As moshavniks mechanised privately in
the 1960s, in order to supplement inadequate supplies of
labour from their families and to meet their energy needs
timeously, they were also tempted into selling both their
surplus (over and above their marketing quotas allocated by
the co-operative marketing organisation) and increasingly part
of these official quotas themselves, on the private market,
thus undermining both the ideology and the organisation of the
moshavim, particularly their ability to provide improved
collective welfare facilities through taxes on marketing.

The problem of sharing machinery is always a rostering
one. Few farm machines (except possibly tractors) are multi-
purpose: they are designed to do specific tasks at specific
points in the agricultural cycle. Given their limited period
of usefulness, every farmer wants his own, so that he is not
inconvenienced, nor his yields jeopardised, by having to queue
for shared equipment. Every farmer wants his lands prepared
before the rains begin; his planting started immediately after
the rains; his herbicides applied immediately after germina-
tion; his crops sprayed as soon as pests are detected, and
harvested at optimum moisture contents. He (or she) does not
wish to forego output by late ploughing, late planting, un-
timely pesticide applications, or herbicides applied too late
to prevent weeds from using nutrients intended for the crops.
Nor do farmers wish to dry their crops beyond permissible
moisture levels for storage, and so lose weight which has a
cash value; or have their grains harvested so early that
marketing organisations penalise them for excess moisture. But
when they have to take their turn in a queue for machinery,
all of these undesirable things happen to them. Hence their
scramble to mechanise individually, where the larger system
permits this. In Israel, the moshav ideology alone was too
weak to prevent such mechanisation. In fully socialist systems
where the ideology of co-operation is supplemented by tight
controls on the production and marketing of agricultural (and
other) machinery, the state may be more successful in ensuring
the most rational use of scarce resoures. As Hann (1980:80)
notes of Hungary, specialist co-operatives controlling machinery generally satisfied local demand for the most essential
of services, except at isolated peaks'. Individual investors
attempting to use their machinery to extract labour rather
than cash from neighbours wishing to hire it, were therefore

70

generally unsuccessful.

Mechanisation does not occur in a vacuum. It is affected not only by government policy (especially in centrally-planned economies) and the provision of technical information (by government or private extension agencies), nor merely by the labour bottlenecks experienced by individual producers. More importantly, mechanisation as a form of innovation is affected by the socio-cultural and political environment of the local community within which it takes place. In some societies, like those of Northern Italy (Vincent 1973), those individuals with an existing reputation (especially in farming) were the best-placed to introduce new techniques (such as mechanical milking) which others followed. But in village Mexico, their existing status in traditional spheres of prestige precluded older men from demeaning themselves to learn new skills (Acheson 1972), particularly in the field of craft and industrial enterprises. In rural France (Layton 1973), wealthy young farmers who had mechanised their production tended to be admired by their peers, but denigrated by their elders. On the whole their position was unstable and ambiguous, because of their repeated positive responses to the external world. However, Layton argued that their isolation was less marked than that of older men who repeatedly rejected mechanisation, whose reasons for such rejection were rational in terms of their own disappearing lifestyle (based for example on the negative effect of combine harvesting on the quality of grain used to bake homemade bread), but not widely shared.

In addition to cultural values and the local rules of political leadership, other factors also affect agricultural (and industrial) mechanisation. Important economic factors include the costs of such investment relative to local incomes as well as to expected returns; the existing level of capital accumulation; the forms of local capital and the ease with which they can be converted into cash; consumption needs and costs relative to savings; and the structure and absorptive capacity of the market for the increased output resulting from mechanisation. Operating and maintenance skills are also important, as is the composition of social overhead capital (roads, water supplies, electric power, communications, fuel availability) in that particular area. In many peasant societies, arguably the greatest constraint on individuals' capacity to mechanise is the `low level equilibrium trap' balancing existing output against its consumption in a relatively isolated system. In urban contexts, this trap balances existing output against the financial capacity of the poor to pay for a more expensive product. In such situations, until this equilibrium is upset (for example by new marketing possibilities), labour bottlenecks will remain relatively unimportant

71

in the productive system.

Labour Requirements and Household Composition

Where, as in most peasant societies, farming depends on the amount of human labour available, and is geared to household subsistence (whether directly or by exchanges on the market to acquire essentials not produced), there is a close relationship between the size and composition of the household and the area of land it uses for cultivation or stock-raising. Alexander Chayanov, an agricultural economist who eventually fell victim to Stalin in 1939, first demonstrated this relationship from the nineteenth-century provincial zemstva surveys of the Russian peasantry. From these very extensive time-series data running from 1882 to 1911, and assuming that no labour was hired, he modelled the relationship of the area sown to the ratio within the family between producers and consumers. At first, following the establishment of a new family by marriage, this ratio is 1:1 and the area sown depends on the labour of the man and his wife. Later, as children are born and less of the wife's time is spent in the fields, the area sown declines slightly as the producer: consumer ratio falls on the basis of the husband's labour only. This ratio bottoms out at nearly 1:2 in the family's fourteenth year of existence, when none of the children is yet old enough to produce effectively. Thereafter this ratio rises, as the older children start to work on the farm. At this point, the family can start to expand its sown area as more and more labour becomes available. Later still, when all but the youngest children have married and left the parental home, the sown area once again contracts to meet the smaller needs of the ageing parents.

Chayanov's model applies in the first instance only to monogamous societies. It needs modification to account for those African societies in which the majority of labour inputs to agriculture come from women and where the producer:consumer ratio is maintained at a fairly high level through multiple marriages. Nor, indeed, is the producer:consumer ratio the only factor which influences the amount of land cultivated. Of greater importance, perhaps, is whether or not unused land is available to be taken into cultivation. Where it is not available, expansion is not a viable strategy, and intensi-fication is more likely to occur, as Netting (1965, 1968) has shown for one section of the Kofyar people of Nigeria.

Historically, the Kofyar for reasons of defence inhabited the steep slopes rising to the Jos plateau. Here they developed an intensive agricultural regimen of terracing and deep manuring small gardens (in the early 1960s averaging 1.2 acres) on the hill slopes. Although this system was labour-intensive, the Kofyar, like the Torbjers in the Swiss alps, had established an equilibrium between the productive capacity of their ecosystem and their population, which was based on relatively small families (averaging just over 5 people), fission rather than extension of growing families, non-partible inheritance, and hard work.

But when, after 1930, some Kofyar descended into the surrounding plain to hack additional grain farms out of the virgin bush, they adopted the entirely different productive strategy of expansion. They cropped extensively on a shifting basis, fallowing rather than fertilising their fields. Nearly one-third began to hire labour. Over 60 per cent married polygynously in order to ensure their labour supplies. They extended their families rather than encouraging them to split, and allowed the land to be inherited equally by all the sons in a family. A very different type of family organisation emerged from that of Kofyar tradition in the hills.

Clearly, we are faced in such examples with strategies for recruiting labour which are set primarily within the cultural context of marriage and reproduction, rather than hiring practices. As Boserup (1970) and Goody (1976), among others, have argued, constituting marriage through the payment of bridewealth (from the groom and his family to the bride's father), reflects a situation in which women's labour is critically important to agricultural production. In such systems, marriage itself constitutes the social relations of production.

However, we should not then simply assume that women are exploited as unpaid workers. Perhaps most women may be in this situation, but at least a minority also exercises a new authority over production through this male strategy of polygamy. For example, Hill (1963) noted that successful cocoa farmers who managed to buy or inherit a number of strip farms, often married polygamously and installed a wife as manager of each separate farm. In the early stages of farm development, before the cocoa began to bear in the fourth or fifth season after planting, labour was drawn exclusively from family sources. Later, casual labour (often female, as in most commercial agriculture) was hired for cash on a daily basis, or contract workers were employed for plucking, before permanent, `annual´ workers were taken on in the abusa system described earlier. They were remunerated with cocoa pickings until the trees came into full bearing at fifteen years. It was at the stage of partial bearing that wives tended to be installed as managers. After all, wives have a greater interest in the final product than do hired workers or share-croppers, even if their share does not equal that of their husbands. Cheater (1981) has also remarked, for undivided freehold farms in Zimbabwe, on the influence of senior wives in polygamous marriages, not only on production decisions, but also on the organisation of field and domestic labour from junior wives. Wives as managers of resources and labour, then, occupy a position within the productive system which in a sense mediates between those who control the means of production and those who provide labour.

If one is concerned to effect equitable rewards to agricultural labour, then, as many socialist governments have been, it is not enough simply to reform landholding and to legislate on wages and conditions of service. Formal conditions of labour rarely apply to casuals and never to the work of family members, which is the most important source of labour for individual or collectivised peasant farming. Moreover, inequities in rewards to labour may be built into collectivised systems, as a concession to male views or as a result of the dominance of male decision-makers. The attitude of Tanzanian resettlement officials has already been noted. Of greater significance, perhaps, was the case of Chinese collectivisation, which rewarded a woman's working day with eight work points, compared to the male standard of ten, while not rewarding domestic labour at all. More recently, in the `responsibility' system based on the household unit, the traditional dominance of men as decision-makers has effectively been restored, with no safeguards for dependant family workers concerning the distribution of their labour product or the money derived from it.

Croll (1979, 1983) has noted that attempts to change the relations of peasant production which leave the family and household intact, will not improve the control of women as producers over their product. But external intervention in the structure of the family is a challenge to the fundamental ideological precepts of the culture in question. As Godelier (1978) observes, such ideel realities as the `proper' work of men and women, and the `proper' rewards to that work, do indeed structure the relations of production. They are also stubbornly persistent, even in the face of revolutionary political change, urbanisation and industrialisation.

74

CHAPTER FOUR

INDUSTRIALISATION AND PROLETARIANISATION

Increasingly in the third world, both individuals and local societies are being drawn into larger economic systems at national, regional and international levels. Peasant economies are being `articulated´, as marxist jargon has it, with international capitalism, collectively through their production of industrial crops sold on international commodity markets, and individually by means of waged employment in enterprises which mine, farm, trade, transport or manufacture for the world market.

Often marxists write, rather carelessly, as if wage labour alone were the hallmark of the `proletarian´. For Marx (1867/1976) himself, the process of proletarianisation was more complex and the status of `wage labourer´ merely the final outcome of this process. While the details will vary from one society to the next of precisely how proletarianisation is achieved, in Marx´s view it must always involve the separation of agricultural producers not merely from ownership or control of the land, but also from usufructuary access to it. Only when they are stripped of their independent means of subsistence will landless peasants seek wage labour; and often enough they will not find find it, instead swelling the ranks of the urban `reserve army´ of unemployed work-seekers, whose desperation to survive will threaten the job security and wage levels of those lucky enough temporarily to have jobs.

While this model may or may not be an accurate reflection of the history of industrialisation in western countries, in most developing economies of the late twentieth century wage employment has not resulted from outright landlessness. Urban workers have not moved from being independent peasants yesterday to waged proletarians today. In the Pacific, Asia and Africa at least, many men and fewer women have instead migrated to towns, seeking temporary though often long-term employment, in the pattern known as recurrent or circulatory labour migration. While working, these men have left their wives and families behind at home to safeguard their land rights and actually work their land. One historical reason for this pattern was the setting of wages in `the colonies´ well below levels on which families could survive; another was the control of entry into towns and the provision of bachelor accommodation only; a third the reaction of men to these conditions, which made towns `unsafe´ for the honour and dignity of women whose sexual services were in such short supply, and therefore caused the men to prefer to leave their own wives and daughters in the moral safety of the countryside. All three factors combined to perpetuate the `double-rootedness´ of wage workers whose jobs tied them to the employment centres while in every other way they were simultaneously linked to their rural homes. This system, it is argued, has become part of the process whereby the capitalist mode of production has crippled previously viable precapitalist economies, while simultaneously bolstering its own profitability, by requiring them to meet the costs of `social reproduction´ (that is, of subsistence for workers´ families).

Waged jobs have never been plentiful in developing economies relative to the total population, or even to the adult male population. As the cash needs of their families have expanded steadily, the early male response of shunning colonial wage labour has in two generations turned into policies of protecting nationals against foreign competition for what jobs are available. The unemployment crisis in the developing countries of the 1980s is far worse than in the developed world. Not surprisingly, then, workers especially in Africa have maintained their rural land rights as an ultimate security against losing valued urban jobs, in the context of unemployment insurance and social welfare benefits that frequently do not exist.

Circulatory Labour Migration

What was it that caused a man to spend his working life shuttling between town and countryside? Why did he not choose one or the other locality permanently?

Early attempts to answer these questions yielded single-cause answers: rural poverty forced people out of peasant agriculture; the `bright lights´ of urban glamour attracted people into these burgeoning centres. By the 1940s, however, social anthropologists like Schapera (1947) were beginning to offer more complex answers. Certainly the countryside was impoverished, but among the Tswana, who had begun to migrate to the South African diamond mines in the 1870s, a stint underground had come to substitute for more traditional forms of initiation, without which experience a man would not be able to persuade any desirable girl to marry him, nor pay the rapidly-inflating bridewealth.

Clearly, as Mitchell (1959) first discerned, there existed `centrifugal´ forces spinning men out of the countryside, but these were combined with `centripetal´ factors attracting them back again. At first Mitchell saw the centrifugal forces as economic and the centripetal ones as social, both from a rural perspective. In his later (1969) model, he decided that economic, social and political factors affecting labour circulation might fall under either centrifugal or centripetal headings, that both centrifugal and centripetal forces operated from both urban and rural ends of the circulatory cycle, and that all of these factors were integrated with one another over the working life of any individual migrant. His final model of recurrent migration was, therefore, based on the life-cycle of a male migrant.

According to this model, the migratory cycle begins around the minimum age stipulated in law for adult employment, roughly 18 - 20 years in Southern Africa, after a youth has acquired his identity document. Having left school much earlier, there is pressure on him at this age to seek work, to contribute to the expenses particularly of his younger siblings' education, and to start saving toward bridewealth even if he is not at this stage seriously thinking of getting married. So off he goes to look for work and the model requires that he be lucky enough to find it. In his mid-twenties, his marriage interests become more important and, together with his labour obligations to his ageing parents, cause him to return home to work the fields, seek a wife and start his own family. Almost immediately after marriage, however, his incomplete bridewealth and the consumer demands of his wife and children, as well as those of his parents and affines, for clothes and other commodities, push him back to urban employment. In turn, once back in town, he is pulled back into an extended rural sojourn by his acquisition of his own fields at home as a married man with children, the desirability of acquiring his own draught power for tillage, the construction of a home independent of his parents, and his growing family. But by the time he is about thirty, the costs of tax and clothing and educating his family cause him to return to work for the third time, for a more extended period that is interrupted briefly in his mid-thirties to help his retiring parents and parents-in-law with their farming, to repair their houses and to repair and extend his own. His fourth and final work period is geared to accumulating rural capital in the form of livestock and equipment before his own age endangers his chances of retaining or finding urban manual employment again. In his mid- to late-forties, therefore, he retires home for good, and may be replaced in another migratory cycle by his eldest son.

This model may have characterised Southern African migratory reality up to the 1950s, with its legislation requiring black foreigners to terminate their employment at regular intervals. But by the 1960s, studies of individual workplaces elsewhere were beginning to suggest much longer average spells in employment than this model allowed for. By 1965 in Kampala, Uganda, for example, the median length of service among East African Railways and Harbours workers was 12.0 years, compared to 9.5 years among workers in a local tobacco factory (Grillo 1973:14). More recently, in a country where the state controls over migration were relaxed in the 1960s, Cheater (1986) recorded an average length of service of 8.9 years in a Zimbabwean textile factory. These figures were related to the acquisition of skills among workers, as well as to a change in the nature of labour migration. What seemed to be happening, at least in some cases, was that over long weekends and for their annual holidays, workers commuted by bus to rural homes within a four-hour travel radius of their employment centres, rather than regularly throwing up their jobs to return home for more extended visits.

This `stabilisation´ of workers in towns, therefore, did not necessarily lead to `urbanisation´ in the sense of permanent urban-rootedness, but was entirely compatible with final retirement in the countryside. In some cases, as Grillo (1973) has shown for railways employees, the requirement of mobility on the job and the provision of railways housing reinforced workers´ identification with their rural homes and actually channelled their financial investments there rather than into urban property. In other places, a similar provision of rented municipal housing had the same effect. But even wealthy urban businessmen in Africa also tend to invest in rural land, often but not exclusively to farm commercially. The ideological pull of the land remains very strong, not only among those whom we might call semi-proletarianised workers who oscillate between rural and urban localities.

The effects of labour migration on the towns have centred on the demographic imbalances it created. In colonial Africa, male:female ratios of 2:1 were common, leading to problems of prostitution; sexually-transmitted diseases (which were also passed on to rural wives by visiting husbands); and violence against and the brutalisation of those women who did make their way to the towns (who had often been outcast from their rural homes as a result of barrenness, divorce and/or witchcraft accusations).

The effects of circulatory migration on the countryside were much more varied, depending specifically on the traditional division of labour and more generally on social organisation. Where the absence of men made little difference to cropping (for example, among the Lakeside Tonga of Malawi, where cassava was cultivated almost exclusively by women), remittances in cash and kind raised the standard of living and helped to capitalise rural production. But where the labour of

78

men was critical to the agricultural system, whether or not their absence affected production detrimentally depended on how production could be re-organised, if at all, to minimise the impact of their absence.

Among the matrilineal Bemba of Northern Zambia, where the men traditionally lived with their wives´ matrikin and were all strangers to one another within any given village, the loss of the men´s labour to the Copperbelt mines was disastrous. Traditionally the Bemba men pollarded branches from trees and dragged them into a circle for firing, to provide potash to the soil and to kill weeds and pests by the heat. Since it was undignified at the least for women to climb trees in order to undertake this task, they simply chopped the trees down, thus leading to rapid deforestation, soil erosion and the dessication of their agricultural land.

The chitimene system was also practised by the patrilineal Mambwe, neighbours to the Bemba, whose villages were composed around a core of related men. Among the Mambwe, in contrast to the Bemba, Watson (1958) described how the absence of some men was compensated for by their brothers and other male patrikin co-operating in the task of firing for the absentees´ wives, so that production continued much as it had always done, in what was and still is agronomically the most efficient way of using these particular soils.

The withdrawal of men´s labour impaired rural production, then, if women were for whatever reason unable to take over male tasks, or if the existing social organisation was incapable of restructuring work on the basis of co-operation among normally independent households. Agriculture was also affected negatively where the women were unwilling or unable to take over the role of decision-maker on issues of production, which then had to be deferred until the men returned or could be contacted at work. However, sub-Saharan Africa is generally an area of `female farming´ (Boserup 1970), in which examples such as the Bemba are relatively rare. The contemporary crisis of African agriculture is essentially one of post-colonial pricing policy, rather than a hangover from colonial labour migration. By and large agriculture survived the colonial period, with its extensive labour circulation, though not very well. One can of course argue that without this undermining of agriculture during colonialism, the impact of post-colonial policies would not have been as severe as it was. What is not at issue, however, is the fact that, since before the colonial period proper, peasant agriculture has been assaulted in various ways by the assumption that the economic future of the developing world lies with industry, not agriculture.

Enskilling Labour

Peasant economies, as Firth (1971) has indicated, are not purely agricultural. They also include stock-raising, fishing, trading and craft work, all of which, like agriculture, have been adversely affected by the `culture´ of industrialism. Let us examine craft work as an example here, the products of which have increasingly become tourist objets d´art as their usefulness as tools and domestic utensils has been replaced with more durable, if less attractive, mass-produced manufactures, often imported. Marx (1867/1976) first noted the alienation of the traditional craft worker in Europe and the UK, as machines nullified the skills he had acquired over a long apprenticeship. Subsequently other precapitalist craft workers have been similarly affected.

In West Africa, for example among the Yoruba of Western Nigeria, traditional crafts included metalwork (in gold, iron, tin, bronze and silver), woodwork, weaving, pottery and music, as well as service occupations like healing and divination. During the early colonial period were added `new´ crafts such as cobbling, tailoring, repairing bicycles, building construction using new techniques, and taking in washing (by those who owned flat-irons). In the same period, the `industrial´ crafts of machining, fitting, electronics, printing and so on also became part of the Nigerian economy.

How were these skills acquired and practised? In the case of traditional crafts, as Lloyd (1953) has described, their organisation differed between large and small centres. Large towns, of 20,000 people or more, supported full-time specialists in these fields, whereas in the smaller centres and villages, part-time practitioners were linked into the urban, lineage-based craft organisations. Craft skills were lineage property, usually transmitted from father to son or by other patrilineal links, though occasionally a man might train his sister´s sons. Craft affairs were controlled, as part and parcel of the wider lineage affairs, by the lineage head, or bale. So problems of workshop maintenance, work standards and product pricing, like those of land allocation and marital conflict, were resolved by lineage meetings under his chairmanship. In the event of conflict among practitioners of the same craft in different towns, it was their respective lineage heads who handled these disputes and, if necessary, took them to the town oba or `king´ for ultimate resolution. It was the lineage head, too, who was responsible for propitiating, on behalf of his craftsmen, lineage ancestors as well as those gods who stood in a special relationship to that craft (Ogun, the god of iron and of war, for example, was particularly significant to hunters, carvers and iron-smiths). One can see,

80

then, why Lloyd (1953:34) remarks that there was `no division in the minds of the craftsmen between their social and economic activities´, all of which fell within the framework of lineage organisation. But with the exception of weaving the traditional Yoruba robes, most of these craft skills fell into disuse as their products (knives, guns, doorframes, pottery, weaving looms) were displaced by imported or locally-produced manufactured equivalents. For decades, Yoruba youth wanting to acquire skills have opted instead for the `new´ skills and industrial trades.

The new crafts required relatively sophisticated tools (saws, planes, sewing machines and so on), which required a capital outlay in cash and without which the new skill could not be practised. The corollary of this dependence on tools was that anyone who had the cash could buy them, so these skills, unlike the traditional ones, could not be restrictively controlled by the lineages. Instead, craft guilds (not dissimilar to those of mediaeval Europe) began to emerge soon after the first world war. Membership of these guilds was enforced on all craftsmen by edicts of the town obas. These guilds regulated prices, work standards, apprenticeship training, intra-trade competition and professional ethics: carpenters, for example, were fined by their guild for soliciting coffin custom at houses where deaths were known to have occurred. The guilds also promoted social as well as occupational harmony among their memberships. Like the trades unions which originated at roughly the same time, the craft guilds set much store by their bureaucratic organisation, resting on the literacy not only of the guild secretary but also many of the younger members.

The apprenticeship system which was controlled by these guilds linked trainees to master-craftsmen registered with the guilds. Written contracts specified the details of the training to be given, the fees, and the arrangements for the apprentice´s board and lodging. Living with the master increased the costs and the work hours of the apprentice, but also enabled him to acquire greater experience than he would if `living out´. The scale of fees for training was recommended by the guild, but fees could be varied downwards for kin and friends. At the end of the apprenticeship contract, the trainee graduated to journeyman status through his `freedom ceremony´, at which his father or his master would present him with the tools of his trade as a gift.

Peil (1970) has noted that parallel arrangements existed in the formal apprenticeships for industrial trades in Ghana. A firm might register a youth as an apprentice fitter, for example, with his formal training coming from the local polytechnic, but unless he also entered into an informal agreement with a skilled journeyman in that firm, he was unlikely to be taught the necessary practical skills of that job. Although the wages in industrial apprenticeships were higher, and although the Ghanaian government conducted formal trade tests at the end of the training period, Peil (1970:138) suggested that `training on the job seems to differ little from a non-industrial apprenticeship´

These non-industrial apprenticeships have become extremely important all over Africa as unemployment rates have risen and self-employment has increased. However, the extent to which practical skills are reserved to themselves and regarded as a financial resource by the formally-employed seems to vary. In a Zimbabwean textile factory, for example, Cheater (1986) found that weavers were quite willing to train others to use their fully-automated looms. In the same way as master craftsmen benefitted from the labour of their apprentices, so these black weavers benefitted from the labour inputs of their `assistants´, whom they were training with the knowledge and approval of the white manager. They could leave their looms while formally on shift and slip off for a smoke or a chat, while the looms´ output accrued to themselves. Since their `assistants´ had to wait for a weaving vacancy to occur before they could move up the pay scale, training them represented no threat to existing weavers, who did not charge for this training. Although Zimbabwe also had informal apprenticeships of the type described earlier, it would seem that by the 1980s these had not yet penetrated formal factory organisation as in Ghana. Whether they will in future is an open question.

Employment and `Petty Commodity Production´

Formal apprenticeships, like formal jobs, are scarce in contemporary Africa (where the proportion of formally employed workers in the total adult population rarely rises above 25 per cent), and elsewhere in the third world. Arguably, too, neither formal training nor formal jobs are related to the productive needs of the majority of third world populations, the poor. King (1977), for example, has shown that the proliferation of informal training in Kenya in the 1970s was related not only to the difficulties of getting a formal job, but also to the needs of poor consumers, who could not afford to pay for the products of `high-tech´ industrial enterprises. `Low-tech´ production is an area in which generally neither governments nor those with capital to invest are interested. Informal training, then, is a natural corollary of `informal´ employment, or petty commodity production by the self-employed. Its appropriation of labour from poorly-paid ap-

82

prentices, often under sweat-shop conditions, is, in the views of those involved in it, counter-balanced by the transfer of skills which enable people to survive by supplying an existing market.

This `informal sector´ of developing economies, together with its training systems, seems from western history to be an inevitable part of the industrialisation process. Many contemporary marxists regard it, like labour migration and peasant agriculture, as an auxiliary mechanism whereby the profitability of capitalism is protected, in this case by helping to ensure the survival of the urban industrial `reserve army´ of the formally unemployed. Some, like Marx himself, go so far as to regard petty commodity producers as part of the criminal lumpenproletariat, but most seem content to regard the `petty commodity mode of production´ as being articulated with capitalism in a subordinate relationship that does not permit it to develop any further.

Long and Richardson (1978), however, showed that in Peru of the 1970s petty commodity production was integrally tied into the repair sector, and to a lesser extent (through `putting out´) the manufacturing sector, of the so-called `formal´ economies, and had an internal dynamic of its own. Informal input supply and marketing systems were sometimes centralised. More often, however, in highly competitive situations, these systems were `co-ordinated´, among producers in similar positions, by social networks based on kinship, compadrazgo (ritual kinship) and village ties. Along these networks flowed more or less balanced exchanges of economic information and financial assistance.

In a similar study of Minangkabau blacksmiths in a town in West Sumatra, Kahn (1975) has detailed the low productivity of small workshops in which the owner, as one of the work-team, received only marginally more than his employees while bearing all of the risks of production and marketing. (Long and Richardson found, in similar workshops in Peru, that workers might also use the owner´s equipment for their own production during their free time.) Kahn noted that the market for such products, among local peasants, allowed only a small margin of price flexibility, mainly because of competition from cheap, imported steel goods (knives, machetes, sickles, axes, plough shares and hoes). The market thus prevented forge-owners from upgrading their productive technology, because small improvements in the quality of their products would not have been sufficient to make these competitive with manufactured imports, nor could the increased costs of these relatively minor technological changes be passed on to customers. The forge-owners could not increase their own profits by paying their workers any less, without running the risk of losing their workforce. There was, therefore, no way in which the blacksmithing entrepreneurs could accumulate sufficient capital to revolutionise their productive techno- logy and make the quality of their output competitive with imported steel tools. They were caught in this classical `low level equilibrium trap´ because, Kahn argued, they were integrated into an international market even while <u>not</u> producing for it.

In South-East Asia, Latin America and Africa alike, this problem dogs attempts to upgrade the small-scale production of goods and services, whether by encouraging producers to form co-operatives or by providing government financial assistance at special rates of interest to those whom commercial banks regard as too `high-risk´ to qualify for normal loans. As Kahn (1975:144) notes, the problem is a structural one, intractible to solution at the individual level. While it affects all petty producers, men and women alike, one effect of this structural problem is to criminalise the activities particu- larly of <u>women</u> who try to survive individually.

As we have already seen in chapter 3, women may have access to land through related men, but only rarely control the means of farm production in their own right. In patri- lineal African societies, girls are less likely to be educated than their brothers (because fathers see no point in educating a daughter whose earning capacity, on marriage and the payment of bridewealth, accrues to others). Women are consequently less employable than men. In agriculture, if formally employ- ed, women are usually casual, daily-paid plantation workers. In the cities, their main unskilled employment possibilities lie in domestic service. However, they may have to earn an independent income in order to survive when their informal access to farmland is withdrawn. It is, therefore, hardly surprising that women are involved more often in petty com- modity production than in formal employment. A substantial proportion, if not a majority, of all households earning their income from self-employment are headed by women. `Matrifocal´ households have, in the past three decades, become almost as much a feature of urban Africa as of the Caribbean. But why the activities of self-employed women should be deemed more reprehensible than those of self-employed men, is not immed- iately self-evident.

Perhaps one answer lies in the work of Nelson (1979) and Obbo (1981), who showed independently, in the two East African cities of Nairobi and Kampala, that self-employed urban women survive in contemporary times by selling services and products that are associated with married female status. Brewing and distilling, marketing fresh or cooked foodstuffs, or exchanging sex for cash or more general financial support, are the methods by which women survive independently of men. Because they have little capital, except after having pursued one of the above occupations for some years, few women enter the kinds of capitalised self-employment associated with men, as store-owners or large-scale dealers in `formal sector´ products, makers of simple metal products, or even as transporters or fuel suppliers. Perhaps it is this commercialisation of marital goods and services that causes men to stigmatise women´s self-employed occupations as semi- if not il-legal.

The `criminalisation´ of women´s strategies for independent survival is reflected in their frequent harassment by police. Perhaps both stigma and persecution also relate to male attempts to reassert domination over women who have grasped individual control of both their productive and reproductive capacities, while men even in self-employment remain generally more subservient to the authority of society and to the control of their workmates.

Social Control in the Workplace

The studies conducted by Elton Mayo and his associates in the 1920s and 1930s at Western Electric´s Hawthorne plant in Chicago, USA, first revealed the existence of informal, social relations on the shopfloor which parallelled and to some extent contradicted the formal work hierarchy. In the context of the Great Depression, workers (especially in small work units like the bank wiring room) evolved a system of controlling their collective output to ensure (in their own perspective) that increased productivity would not threaten their jobs. Sanctions were applied not only among themselves to prevent rate-busting, but also to their supervisors to ensure that they did not bring this situation to the attention of management. Such was the control exerted by the work group that it did not permit individual workers to respond to material incentives offerred by management to increase output. Subsequently, many other studies have shown that managerial authority is not the only source of power in the workplace. Nor, in unionised enterprises, is the influence of shop stewards its sole supplement. In the traditional Yoruba towns of West Africa, we have already seen how craft workers were ultimately controlled by their lineages, represented by the lineage heads. On Norwegian fishing trawlers, we have already noted how the ultimate control of the skipper was counterbalanced by the need for equality among workers in a high-risk occupation. Now let us examine more explicitly how social factors enter into the control of behaviour in the workplace.

85

We should start by noting that the more isolated the workplace is from the influence of the encompassing society, and the more closely it approximates what Goffman (1961) has called a `total institution´ closed to the outside world, the more likely it is that workers will exercise dominant control over their own behaviour. Especially where the enterprise is spatially isolated (mines and fishing trawlers are the classic examples here), workers´ social lives are very closely integrated. Such communities can make the individual´s life very miserable if he or she does not behave as expected. Crossing a picket line, or even expressing an opinion contrary to that of the majority, may result in effective ostracism. However, some enterprises (like railways, with their own housing schemes to cater for the work requirement of constant mobility) may be spatially and socially isolated from the larger society, but prevent the growth of such a community ethos among the workforce by frequent transfers of workers among stations. In such circumstances, competition and control among the workers tends to be confined more narrowly to small work units, while off-duty social relations link men of the same rank and status at work, sometimes over long distances in friendships down the line of rail.

Grillo (1973) noted in his study of the East African Railways and Harbours organisation in Kampala, Uganda, that the `loco shed´ had the best-developed sense of corporate identity as a work unit. Not only was it stereotyped as `troublesome´ and `militant´, depending on the viewpoint of the speaker, it was also reputed to harbour witches. The responsibilities of the drivers´ job contributed to their beliefs that others, jealous of their position, might attack them mystically, for driving errors leading to accidents, whether fatal or not, resulted in official enquiries and retarded promotion. Other elements, for example of competition for jobs between different ethnic groups, also entered into these beliefs in and accusations of witchcraft.

However, there was another, more important reason why the loco shed had its reputation for being witch-ridden. EARH displayed the normal tension on railways between footplate staff and all others, but among the drivers themselves there were tensions specific to a railway in a recently-decolonised, developing economy. The five years following the attainment of independence of Kenya, Uganda and Tanzania between 1961 and 1963, saw the rapid Africanisation of senior posts in the EARH formerly held by whites. Job opportunities for blacks expanded in all sections. Senior black drivers with twenty or more years of experience but little formal education, who failed to pass conversion tests from oil-fired to diesel engines, found themselves competing for the prestige lines with much younger but more educated men, promoted to drive the new locomotives shortly after leaving the EARH Training School in Nairobi. In this context, the older drivers were on the defensive. Their belief that younger and somewhat junior drivers were bewitching them reflected their insecurity under changing circumstances and their problems of attaining further promotion. In turn, the belief that they bewitched their juniors perhaps reflected their desire to reinforce their own position in the hierarchy of status based on age.

Age remains an important hierarchical principle in contemporary Africa, although the age-grading systems described in chapters 6 and 8 no longer exist in that form. Among unskilled and even among more skilled workers in Africa's mines and factories, hierarchical idioms based on age and kinship form part of the structure of social control in these workplaces. Sometimes management has used kinship ties to existing workers as a strategy for recruiting new workers, and then expected senior kinsmen to control their juniors. Among unrelated workers themselves, a hierarchy of respect and personal service has often been established in the idiom of kinship. Kapferer (1969) noted that in a beneficiation plant in Kabwe, Zambia, younger workers addressed their elders as `father´ and ran errands for them as befitted the position of `sons´. The use of this classificatory kinship terminology cross-cut ethnic differences among these workers, while emphasising the generation gap. Such mechanisms for establishing a rank order among workers at the same level of employment, often contradict other possible differentiating factors. For example, younger workers generally have higher levels of formal education than their older colleagues, but the use of kinship idioms to emphasise age differences does not permit education or greater work capacity to upset this informal age ranking, which subordinates the young to their elders.

Occasionally age ranking as a mechanism for subordinating younger workers may be reinforced by implications if not outright accusations of witchcraft. We have already seen in the case of the EARH drivers that witchcraft accusations ran both ways between older and younger men, reflecting competitive tensions as' well as attempts by older drivers to control their junior colleagues. Kapferer´s (1969) work clarified how the witchcraft of older workmates was more generally feared by their juniors. Towards the end of a working day, when his greater work capacity posed no threat of rate-busting, a relatively young, fit, strong and hard-working stripper in the cell room of a zinc titration plant was reprimanded by an older work-mate for working too fast. The young man escalated this reprimand into an implication of witchcraft directed at himself. Partly because he found himself isolated in this

87

conflict and bereft of support from other workers in the cell room, three days later he successfully applied for a transfer to a lesser-paid underground job in the mine itself, thus removing from the cell room a potential threat to the routine of work whereby strippers were paid for an eight-hour day when the work actually took them only four hours. We see here an example of the process whereby older, weaker and less fit manual workers manage to control the work behaviour of their chronological juniors, by bringing into the workplace cultural beliefs and behaviour patterns from traditional African society.

Control of workers and the work process, then, is not fully in the hands of management. Workers, particularly those owning `means of production´ in their own right (such as employed tailors with their own sewing machines at home), may exercise an important, though normally unacknowledged, influence over their own work behaviour, the work behaviour of their workmates, and output. They may also jeopardise the employment and remuneration of other, less influential workmates, if such behaviour serves their own specific interests.

In the Kabwe clothing factory studied by Kapferer (1972), for example, the hourly rate of pay varied only marginally among different categories of workers. This caused dissatisfaction among the more skilled, especially the tailors, even though, in addition to their weekly wages, the tailors also benefitted from various `fiddles´ within the factory, which centred, as might be expected, around factory stocks of thread and cloth, but also included the recording of hours worked. In seeking to organise industrial action, however, the tailors were initially frustrated by the reluctance of unskilled `target workers´ to jeopardise their own employment by going on strike. Over a period of six months after their failure to bring the factory out, the tailors deliberately set about creating social and financial ties with their unskilled colleagues, in order to be able to bring personal pressure on them to support strike action in the future.

It is this type of action that has led some marxists to distinguish, within the general class of labour in developing economies, a sub-class of skilled, formally-employed, often unionised, and well-remunerated `labour aristocrats´, who are prepared in their own interests to collaborate with the class interests of capital. Originally this concept of a `labour aristocracy´ was applied to white artisans in racially segregated economies. Later it was extended to `strategic´ workers who used their positions of advantage in their personal rather than in their so-called `class´ interests. More recently, some, like Peace (1975), have argued that this theoretical `labour aristocracy´ does not exist in practice, because their distinctiveness in terms of skill is overridden by the social and financial ties among everyone trying to make a living in an unpropitious environment. And certainly there is at least one sense in which it is difficult to distinguish `formal´ from `informal´ income-generating activities, for they are closely intertwined.

Moonlighting, `Parallel Employment´ and Informal Rewards

From the considerable degree of underwork relative to their pay in the case of the titration plant strippers, we can infer that the tactical use of traditional controls over work relations on the African shopfloor relates directly to the total rewards of the employment system. Mars (1982) has emphasised that all jobs have a `fiddle potential´, whereby the formal pay and fringe benefits comprise only part of the total package. Perks, tips, additional work and even consultancy may be the informal rewards of a formal job. But in addition, there are rewards to be gained from illegal occupations (organised crime, prostitution); from the `social economy´ of household barter exchanges of goods and labour; from the `black economy´ of unregistered work and moonlighting in second jobs; and from the `hidden economy´ underlying formal employment and involving theft, short-changing, overcharging legitimate expense accounts, overloading and under-delivering goods, and so forth. The hidden economy, relative to the formal economy, is the submerged part of the iceberg, integrally part of the structure but normally invisible, hence its designation.

In `advanced´ capitalist economies, the extent to which all economic activity is monitored and taxed varies. Mars (1982:11ff) noted that the UK Inland Revenue estimated for 1980 that some 7.5 per cent of the Gross Domestic Product was `black´, costing the department up to £3.5 billion in uncollected taxes that year. In the USA the figure may be as high as US$200 billion or 10 per cent of Gross National Product, with some 4.5 million workers existing purely on unrecorded and untaxed jobs. In Italy, the figure for unrecorded economic activity approaches 20 per cent of the total, which brings it closer to - but still a very long way from - estimates for such activity in third world economies. In Zaire and Uganda, for example, recent estimates have suggested that up to two-thirds of all economic activity is located within the social economy, or is `black´, `hidden´, `informal´ or even criminal in nature (MacGaffey 1983).

How do the work activities of individuals add up to such

staggering totals? Firstly, in underdeveloped economies, the recording system is poorly developed. It also usually refuses to acknowledge peasant agriculture, indigenous trading or self-employment in petty commodity production as `economic activity´. Secondly, these figures often include the truly spectacular activities based on transnational corporations´ `slush funds´, such as those of Lockheed which ultimately caused Japanese prime minister Tanaka to resign in disgrace. Thirdly, especially in the USA, the activities of the Mafia and other drug smugglers also inflate the figures.

But for the most part, these figures reflect what Mars (1982:1) has called `the normal crimes of normal people in the normal circumstances of their work´. In some jobs, the incumbent may fiddle in the individualised style of what Mars calls the `hawk´. With some stage-setting assistance from fellow workers, individuals may also fiddle in `donkey´ jobs (such as those of supermarket cashiers), or as `vultures´ (in the restaurant trade, for example). Or fiddling may be a group affair among `wolfpacks´ of dock workers or refuse collectors.

These distinctions of type may on occasion be somewhat blurred when the same individuals fiddle in different work capacities. In the case of the stripper `wolfpack´ in the Zambian zinc titration plant, for example, their underwork was the result of a definitional error by management, but they defended their right to go when finished their established quotas, rather than negotiating increased pay for working a full eight-hour day, because they used this time, as `hawks´, on supplementary income-earning activities. As Mars (1982:205) points out, `it is no use officially paying a man an additional £50 a month that is taxable if this prevents him from unofficially earning a tax-free £50´. Similarly, in the clothing factory in Kabwe, the skilled tailors collectively refused to work overtime at the factory on rush orders, instead preferring to take work home to their own sewing machines on a piecework basis, thereby also depriving their workmates of opportunities to earn additional income through overtime. As `hawks´ both tailors and strippers may have made marginally more money from this strategy of parallel self-employment. However, they did it mainly to retain some control over production, and some degree of leverage over management, in their own hands. `Worker participation´ may thus take different forms in different situations.

Unionisation and the Relationships between Capital, Labour and the State

Industrialised production, whether in agriculture, mining

or manufacturing, stretches back just over a century in Africa, to the discovery of diamonds in Kimberley, South Africa, in 1871. On this continent, industrialisation occurred within a colonial context which, for a number of decades, banned the formal organisation of indigenous workers. In most of English- and French-speaking Africa, trades unions for African workers were legalised only after the second world war, although unregistered oganisations date back to the 1920s. Immigrant white workers, of course, brought their own concepts of worker participation with them and set up racially exclusive organisations at a much earlier stage. Ironically, in the most industrialised country of the continent, South Africa, the legalisation of informal, unrecognised unions among black workers occurred only in the 1970s.

In Africa, contemporary trades unions have had a number of predecessors, as Epstein (1958) has described for the Zambian copperbelt. The first of these copper mines opened in 1926 and five years later instituted a system of `tribal elders´ to deal with problems affecting their migrant workforce. Later this system developed two variations, one in the mine `compounds´ and the other in the municipal housing areas not controlled by the mines but falling under the jurisdiction of the colonial government.

On the mines, these elders were elected by workers belonging to each of the twenty or so major ethnic categories. They acted as an official channel of communication between workers and mine management, tried cases of dispute as recognised court officials, and maintained a link between the chiefs in their homes of origin and the mines. As Epstein (1958:43) notes, this system rested `on the common assumption that the social ties, the norms, and the values which had served to regulate behaviour in the tribal societies from which all the new urban dwellers had come, could continue to operate in the different conditions of an industrial community´. The tribal elders were rewarded with certain privileges, including somewhat improved mine housing, extra food rations and `gifts´ at Christmas. Perhaps because the majority of them were fairly closely related to chiefs in their home areas, they commanded respect and for a time the system worked well.

However, as early as the first industrial dispute in 1935, it became apparent that, although tribal elders might be highly efficient in easing the social problems of migrant workers, they were irrelevant to work interests and were not seen by the workers to be an appropriate channel for negotiating with management about their wages and conditions of labour. It was suggested then (by the Ndola district commissioner) that worker organisations should be legalised, but nothing came of it until 1947. Indeed, by 1940, when the next industrial unrest among black workers occurred immediately after a strike of white mineworkers, not all of the mines even had tribal elders. However, a revised system of `tribal representatives´ was then instituted to deal with work negotiations as well as social life. The better-educated black clerks and supervisors for a while set up parallel organisations of Clerks´ Associations and Boss Boys´ Committees, and in 1946 Works Committees were introduced. Each Works Committee was composed of representatives from all of the different departments within the individual mine, and handled matters such as working hours, mine safety, canteens and routine shopfloor issues. However, the Works Committees were generally not empowered to deal with negotiations about wages or conditions of service, which affected all of the mines collectively.

In 1948, then, following the 1947 secondment by the Colonial Office of a British trade unionist to assist in organising black workers, the African Mine Workers Union was formed, some months after shop assistants, general and railways workers had organised themselves. Explaining this apparent reluctance to unionise themselves, Epstein noted the generally unfavourable stereotype of `barbarism´ which then attached to black mineworkers in the black population; the opposition of the more educated and skilled workers on the mines; the miners´ suspicion of the British unionist sent to assist nascent black unions; and the black miners´ rejection of overtures for their membership by the white mineworkers´ union. With great effort, however, the AMWU built up its membership and in the early 1950s called a strike during which the `tribal representatives´ were used by management to persuade workers to return to work. Having had its attention drawn to the continued presence of this rival institution, the AMWU in 1953 managed to have the older system abolished. Epstein hints at a `generation gap´ separating the young, relatively educated leaders of the AMWU and the gerontocratic tribal representatives, as part of this conflict. Thereafter, in the context of the mineworkers´ strategic significance in an undiversified economy, the union went from strength to strength. By the 1980s, the Zambian Mineworkers´ Union had become the most powerful in the country, well able to resist attempted government erosion of its members´ economic interests in order to stabilise the national economy on the terms set by the International Monetary Fund. It was not impressed by appeals to tighten belts from those `who wear elastic belts´. As the Zambian economy deteriorated, the strength of the union apparently grew, in contrast to the wavering patterns of support in its early days.

Like other unions in Africa, the AMWU on the copperbelt

92

initially attracted varying support. When fighting militant battles against racial discrimination, and after successfully having negotiated better remuneration and working conditions, it enjoyed the paid-up support of a majority of its potential membership. As these successes faded into history, workers stopped paying their dues, especially in workplaces that did not operate a check-off system, and started muttering about how the leadership misused union funds. Epstein (1958:112f) noted wild fluctuations in membership over six months, ranging from 80 to around 20 per cent. More recent studies of longer-established unions in East and Central Africa (Grillo 1969, Cheater 1986), suggest that a comfortable majority (ranging between 60 and 75 per cent) of formally-employed workers may normally be unionised.

In the process of decolonisation, the removal of racial discrimination came fairly easily and could be (and was) claimed as a union victory. More intractible to union manipulation were the issues of work and wages. Hence there seems to be an overall pattern to union activity on the African continent to date, whereby long periods of apathy have been interspersed with militant, usually strike, action. Which - if either - fairly represented the state of worker consciousness in this part of the world, is difficult to say. However, this pattern reflects the underlying tension between the unskilled majority of unionised manual workers and the relatively educated, skilled-clerical-administrative minority. Strategies to improve their working conditions have varied between these two sections of the African workforce.

Historically, the educated minority has shown an early interest in union organisation and especially in union leadership, which it has used to achieve individual job and sometimes political mobility, before discarding union membership in favour of `salaried staff associations´ or the equivalent to protect its own interests. In contrast, the unskilled majority has generally favoured union militancy and strike action to achieve improvements for all members, often against the better judgement of educated union leaders.

However, it is important to note that the vast majority of unskilled workers in Africa have never been unionised. Like the `cotton boys´ in the textile factory studied by Kapferer (1972), young `target workers´ have shown little interest in unionisation. Indeed, with alternative organisations also seeking to protect worker interests, sometimes more successfully than unions, there is little reason why they should.

Particularly during the colonial period, welfare associations, teachers´ associations and other proto-political bodies

93

were pushing quite as hard as trades unions for the removal of racial discrimination, not only concerning the terms and conditions of employment, but also in the marketing of farm produce. As Cheater (1984) has shown in detail for Zimbabwe, there was usually considerable overlap in the leadership of such organisations, which was drawn from the tiny pool of `educated people´. Later, when it became legal, many of these leaders entered formal politics. Arguably, it was party political pressure, more than union or association activity, which, in conjunction with metropolitan decisions, hastened the demise of structural racialism in colonial territories. Certainly both union officials and ordinary workers, in the immediate post-independence era, have looked to black governments to support them politically against capital and its management, manipulating the idiom of racial conflict to gain this support. However, as Kapferer (1972) and Cheater (1986) have shown, this support has not been readily forthcoming.

The main reason for this failure of newly-independent governments to support their own political supporters in their workplaces, is less the distinction between the politics of opposition and the politics of government, than the class alliance between capital and the state. The state subsists off taxes and, as we have seen earlier, only a minor fraction of the total economic activity in developing economies is recorded and taxed, thus hampering state activities. Those who control the state, therefore, cannot afford to erode any further the `formal´ economic base off which the state is supported, without endangering their own position, which is further complicated by their necessary participation in international markets, and their necessary submission to international financing institutions. Together, these links have led to the charge that those who control the state, as the `comprador bourgeoisie´, collude with international capital against the class interests of their poor citizens. Such an analytical framework perhaps helps to explain the findings of anthropologists like Kapferer (1972). He recorded the dismay of a militant worker in Kabwe who appealed to the Resident Minister for assistance in the workers´ dispute with the Indian management of the clothing factory. But the worker was lectured sternly on the workers´ responsibility to keep production lines moving and threatened personally with being stripped of his party position as branch treasurer should the workers strike. At a later stage, the Resident Minister´s office made quite clear that it would not be drawn into disputes that were the `proper´ preserve of employers and unions alone.

So while the rhetoric of politicians addressing rallies may lead workers to assume that government is on their side against employers, especially of a different race, the actions of the government bureaucracy dealing with labour issues may be very disillusioning. Even where ostensibly socialist governments genuinely attempt to strengthen workers in their dealings with employers, the outcome is often different. Zimbabwe, for example, set up `workers´ committees´ after independence, which were initially presented as revolutionary intrusions into the decision-making rights of management. By 1984, however, the minister responsible for their introduction had publicly denied that these committees were intended to put `power´ into the hands of workers (Cheater 1986). In the interim, in at least some industries, these new committees had seriously undermined the ability of the unions concerned to defend the interests of their members, at the same time that government influence over all unions, through the newly-established Zimbabwe Congress of Trades Unions, was increasing. Under such circumstances, the structural relationships linking government, labour and capital are very complex, and hardly amenable to an orthodox marxist analysis based on the ownership or non-ownership of the means of industrial production, though the idea that the state is the executive of the owning class is not irrelevant.

The Growth of Worker Consciousness?

Throughout the history of industrialisation in Africa, there has been something of a mismatch between ideas (of the workers themselves, as well as about them by others) and actual behaviour. As workers were migrating to the mines, those who offerred them employment, accommodation and recreation thought of them as `tribesmen´, and treated them as such on the mines, constructing new modes of `tribalism´ in the town setting. This reconstruction of tribal identity has been problematic, for in responding to it as an urban reality, African workers have been seen by outsiders as cleaving to `primordial´ loyalties and failing to adapt to the `universalist´ principles on which urban-based bureaucracies are supposed to work. So, as the Zambian mineworkers themselves rejected the system of `tribal representatives´, this view saw them as constructing their trade union in turn along `tribal´ lines. `Tribal´ ties, in this view, cannot be transcended. They will dominate everything, from job recruitment to trade union politics, and prevent the growth of class consciousness among workers in the same structural position. Class awareness will be subordinated to ethnic consciousness.

Certainly there is a sense in which ethnic stereotypes exist in Africa, as in Europe and elsewhere. In Central Africa, these stereotypes are still closely associated with

95

inter-tribal `joking relationships´, in which those linked by such standardised ties are not permitted to take offence at their collective denigration. But in his careful examination of the internal politics of the Railway African Union (Uganda), Grillo (1969) was able to show that accusations of `tribalism´ (always made against a rival faction, never admitted to by one´s own) were essentially a tool to discredit competitors in the leadership arena. The substance of political support within the union was generated not through ethnic ties, but by a form of `clientship´ based on departments and sections of the railways organisation. If the head of a section supported one faction within the union, so did most of his subordinates, whether or not they belonged to the same ethnic group as the section head or the union politician.

Grillo (1969:303) also made the point that `[i]n recruitment preferential treatment is given to a kinsman or neighbour from home, and the fact that a work-seeker is of one´s own tribe is not, of itself, a sufficient reason for finding him a job´. Clustering of workers of the same ethnic identity in the same work department, then, has normally resulted, not from `tribalism´, but through chain migration from particular villages, as both Grillo (1973) and Cheater (1986) have shown in detail. `Nepotism´, in other words, has been an important feature of African industrialisation.

Like `tribalism´ in the sense of establishing a new `tribal´ organisation in the towns, nepotism among Africans has often been connived at, if not encouraged, by non-Africans. As mentioned earlier, international companies and white managers have often found it convenient to use existing kinship as well as tribal ties to control workers´ behaviour in the urban workplace. Indeed, the entire concept of `tribe´ as a political entity seems to stem from a combination of the administrative practicalities of `indirect rule´ in British colonies, and the analytical constructs of anthropologists. Under these circumstances, the view that Africans themselves cleave to a `tribal´ ideology seems more than a little unfair.

But if `tribalism´ among African workers is a mythical reality deriving from the colonial experience, are workers in developing countries conscious of themselves as a `class´? Can we agree with the economic historians who have interpreted strike action and the growth of trades unions as sufficient indication that there is a `working class´ capable of defending workers´ class interests, irrespective of their other diverging interests? Or is the reality closer to Lloyd´s (1966) assertion that, in the classic marxist sense, classes have not existed and do not yet exist in Africa?

96

Answering these questions involves not merely finding but also interpreting data. It is possible, for example, to argue a marxist line that avers the existence of `objective´ classes even though the people comprising them remain unaware of their existence, and therefore require `conscientisation´ to bring about the workers´ revolution. Here, however, we are asking explicitly about the `subjective´ class awareness of individual actors as members of a class in society, and we cannot avoid evaluating their own motives for behaving as they do. Anthropologists have in the past generally preferred to attribute motives on the basis of observed behaviour, rather than to ask directly, not least because actors´ own perceptions often do not fit the motives attributed to them by others. So if a man strikes because, he says, his wife nags him into doing as the others do, is he (or she) exhibiting class awareness or not? If a worker joins a staff association rather than a union because, he says, employers never listen to militants and they are therefore ineffective, is he splitting worker solidarity and pursuing his own personal interests, or will his strategy in fact result in larger gains for all workers? If a worker threatens his fellow-workers with redundancy as `an economic fact of life´ if they do not work harder in a recessionary situation, is he conscious of his class position or not?

Anthropological evidence concerning the issue of class consciousness is difficult to interpret. On the one hand, Epstein (1958) showed how union membership fluctuated in response to the union´s effectiveness in getting individual workers more of what they wanted. On the other, Cheater (1986) described how workers fought among themselves and agreed to destroy some of their own jobs in a crisis situation in order to prevent greater catastrophe. No anthropologist has yet attempted the problematic analysis of how the self-employed women described by Obbo (1981) and others might be accommodated within an orthodox class analysis, objectively or subjectively.

It would seem that workers, like everyone else, select the most appropriate response, in the light of their personal requirements, to different situations. Personal interests do dominate those of the collectivity or class, and may explain equally well both strike action and collaboration with management on a redundancy programme. Yet such action does not necessarily mean that the individual does not identify himself with the larger unit. It may merely reflect the perfectly normal gap between what people say is right and what they actually do in order to survive. Maybe, then, on the issue of class consciousness, we have in the past been asking the wrong questions, from the wrong perspective, in the wrong way.

CHAPTER FIVE

RELATIONS OF APPROPRIATION IN SYSTEMS OF EXCHANGE

In previous chapters we have noted, in examining a wide range of ethnographic material, that a simple split between the owners and non-owners of the means of production does not often yield `classes´ in the marxist sense. Yet there is systematic inequality in these societies, whether we regard it as class-based or not. So the question is, how do such inequalities arise, if not from the relations of production? In many cases, they may be generated in the distribution of the products of human labour, through what we may distinguish (from the `relations of production´) as `relations of appropriation´. Marx regarded relations of appropriation as part of the social relations of production. However, in precapitalist systems, this approach may lead us to overlook other, more differentiated relations of appropriation. It may also lead us into dangerous theoretical territory.

The Division and Exchange of Labour

Relations of appropriation may be structured by the ways in which work is divided. In turn, the division of labour often reflects specific `ideel realities´, or ideological assumptions about the propriety of particular types of work being associated with particular types of people. It is in fact rather rare in `precapitalist´ economies to find the situation envisaged by Durkheim (1893/1964) in his concept of `mechanical solidarity´, whereby the work is so undifferentiated that anyone can do it and one worker may at any time substitute for another of similar age and sex.

Economists such as Adam Smith and sociologists like Durkheim have regarded increasing specialisation in the way in which work is divided, as contributing to the efficiency of production and the collective accumulation of wealth in the process of `development´. Such functionalist perspectives have been shared by social anthropologists who, following Durkheim, have also interpreted the division of labour as a mechanism for integrating society. This integration is achieved by creating interdependencies among producers of different goods and services. These interdependencies often transfer much of the value of work from those who do it to those who control it. Marx emphasised the importance of this transfer in structuring capitalist economies, but it also characterises `precapitalist´ societies, as can be seen from the Gikuyu of Kenya.

98

Kenyatta (1938:78) emphasised that `work reciprocity [was] the fundamental principle governing the relationship between a man and his neighbours´ and defaulting on reciprocal obligations was punishable by a system of fines. Here we are dealing with the obligation of reciprocity among men. But when we examine the work relations linking men and women in Gikuyu society, the story was different. Kenyatta (1938:54) characterised domestic labour as `naturally fall[ing] within the sphere of women´s activities´. But he also noted that men who undertook women´s work were systematically ridiculed by both men and women. `Women are afraid of a man of this character, for they say that if he could perform women´s work, what is the use of getting married?´ A rigid division of labour based on sex, then, very often underpins the institution of marriage. In turn, marriage reinforces the allocation of tasks by sex.

It is within the framework of marriage, too, that the most fundamental transfers of value may occur. Usually, the value of a wife´s work accrues to her husband rather than vice versa. Among the Gikuyu, this process of transferring labour-value worked as follows. Regarding agricultural tasks, men broke the soil while women prepared the ground for planting. Although planting was done by both sexes, men planted the `male´ crops (bananas, yams, sugar-cane, tobacco) which regularly found their way into local markets; while women planted the grains and legumes which provided family subsistence, over which they exercised some degree of control regarding storage and use. A man could not sell grain without his wife´s consent, whereas it was no concern of her´s what he did with his own crops. Weeding, like planting, was differentiated between the sexes by crop, but the harvesting of all crops was mainly the responsibility of women. Overall, then, there was some balance in the allocation of agricultural tasks, but (as in most other parts of savannah Africa), the women´s agricultural work took longer and, in addition, they ran the households. They carried the `double burden´ of productive and domestic work.

Realising and investing the value of surplus crop production occurred in two ways, both of which depended on marketing in the first instance. The proceeds of marketing could be invested in livestock, and livestock in women (through bridewealth). In turn, the direct labour of women produced more marketable surpluses; and their labour in brewing also allowed men to mobilise the labour of other men. Women´s crops were less marketable than those of men, for only the grain and beans surplus to the family´s annual requirements were sold. Even where women were able to sell their craft products, notably pottery, their other work obligations did not usually

99

leave them sufficient time to produce such goods in marketable quantities. And should a woman by some freak chance manage to acquire cash in the face of these hindrances to her marketing, she could not invest it in livestock.

Gikuyu mythology offerred an explanation for why women were forbidden to own or tend livestock. In the beginning, the Gikuyu high god, Mogai, divided the animals equally among men and women. But the women, responsible as they were for feeding their families, started slaughtering their livestock with blunt wooden knives. The surviving animals deserted, and Mogai refused to help the women regain them from the forest. Instead, he rewarded the men, whose animals were increasing at a somewhat embarrassing rate, with the knowledge of iron-working which would enable them to slaughter their beasts humanely. Women were still to be excluded from owning live-stock. In addition, to judge from Kenyatta's account, the men seem to have interpreted Mogai's instruction to share their new tools `with your unfortunate womenfolk' as a licence for the smithing clan to use its wives and children as unskilled labour in their iron foundries.

As a result of Gikuyu women's difficulties in marketing their surplus products and their exclusion from stock owner-ship, they were unable to use the accumulatory spiral of crop surplus -> livestock -> wives -> labour + beer -> crop surplus which was open to men. Instead, their labour within marriage underpinned this spiral. Kenyatta's insider, male, functional-ist perspective suggested that the Gikuyu women accepted as `proper' the culturally-defined division of labour and the investment pattern which discriminated against them. Later fieldwork by a female anthropologist, however, yielded infor-mation on intra-marital conflicts which suggested that women were well aware of the significance of money and investment in the process by which they were subordinated to their husbands. Clarke (1980) noted that women who did manage to retain and control the product of their own labour, refused to be sub-jected to normal expectations of wifely obedience because they, too, `had money'. But in general their lack of access to `money' resulted from the marriage system, which also deprived women of primary rights to till mbari land independently of men. One could argue, then, with Marx, that the relations of appropriation in Gikuyu marriage merely reflected the division between those who owned productive property and those who did not. But then we imply the constitution of economic classes on the basis of gender and marriage!

While marriage may be one way of structuring assymetrical exchanges of labour, it is by no means the only one in `precapitalist' economies. Of perhaps equal importance is the

100

very widespread institution of the `work party´, in which the host provides beer (or other alcoholic refreshment) in return for the work of those who attend. Their labour ceases when the refreshments run out, so the careful host husbands his drink until as late an hour as possible. As we have already seen among the Gikuyu, the work of preparing the beer normally falls on wives. Discounting this labour, Barth (1965) estimated that in Darfur, the conversion of millet into beer for a work party tripled its value in terms of labour mobilised. Therefore, in a system where beer is the only reward for labour, the work party may be a very effective way of appropriating labour. And in Darfur, Barth indeed found a clear distinction between the successful, who hosted more work parties than they attended; and the unsuccessful (the elderly, the disabled and those with a penchant for beer) who regularly transferred their labour to others through this institution.

Commercial farmers, however, may cost the work party differently to the millet-cultivating Fur. Freehold farmers in Msengezi, Zimbabwe, regarded the work party as an inefficient institution, for a number of reasons. Firstly, they believed that the labour of their wives could be more effectively deployed weeding or harvesting than brewing during the worst seasonal labour shortages. Secondly, they regarded the work efficiency of beer-drinkers as low. Thirdly, even free beer did not mobilise labour on the scale they required to work an average of over 35 acres planted mainly to hybrid maize and cotton.

Historically, in Southern Africa beer was not, apparently, an adequate return for labour. A number of anthropologists have argued that the beer was ancillary to the <u>reciprocal</u> exchange of labour in this part of the world. More recent fieldwork, however, has suggested that this interpretation perhaps reflected cultural ideals rather than empirical practice. The Msengezi farmers, for example, had devised a new term, entirely different from the work party or <u>nhimbe</u> in Shona, for exact exchanges of labour on a regular basis. But even this <u>machangano</u> arrangement had been unsuccessful in meeting the labour needs of commercial farming. It is possible, therefore, that work parties and exchanges of labour, properly costed, do not in fact permit the appropriation of others´ labour on a sufficiently large scale to be attractive beyond relatively limited production for subsistence and the occasional marketing of small surpluses. Polygamy appears to be a much better bet!

Appropriation and Investment

For Marx himself (in <u>Capital</u>), the major appropriative mechanism, which was linked directly into ownership of the means of production, was rent. He identified three somewhat different types of rent: labour rent; rent-in-kind; and money rent. The first two (which are often associated with systems of sharecropping) he saw as characteristic of precapitalist systems, while the last he associated with capitalism. Again, however, western concepts of rent have not in the past proved very useful in their application to other systems. As we saw in chapter 2 in the case of Malay fishermen, `rent´ in peasant societies may be expressed as rightful shares in the product, irrespective of the actual quantity of this product. On this basis, `sharecropping´ arrangements have characterised peasant systems of fishing, herding and cultivation alike.

In such systems of fixed shares in variable products, what producers actually retain in relation to their needs depends on the absolute quantity of their product, which in turn depends on environmental factors. A good season will yield a surplus for the producer, even after `rent´ shares have been deducted from the total, and he may invest this surplus in what may become an accumulatory spiral (for example, of money-lending). A poor season, in contrast, will leave him short on his household consumption requirements, and drive him into debt to fund his subsistence. Peasants are more often in one of these two polar positions than in the median alternative, of simply breaking even on what they need to live. Roseberry (1976) has demonstrated theoretically that this mechanism of rent, through its absolute variability despite its fixed proportions, can therefore introduce class differentiation into peasant societies in which landholdings were originally identical. But then the question becomes, what mechanisms permit those who do not break even to continue to subsist?

Clearly, in Asian societies, one answer is the system of village money-lending, in which interest rates (for example, for fishing loans) may run as high as 10 per cent per day. Another is the <u>jajmani</u> system, which defines poor service workers as the permanent clients, paid in grain, of wealthy families. In both Asian and many other societies, a third answer revolves around systems of exchange, including gifts and services as well as trading commodities.

Sharing and redistributing what Marx called `use-values´ may be regarded as essentially political behaviour, whereas trading `exchange-values´ is essentially economic. The products of generosity are usually political influence, if not

102

power or authority, and enhanced social prestige, as we see most readily in the example of New Guinea `big-men´. Indeed, Godelier (1978) has suggested that exchange might have been the primary mechanism by which states emerged in uncentralised societies. He argued that people may undervalue easily-produced, material goods and willingly exchange them for more highly-valued non-material services (for example, in communicating with deities believed to control the conditions of production).

In monetised systems, production surpluses may be accumulated in material form. In what some have called `natural´ economies, however, a surplus product is more likely to be invested in people, though it may also be invested in capital goods (such as livestock or fishing canoes). Indeed, where accumulation proceeds by capitalising labour, it is difficult to separate people (for example, wives) from capital goods. The payment of bridewealth in capital goods illustrates this linkage. In the past, investment in people might be made directly through marriage, or slavery, or indirectly through participation in feasting or systems of `ceremonial exchange´. In the present, perhaps the most common form of human investment is in the education of the young, in the expectation of longer-deferred rewards than was characteristic of past patterns of investing in people.

Spheres of Exchange and Conversion Possibilities

We may agree with Bailey (1971:10) that `Exchange is the essence of social interaction: society exists in that men give each other deference, challenge, pieces of information, money, tribute, service´. However, certain types of goods and services are not normally exchanged against one another in any society. In Tikopia, one did not exchange fishing canoes for food. In Darfur, one did not traditionally work for money. In most societies, one does not tender jewellery in return for medical attention. Goods (and services) may therefore be grouped empirically into separate `spheres of exchange´, within which the transaction values of particular items are reasonably standardised. Between these separate spheres, relative values are much more difficult to determine. Analytically, however, these separate spheres are linked in a total system of circulating goods and sevices, which, in the long term and for the society as a whole, normally accumulate value and capitalise production.

These separate spheres of exchange are not readily distinguished from one another in economies using a formal currency for most exchange transactions. However, in non-monetised economies, traditionally at least two separate spheres existed, in ceremonial and non-ceremonial goods, or luxury and marital goods, as opposed to foodstuffs and household subsistence requirements. Such systems are rapidly disappearing, of course, in `this world of money´, as the introduction or extension of currencies has affected the integrity of the boundaries separating traditionally distinct spheres of exchange.

Within each sphere, items could be exchanged against one another, but they could not <u>normally</u> be tendered against items from a different sphere. In crisis situations, however, exchanges did breach the `normal´ rules. For example, in Shona society, one did not usually exchange marriageable women for food, not least because they had a bridewealth value much greater than that of food. But when drought struck and the food ran out, poorer families did indeed exchange their unmarried daughters for food from wealthier producers´ stocks. In the absence of an immediately marriageable girl, female infants were pledged in later marriage to the family which provided food in a crisis. In this patrilineal society, too, one did not normally pay bridewealth by working for one´s father-in-law, as the biblical Jacob worked for both Leah and Rachel. But if a young man had no hoes or livestock, he provided groom service as the poor man´s substitute for bridewealth - otherwise he didn´t get married. Like any other rules, then, those bounding separate spheres of exchange were not immutable. Nonetheless, they did generate systems of exchange which westerners found difficult to understand.

On the north-west coast of North America, for example, indigenous Indian societies such as the Kwakiutl and Tlingit had a system of feasting and gift-giving which has passed into the anthropological literature under its local name of the `potlatch´. The essence of the potlatch was the distribution of food and valuables to large numbers of people who attended feasts sponsored by wealthy individuals. This system has to be understood against the background of an ecology which permitted the regular production of surplus food and other products; and the decimation of nineteenth-century Indian populations by the diseases of colonialism, which left many chiefly titles vacant, uninherited and `up for grabs´ by ambitious commoners.

In this competitive situation, potlatching was transformed. Originally the potlatch marked, by the ritual exchange of traditional valuables, changes in social status which accompanied the `life crises´ of birth, marriage, death and accession to political office. But in the nineteenth century, potlatching became a means of attaining power by the destruction of wealth. Vacant titles were claimed by those who established their ascendancy over their competitors by shaming them through destroying more valuables. Beaten copper shields and vast quantities of trade goods such as blankets were burned or thrown into the sea at huge feasts. The `new´ potlatch breached the older definitions of acceptable exchanges by enabling `ceremonial´ goods to be converted into political power, and then ratifying this power as the legitimate authority of traditional office. Which is not quite the same as requiring millions of dollars to run for the presidency of the United States of America, but there are certain similarities!

If property-conscious westerners found the potlatch difficult to understand when they first encountered its modified form, the `kula´ of Melanesia was even more incomprehensible. The `kula´, which is best translated into English as `ring´ or `circle´, linked and still links a number of small island groups off the eastern tip of Papua-New Guinea in another form of ceremonial exchange. Malinowski (1922) wrote of the kula from a Trobriand perspective, but six other island groups also participated in the exchange system: the Engineer group, Misima, the Laughlans, Woodlark, the Marshall Bennett and d´Entrecasteaux islands.

The kula takes its name from the formalised, ceremonial exchange of two types of shell ornaments: the red necklaces or <u>soulava</u> and white armbands called <u>mwali</u>. These valuables are made from scarce, imported, highly-valued raw shell from the Port Moresby area of mainland New Guinea to the west and from Sudest and Rossel islands to the south-east. The shell is apparently manufactured into necklaces and armbands by a number of craftsmen in different stages. New valuables therefore work their way into the exchanges gradually; they do not upset the system by suddenly appearing, complete, as new and high-ranking ornaments.

The necklaces travel clockwise around the participating islands while the armbands move in the opposite direction. The exchange is deferred. On one trip I go to collect a valuable from my partner. Later, he will visit me to receive an article of the opposite type but of equivalent ranking in the system. If either of us tries to cheat on the equivalence, there is nothing the partner can do immediately, for it is unseemly to haggle over kula valuables. However, such behaviour generates mistrust which, in the long run, may ease the cheat out of the system altogether.

At the time that Malinowski studied it, the kula was a closed system, an affair of aristocrats and chiefs. Only successful or up-and-coming `big-men´ commoners managed to break into the system by acquiring a valuable from an existing member wishing to sponsor promising young men. Normally valuables were enclosed within the existing status circuit by confining their transfer to kula exchanges, marriage, inheritance, anticipatory inheritance, or (in the matrilineal system of the Trobriands) gifts from father to son. It was impossible to acquire a kula valuable by offering trade goods in exchange, and the necessity to know the kula magic militated against entry to the circuit through the illegitimate acquisition of a valuable (by theft, for example, or barter access to the raw materials). Participation in kula exchanges thus reinforced existing socio-political differentials in these island societies, and confirmed the importance of political authority in enabling necessary trade to occur.

In addition to the exchange of kula valuables by chiefs, aristocrats and `big-men´, the kula also used to support extensive inter-island trade among the commoners, in both foodstuffs (yams, taro, bananas, pigs) and manufactured goods (pottery, axe-blades, canoes). Trade (<u>gimwali</u>) was the antithesis of kula exchanges in its fiercely-negotiated barter deals. The kula valuables and the trade goods were emphatically in different spheres of exchange, but without the protection of the kula, trade would not, in the past, have been possible between these autonomous islands which were politically and mystically hostile to one another. Trade was important, because some islands in the system had poor soils and a food deficit. They did, however, produce craft goods. More recently they have been disadvantaged, in inter-island trade, by the increasing availability of imported trade goods.

The maintenance of distinct spheres of ceremonial and trade exchanges in Melanesia, then, helped to perpetuate the system of political ranking and social differentiation, even if chiefs and aristocrats shared a similar standard of living with their subordinates. The appropriation of kula valuables by the `ruling class´ (if we may call it that) defined their functional importance in these island societies. We are dealing here with a system of collective appropriation of material objects that have a primary ideological significance in defining `the proper order of things´, rather than with the appropriation of the products of human labour, which is doubtless why the kula has persisted. As yet, apparently, the conditions have not arisen that would enable the separation of kula and trade spheres to be breached, as happened to the potlatch a hundred years ago.

Convertibility and Monetisation

In maintaining the integrity of their ceremonial sphere of exchange, these Melanesian islands are somewhat peculiar. All over the developing world, those spheres incorporating marriage exchanges in particular have been systematically commercialised by allowing money to replace traditional luxury goods. Douglas (1965) has described the impact of such changes among the Lele of Kasai province, Zaire, Central Africa. She has argued that the goods traditionally used in ceremonial payments, such as marriage, should not be regarded as money at all, but rather as coupons or licences controlling participation in that sphere.

Lele society was a gerontocracy, in which the old men not only aggregated power to themselves, but also monopolised the marriageable women in polygamous unions. Men could not expect to marry individually much before the age of forty years, but before this their sexual needs were accommodated by the institution of the `village wife´, who was married to a group of `bachelors´. Bridewealth for the village wife, in the standard form of raffia cloths woven from tree-bark, was paid by the village elders. Her children, like all others, belonged to their mother´s matrilineage. When her `husbands´ married individually, they had to provide the raffia cloth themselves for their bridewealth payments.

Raffia cloths, as rationing coupons, were the means by which Lele elders controlled the distribution of women in marriage. The raw material for raffia cloths literally grew on trees, and weaving the cloths was a male prerogative. The reason why younger men did not simply weave their own bridewealth in the required quantities was that fines, fees and levies determined by the elders consumed most of the products of the younger men´s labour, and delivered the raffia they made into the hands of the elders. For the large quantities required for bridewealth, then, the younger men had to rely on the elders´ contributions. `These senior men thus found themselves at the issue-desk [for coupons], as it were, and did not fail to take full advantage of the patron-client opportunities of their situation´, as Douglas (1965:132) noted.

As younger Lele men migrated to the copper mines of Southern Zaire and brought Belgian francs back home, we might expect this hard currency to have undermined the elders´ control of the raffia rationing system. In practice, the elders devised counter-measures. A three-way exchange rate, linking raffia, francs and goods, had emerged fairly early in the colonial taxation system and an `official´ exchange rate (of 10 francs to one raffia cloth) governed barter exchanges.

However, for valuable goods in such barter deals, for example livestock, an `unofficial´ exchange rate discounted the <u>raffia</u> value by 10 per cent <u>if and only if</u> raffia was tendered as payment. This discount had the effect of pushing up the price of raffia in francs, which only the young men were in a position to tender. Douglas (1965:141) regarded this practice partly as discounting for cash, but mainly as a mechanism `to protect the pattern of wealth-holding within the economy´, on the one hand by stemming the flow of raffia to young men, and on the other by channelling the francs into the hands of the elders. The Lele elders seem to have been particularly astute in their manipulation of two exchange media. Other societies have seen their traditional patterns of control more thoroughly undermined by the monetisation of ceremonial payments. One wonders whether the Lele elders themselves were able to continue to block the convertibility of ceremonial goods beyond the 1950s, when Douglas observed their system.

In contrast to the Lele, among the mountain Fur of the Western Sudan, bridewealth payments have long been monetised, and for generations they have been involved in a system of periodic (weekly) markets. However, when Barth (1965) visited Darfur in 1964, he noted that cash was little used in the Fur villages themselves, men requiring perhaps £8 annually for their subsistence needs and women maybe a third of this figure. Very little millet (the staple grain) was sold, the majority being retained for home consumption and the making of beer. (Notwithstanding Quranic prohibitions on alcohol, beer was very important in this Muslim society.) Tomatoes and wheat, however, were raised as cash crops, and garlic and onions were both consumed and sold, as were the products of the new, irrigated fruit orchards.

It was, therefore, possible to identify two spheres of exchange, one monetised and the other not, but these were not impermeable. Indeed, the exchanges of value between them were the subject of entrepreneurial experimentation and sometimes yielded enormous profits. One man, for example, expended £3.8.0 in mobilising labour for his tomato crop by using the traditional work party, and sold his crop in the weekly market for £38.0.0. Barth argued, therefore, that it was important to understand not merely what the spheres of exchange were, but also how value flowed through the whole system, leading finally to its accumulation (usually in the form of livestock), or to its ultimate consumption (the pilgrimage to Mecca being the most important way in which accumulated value was removed from the Fur economy).

If we look more carefully at the non-monetised sphere of village subsistence, we see a system of fully-individualised

108

production, in which men and their wives were completely
independent units. The husband had to provide his wife and
children with clothes and other purchased needs, while the
wife was obliged to brew beer for her husband from millet that
he provided, but each maintained separate fields, grain stores
and `purses´. This system in fact made men more dependent on
women than vice versa, for only women could brew beer. In the
absence of a wife, a man had to appeal to his mother or sister
to undertake this work for him, if he wished to mobilise
labour to work in his fields. Women, in contrast, did not need
the services of men to organise their own work parties.

Beer was the key to deploying labour, for it was regarded
as shameful to work for cash. Even the Sudanese government
initially had difficulty in recruiting Fur men to posts in the
Forestry Department that paid ten times the daily value of the
beer a man consumed at a work party. Barth admitted, however,
that this calculation - like those of Fur men themselves -
omitted the value of the female labour expended in brewing,
based as it was on the simple conversion of millet to cash at
market prices. Even in a system of egalitarian access to land,
then, mechanisms such as brewing for a work party within a
single sphere of non-monetised exchange, may permit men to
appropriate value from women´s work. And Barth (1965:155-6),
like Nelson and Obbo in East Africa, also noted that the sale
of their beer at the weekly market laid women open to charges
of immodesty and immorality, `because the making of beer is an
intimate female service appropriate only in a close, domestic
context´. It would appear, then, that it may be easier for men
than for women to convert the value of their products between
separate spheres of exchange, and to profit from doing so.

Gift Exchange

So far we have examined exchanges of goods and labour
that may be described as obligatory in some sense. Exchanges
of bridewealth and of labour within marriage are defined and
enjoined by custom. Even the kula valuables have their status
and routes generally determined by the system rather than by
the actions of specific individuals. When we look at the
apparently voluntary exchange of gifts between individuals, we
see again an underlying obligation.

Here the best place to start is with an individualistic
society such as that of the United Kingdom. In such an
`advanced capitalist economy´, we might expect gifts to be
peripheral, in contrast to their importance in precapitalist
societies such as the Trobriands, where after every harvest
men customarily despatched gifts of yams to their married

109

sisters, to reinforce the bonds of matrilineal descent. Gifts are important in the UK, however, not merely in social relationships, but also to the national economy.

In most historical and contemporary societies, the giving of gifts has marked changes in social status, the so-called `life-crises´ of birth, naming, coming-of-age and marriage. Gifts also celebrate, in contemporary societies, individual achievements (such as graduation) and birthdays; and society´s festive days (Easter, Ramadan, Diwali, Christmas, the Chinese spring and autumn festivals, and very many different new years, among others).

Celebratory gifts for these occasions may be drawn from the existing range of commodities produced. However, in affluent societies there is an independent economic niche for both manufacturers of and traders in items that Davis (1972) called `gift-goods´, notably greetings cards, gift-wrapping paper, flowers, perfumes, jewellery and children´s toys. More utilitarian consumer durables and alcohol may also be given as gifts, but their production and distribution is not subject to the same pecularities of demand that the `pure´ gift-goods experience.

Aggregated gift-giving in the UK (and in other western countries) is big business. In 1968, nearly 120,000 workers were employed in manufacturing gift-goods and earned over £115 million in wages. The value of raw materials used exceeded £195 million, while the ex-factory price of the finished gift-goods was estimated at nearly £660 million. Expenditure on gifts, at £1,140 million, totalled some 4.3 per cent of all consumer expenditure in the UK. And these figures - which exceed the government budgets of poorer third world countries - were conservative. They excluded charitable donations, business promotions (such as the drug manufacturers´ free samples to doctors and the ubiquitous pocket diaries and other `advertising´ material), as well as business lunches and other entertainments, and the kind of gifts that landed Mr. Tanaka in such political trouble.

In seeking to explain how small gifts add up to such staggering totals, we must return to the element of obligation. `There are no free lunches´, as the saying goes and, contradicting Malinowski, there are no `free gifts´ of other types either. The French anthropologist Marcel Mauss was the first to analyse the mechanics of gift-giving and to point this out. Mauss (1923-4/1966) argued that gifts actually involve not one obligation, but three: the obligation to give, the obligation to receive, and the obligation to return or repay.

The obligation to give is defined by the wider society. It is a cultural obligation to give gifts on certain occasions and to pass on ceremonial goods like the kula valuables. In some societies, the obligation to give permeates most if not all face-to-face social relations. For example, all hunting societies have specific rules for dividing the product of the hunt. The hunter who kills game must give specific portions to persons related to him in specific ways. Not to give is not merely to be selfish, but to reject participation in this system of social relations.

The obligation to receive is not quite so straight-forward. Who, after all, would `look a gift horse in the mouth´, much less reject it altogether? Well, in the first instance, anyone who does not wish to be indebted to the giver will reject a gift. The young lady not wishing to contemplate marriage will be careful about accepting valuable gifts from would-be suitors. The politician who does not wish to commit himself to supporting a particular company´s tender bid is wise not to accept their gifts. But in many societies, a refusal to accept a gift has more sinister connotations. To reject food may be to imply a distrust not only of its components but also of the intentions of the person who offers it. Many feudal monarchs all over the world employed personal tasters to guard against a `poisoned gift´. (As Bailey (1971) points out, the Germanic stem gif may translate into either `gift´ or `poison´: the two go together.) This distrust may be carried even further, so that a refusal to receive a gift may imply a suspicion of mystical attack, by means of witchcraft or sorcery. The obligation to receive a gift offerred, then, enjoins and reflects trust in social relations.

The obligation to return a gift is more complex than it seems on the surface. Mauss originally thought, based on the Maori concept of hau, that a gift incorporates part of the giver´s personality, which seeks to return to its `owner´ through reciprocation. This notion is now regarded as a faulty understanding of Maori ideas. Generally a failure to return a gift leaves the recipient indebted to the giver. But, as Sahlins (1965/1974) has shown, there are different types of reciprocity, depending on the equivalence of the return, whether the return is immediate or deferred, and how precisely the return is made.

Sahlins has distinguished, firstly, reciprocal or `vice-versa´ transactions from `pooling´ (collecting goods into a political centre) and redistribution. With the exception of certain marriage transactions, these two types may be glossed as direct and indirect exchanges respectively. Reciprocity includes gift-giving and redistribution the payment of taxes

111

and/or tribute in return for general distributions (of welfare payments, or food) when times are hard. In a sense, redistribution proper could be regarded as a form of gift-giving, even though the prior pooling on which it depends is more remote from the `gift´ category.

Secondly, Sahlins noted that the motivation for exchange ranges from simple self-interest, through mutual interest of the parties in each other, to a more detached or disinterested concern for the other. Corresponding to these differences in motivation, we find a range in reciprocation extending from the negative (in which each party is out to extract an unreturned advantage); through a balanced equivalence of value; to positive or `generalised´ reciprocity of an altruistic kind. Negative reciprocity includes such appropriative transactions as those described by `haggling´, `gambling´ and `theft´. Balanced reciprocity is characterised by an immediate return of an equivalent gift (for example, in the direct exchange of sisters in marriage). Generalised reciprocity, in contrast, is open-ended and long-term. The return, as Sahlins (1965/1974:194) puts it, `is not stipulated by time, quantity or quality: the expectation of reciprocity is indefinite´. There is, instead, a `diffuse obligation to reciprocate when necessary´, when the original giver is in need and/or when the original recipient is in a position to repay. The idealised model of generalised reciprocity is that of parenthood or, perhaps, religious sacrifice.

Firth (1963) has identified sacrifice as a specific form of gift exchange linking men and their gods. In exchange for undefined benefits over an unspecified time period, man gives himself (or part of himself) to the deities. He does this symbolically, by destroying his property, in the form of libations of alcohol, offerings of vegetable products, or the slaughter of animals. But sacrifice is not a perfect model of generalised reciprocity, for even here men attempt to cheat. The sacrifice of a chicken, for example, when the donor could have afforded a goat, annoys the Ibo's personal destiny, who may reciprocate by causing a snake to bite the offender. On the other hand, Nuer, who call wild cucumbers `oxen´ and `sacrifice´ them, seem not to be punished by their gods for such `prudent calculation´, and so manage to tip the exchange in their own favour. (Though one would never call such sacrifice `haggling´, the entire institution of sacrifice - not merely these examples - does bear some resemblance to `gambling´.)

We are now perhaps in a better position to understand why gifts comprise such an important part of all economies. An industry with a turnover of over one billion pounds annually, is not an ephemeral speculation in a passing fashion. It is securely founded on structural relationships in society, even if individuals sometimes default on their obligations in these relationships.

Trade, Middlemen and Markets

In the entire range of appropriative relationships, the most obvious, and the one that has been subject to the most efforts to replace it, is that of the middleman or trader who buys from producers and sells to consumers. Particularly where intermediary traders have operated a `closed ethnic shop´ in a foreign society, indigenous governments have made strenuous efforts to replace them, often with co-operative organisations. Lebanese and Syrians in West Africa, Indians in East Africa, Chinese in Malaysia and Jews almost everywhere have had their trading diasporas undermined in an effort to regain for nationals (or the state) the value they have appropriated in the past.

Indignation on the part of national governments about the trading profits of foreigners, however, may be somewhat misplaced. Such governments should themselves bear a far heavier burden of appropriative guilt than they do. In their own systems of appropriation, though taxation, export levies, unequal terms of trade for agricultural as opposed to industrial products, and inefficient marketing monopsonies, they may appropriate so much of the product value that its producers turn to smuggling across national boundaries, or simply abandon certain lines of production altogether. The post-1978 Chinese economic reforms recognised that state appropriations had impaired production in the past and sought, somewhat hesitantly, to diminish them and permit peasants to retain more of the value that they produced. In the 1980s, in an attempt to rehabilitate its agricultural sector, Tanzania abolished the monopsonist co-operative unions that the state had established in the 1960s to prevent the exploitation of its peasantry by Indian traders. While they existed, these unions had extracted a rate of return that the Indians might possibly have envied, had they been as mercenary as they were often painted. The unions, after all, had the weight of state authority behind them in returning to producers less than half of the price that the state realised for their products on its export markets. When anthropologists have sought to understand production and distribution in local societies, they have often ignored this dimension of state action.

But let us examine ethnic trade monopolies in more detail, in an attempt to understand whether it is their ethnic

113

or their appropriative dimensions, or both, which cause indignation in the host society. A useful place to begin is with the marketing of the fish whose production in Kelantan state, Malaya, has been described in chapter 2.

Kelantan fish were landed on the beaches, and sold there to fish-dealers with varying financial resources. For those boats whose total catch (excluding the fish for daily consumption) went to the boat-owner or -financier, there was no bargaining. The catches of independent boats, however, were sold to the highest bidder, almost always one of the larger fish-dealers. The entire catch might be sold as a unit, in which case the purchaser usually enjoyed a bulk discount; or it might be sold in smaller parcels to different traders. Many of the smaller fish-dealers were Malay women; almost all of the big dealers were immigrant Chinese.

The bigger the dealer, the more likely he was to be permitted to buy on credit until the next mosque day (Friday). Poor buyers, in contrast, had to produce cash for smaller quantities. They also usually received the lower-grade fish. Prices fluctuated according to the time of landing, the quantity of particular species available that day, the quantity of fish in general, and market demand at different seasons. In general, prices started low, rose towards midday and fell off by late afternoon. At the end of a day's trading, those who processed fish into paste, or cured it by salting or sun-drying, stepped in to buy up residual stocks at cut prices. By investing labour in prolonging the storage time for which the fish could be kept, they realised a more secure (though still not high) profit than did the dealers in fresh fish. Almost all of the processing labour came from Malay women working on a piecework basis for Chinese fish-dealers.

Chinese profits in the fish-trade were, therefore, somewhat higher than the profits of Malay traders, for three reasons. Firstly, they were able to buy good fish in bulk and sell them in inland urban markets, where the prices were significantly higher than in local coastal outlets. Secondly, by reinvesting at least part of their profits in financing the larger fishermen, they bought the fish at a discounted price and got the benefit of credit. Thirdly, by processing cheap fish using cheap labour so as to make possible its storage and transportation to much more distant, regional markets, they secured a more reliable return to their capital than came from their trade in fresh fish, for which the market swings were more unpredictable.

It is important to note here that the market itself was a constraint on profiteering. As we have already seen in chapter

4, petty commodity producers using unsophisticated technology generally do not earn attractive incomes from `profits´. Enlarging the scale of trade does help to aggregate small absolute profits into large and stable incomes. For this reason, fishermen often prefer to do business with larger and financially more secure traders. But the linkage between marketing and production also enables larger dealers to secure their own position against all other competitors. In Malaya, this linkage separated Malays from Chinese, but in Sri Lanka, the larger and more unscrupulous fish dealers (the mudalali) were themselves local men.

The Hausa of West Africa show more clearly than the Chinese in Malaya the specific strategies which foreign traders may use to protect their own niche in a local market. Hausa involved in `long-distance´ trade are found all over West Africa, from Senegal to Chad, although their homeland is in the north of Nigeria. In most West African cities, they live separately from the host society, in special `quarters´. Sometimes, as in Ibadan (Western Nigeria), the Hausa `sabo´ (short for sabon gari; zongo is the term used in Ghana) originated in an agreement between the local Yoruba and the British colonial administrators that the undesirable habits of the Hausa (and other ethnic groups) necessitated their separation from normal citizens. In other cities, the ethnically-distinct sectors resulted from `home-boys´ sticking together in foreign parts.

The Hausa trading diaspora in West Africa probably still comprises a number of interlinked but distinct commodity `sectors´. In the 1960s, long-distance traders dealt principally in cattle and kola nut, with a number of subsidiary goods, including manufactured imports. These imported goods were generally destined for the rural periodic markets and sedentary traders in large towns and cities, like Kano in Northern Nigeria. Trade in grains and other agricultural products of the northern savannah, however, did not initially go through Hausa traders in periodic markets, but were bought by secluded Hausa wives in what Hill (1969) has called the `house trade´. However, these products might later find their way to southern retail outlets through the long-distance network.

Looking at the principal commodities of the long-distance trade, the cattle were produced by the Fulani herdsmen whom we encountered in chapter 2, while the kola was grown by Yoruba and other farmers in the forest belt. The commissions taken by the buying agents varied between 3 and 10 percent of the value of the purchase. The Hausa traders transported both over hundreds of miles, and national boundaries, to sell in areas where their production was not possible. The price of the final sale, in a situation of unusual scarcity, might be three times the price paid to the producer. However, this price included all of the costs of labour, transport, and customs dues involved in shifting the product from producer to consumer. The value of this trade was very large. Cohen (1969) estimated that in the mid-1960s the cattle trade into Ibadan alone, where 75,000 cattle were sold annually, was worth at least one million Nigerian pounds. The outstanding debt on these transactions totalled over N£100,000. The kola trade out of Ibadan was probably worth even more. Yet none of this trade, or the credit which Hausa traders used and advanced, went through the formal banking system; the cattle were not transported by rail, but driven south on foot; none of the trading arrangements impinged on the modern or `formal´ sector of Nigerian business. How, then, did the system work?

At the core of the Ibadan network were 30-odd landlords who controlled more than half of the housing and storage space in Sabo. Housing was the most important form of Hausa saving and the best index of creditworthiness. One-tenth of all housing in the quarter was reserved for accommodating the mobile trade-agents (the drovers and commission agents in charge of the cattle) and the clerical and domestic workers serving the traders in Sabo. This `hotel´ accommodation, with three meals a day included, was available free of charge to the commission agents who entrusted their business to the landlord who owned it.

The landlords acted as brokers between the mobile cattle traders and the Yoruba butchers who bought their cattle, and between the Yoruba farmers who grew kola and the northern traders on whose behalf they bought it. This brokerage involved extending and guaranteeing credit to buyers. For example, Yoruba butchers were ranked on a four-week credit scale, extending from zero to N£1,000. Each landlord therefore specialised in one of these major commodities, for keeping track of the creditworthiness of his clients was enough to keep him busy full-time in the interests of the trading network as a whole. However, this specialisation did not preclude the landlords from investing in services ancillary to the trade, in travel and lorry transport, as well as housing.

Given that the long-distance trade did not use formal, written contracts or bank guarantees, and that many traders were strangers to one another, the landlords had to devise ways of assessing the honesty of the mobile traders with whom they dealt. Conversely, those who entrusted their business to a local broker, had to know that they would not be conned. This trust was established by emphasising shared Hausa ethnic identity. `Our customs are different´, the traders said, and

116

used their ethnic distinctiveness to draw a definitive social boundary around the trading network. Within this network every individual was vouched for by his behaviour and trackable if he defaulted on his trade obligations. Anyone who did not dress as a Hausa, speak Hausa, attend mosque every Friday, and marry a Hausa girl, was eased out of the long-distance trade and out of the spatial niche in the `sabo´ or `zongo´ from which it operated.

When the conversion of the Yoruba to orthodox Sunni Islam started to blur the division between themselves and their Hausa fellow-worshippers in Ibadan, the Hausa traders converted fanatically to a new and rather obscure Sufi sect within Islam, the Tijaniyya, and ceased to attend the Ibadan central mosque. It should be noted that this `retribalisation´ of the Ibadan Hausa, in a religious idiom, followed their failure to protect their trading interests through secular political activity on behalf of the Northern People´s Congress. As Cohen (1969) pointed out, this `retribalisation´ had little to do with primordial ethnic identity. Those Hausa in Ibadan who were not involved in the long-distance trade were much more prone to marry Yoruba or Ibo women, to abandon the fez and the quftan in favour of western-type dress, and to integrate themselves into local society. But the `customs´ of the traders were certainly `different´, and were used to protect their economic interests. Nor, indeed, are the Hausa unique in this respect, as Cohen (1974) has also indicated in his account of the similar kinds of `custom´ found among brokers on the London Stock Exchange. It would appear that trade requires social trust rather than, or perhaps in addition to, financial guarantees.

From the Hausa example, then, we can understand why host societies may resent traders who encapsulate themselves in ethnic exclusiveness in order to protect their economic interests, and why governments seeking to break a trade monopoly of this kind may attack the ethnic group itself in order to prise open their trade monopoly. In such situations, ethnicity is, in marxist terms, a mystification of the underlying relations of appropriation. However, traders in many societies appear to be more concerned with servicing the long-term social relationships which underpin their mode of livelihood, than with their short-term profits, even where the rate of profit appears to be quite high.

In the Caribbean, as in much of West Africa, marketing fresh produce is the business of women. In Jamaica in the 1950s, small rural traders spent half of their working week in marketing activities, collecting small quantities of their neighbours´ produce on foot or by mule and travelling to and

117

from urban markets by truck. The actual time they spent selling in the market was a very small proportion of their total time in the trade. Their profits appeared to be quite high. Katzin's (1960) figures suggested a rate of profit between 50 and 75 per cent of the buying price. In absolute money terms, however, these profits were small, and were agreed as `fair` (in relation to the prices they realised when selling on to the next stage of wholesaling) by both buyers and sellers. These standard profits, based on stable prices, permitted the trader to restock in the coming week, and to in buy her weekly grocery requirements, including flour, sugar, rice, cooking oil, maize meal, bread, dairy products, salted fish and preserved milk. Because her costs (of transport and admission to market) were fixed, the trader's net profit depended on the volume of goods she could obtain and sell from a large number of peasant farmers, each wanting to dispose of only very small quantities which were surplus to their household consumption requirements.

The concept of a `fair` profit was intended to cover the traders' time as well as direct costs, but it is clear that what accrued to their labour was - as in all other systems of petty commodity production - what was left over after the deduction of their costs. If the quality of their goods was so low that they could not realise their `fair` profit, or if the normally stable prices dipped, their labour might go completely unrewarded. Such `self-exploitation` is a characteristic feature of such systems, in contrast to the fixed costing of labour in capitalist pricing. Over the long term, the concept of a `fair` profit, however high in proportionate terms, is designed to reward the traders' labour at roughly similar rates to those prevailing among the poor whose consumer needs they cater to. As we saw among the Minangkabau blacksmiths in chapter 4, the market sets the level of return to labour and acts as a low-level equilibrium trap.

It is in this context that petty producers and traders emphasise the continuity of their economic niche, by investing in social relationships rather than in high levels of monetary profit. Jamaican country traders, for example, shopped for groceries for those who regularly sold them produce and, since they incurred no freight charges on the journey home from market, charged nothing for this service. They helped `their` producers whenever possible in numerous other ways as well. Similarly, when particular commodities were in short supply, they would reserve part of their supplies, at normal prices, for those wholesalers with whom they did regular business in the urban markets, rather than realising a higher price from those with whom they had no such relationship. They knew that if they wanted to stay in the trade and make a secure, regu-

lar, though small income, pursuing `fast bucks´ didn´t pay.
Social trust was more important, particularly in an somewhat
anarchic physical situation in the markets, where theft and
other illegalities always threatened their slender earnings.

Other social factors also influence trading relationships
and profit-taking. Tolai farmers in the Gazelle peninsula of
North-Eastern New Guinea were well aware that they could
realise the highest final price for their cocoa by selling it
to processing plants controlled by the Local Government
Council. But Epstein (1968) noted that by 1965, 64 per cent of
all Tolai cocoa was being sold secretly to private Chinese
processors. In 1959-60, one-tenth of all households in the
Rapitok parish, where Epstein did her fieldwork, sold their
entire output, while another 26 per cent sold part of their
crop, to Chinese processors. Local newspapers painted the
picture of Chinese traders `milking´ the public fermentaries
by offering prohibited booze and methylated spirits to
alcohol-dependent producers, and of Tolai selling to them in
order to conceal their thefts of cocoa beans from honest
producers. Less prejudiced suggestions included the speculation that individuals needed cash over the weekends, when the
public fermentaries were closed. However, weekend buying, when
introduced, lasted only three months before being discontinued
as uneconomic.

Epstein was able to show that the apparent irrationality
of selling cocoa for a lower price than was readily available,
actually concealed an important social objective. Tolai men
objected to their own matrilineal inheritance customs, whereby
their sons had no rights to their property. As land became
increasingly scarce with the cocoa boom in the 1950s, men were
reluctant to act in any way that might lead to their property
being recorded (for example by registering a cocoa holding or
by selling cocoa through the public processing plants), for
recorded property was subject to matrilineal devolution. Instead, they sold their unrecorded cocoa output secretly and
gave the money to their children immediately, thus preventing
the matrilineage from establishing any claim to it. They were
prepared to forego 10-12 per cent of the total value of their
cocoa in order to remove it from matrilineal control. They
regarded this `cut´ as a fair reward for a service which they
valued. But as soon as the advantage of anonymity was thought
to have been removed from this private marketing, Tolai producers preferred to realise the higher price from the public
fermentaries.

These Jamaican and New Guinea examples illustrate the
ways in which social goals may be traded off against financial
gain, and belie the view that all producers believe that they

119

are being ripped off by all traders. However, there may indeed be very acute conflict between producers and traders. Nupe farmers in Northern Nigeria used to go so far as to accuse those who, like the Jamaican rural traders, bought up their small surpluses to sell in the periodic rural markets, of witchcraft. As Nadel (1952/1970) has shown, there was a particular twist to this conflict, for the farmers were men and the traders were often their own wives.

Nupe society was and still is patrilineal and wives are supposed to join their husbands' families on marriage. Formal rights to lineage land vest in the men, but when Nadel did his fieldwork in the 1940s, the Nupe men, rather unusually, also worked the land themselves, while (as elsewhere in West Africa) the women specialised in marketing. Nadel found that Nupe witches were always women, and were thought to be organised into associations similar to those of the markets. The titled, official head of the market-women's association was thought to be the boss-witch, but, as a reformed character, exercised some measure of control over the nefarious activities of her subordinates. The women's witchcraft (ega) was believed to be unequivocally evil, but some men possessed a similar power (eshe) that could be used to control witchcraft and was, therefore, essentially good, unless it was abused by collaboration with ega. Men, therefore, had the power ultimately to control female behaviour, by means of their secret society which cleansed whole villages of witchcraft.

Nadel interpreted the Nupe material as a clear example of sex antagonism, based on the economic and financial success of the women traders in comparison to male peasant farmers. The men were supposed to be in control of domestic affairs. However, they were often in debt to their wives, whose marketing activities enabled them to meet their husbands' obligations of bridewealth payments for sons' marriages, children's schooling and family celebrations. Furthermore, trading was regarded as an appropriate occupation only for childless women, because it involved working away from the home. However, many married women took it up as soon as their children were fully weaned, and were believed to use contraceptives to prevent additional pregnancies from interfering with their trading activity. It is not clear, from Nadel's brief account, whether the Nupe men merely resented this undermining of their ostensible authority over women in the home, or whether they also believed that their wives, as traders, short-changed them on their own produce, as sometimes occurred in the house-trade among the Hausa. In other words, we cannot be sure that this conflict, which was reflected in witchcraft beliefs and accusations, rested solely on domestic conflicts of authority within marriage, or whether it was primarily a conflict over relations

120

of appropriation between producers and traders in a market-oriented society.

Re-appropriation and `Fiddle Systems´

So far we have been looking at strategies whereby dominant social categories attempt, not always successfully, to benefit from the value produced by the labour of their subordinates. Now is an appropriate time to turn the coin over and return to Mars´ (1982) work to see precisely how those who are so `exploited´ may retrieve some of the value they loose. Here I wish to concentrate not on the entrepreneurial `hawks´ and `vultures´ mentioned in chapter 4, but instead on the `donkeys´ and `wolves´, the unskilled, poorly-paid, low-status manual and clerical workers who are generally regarded as being at the end of the appropriative line. How do they fight back and re-appropriate some of what they lose?

Mars describes `donkey jobs´ as being both subordinated and isolated from contact with fellow-workers in a system of tight managerial control. While `donkeys´ remain powerless if they accept this control, they can also disrupt it. The usual strategies of disruption and re-appropriation centre around withdrawing their labour, temporarily through abnormally high incidences of sick leave and absenteeism and permanently by leaving the job without notice. On assembly lines, however, industrial sabotage is not infrequent, and supermarket tills are often short at the end of the day. Mars cites the somewhat extreme example of a till cashier so alienated by the style of management in her `donkey job´ that she regularly short-changed her till by five times her wage. After changing jobs, she gave up fiddling completely because she liked the new way she was treated as a worker!

Managerial control is much less marked in manual `wolf-pack´ jobs traditionally associated with working-class status, such as refuse collection, mining and docking, but is replaced by control from within the rigid hierarchy of the work-group itself. `Wolfpacks´ are associated with what Goffman (1961) called `total institutions´, isolated from the wider society. The `wolfpack´ organises both the appropriation and the distribution of shares in the appropriated product. Longshoremen in Newfoundland, for example, helped themselves collectively to company-owned cargo to the same value as that of their labour for loading or unloading the boat, knowing that insurance would cover the loss. Any dockworker who individually appropriated personal baggage or individual possessions, however, was stigmatised as a `thief´. Airport baggage handlers clearly have different ethics! The rules of collective appro-

121

priation included not only a ceiling, but also a floor, on the level of predation that the wolfpack determined. The wolfpack was able to organise the appropriation and distribution of goods precisely because it controlled the deployment of its members to specific tasks within the work organisation.

It would seem, then, that re-appropriation, like appropriation itself, may depend on being able to control the allocation of work tasks, if not the definition of the ways in which labour should be divided. We have turned full circle, back to where this chapter began. But on the way, we have noted various points at which other verities, like those of kinship, marriage, ethnicity, and religion, have intruded upon and structured the economic relations of production and distribution. Now is the time to start examining these aspects in more detail.

CHAPTER SIX

ASCRIPTIVE SOCIAL RELATIONS

In examining that level of the superstructure which sits closest to the economic base (see again diagram 1, p. 14), it is useful to begin by distinguishing those roles and statuses which are ascribed to individuals by society, from those which the individual achieves on his or her own account. Ascribed roles and statuses are often related to the biological attributes of age, gender and race. However, they also include the relatively immutable social attributes of ethnic, caste or class origin and kinship. In India, even though caste was officially abolished in the 1950s, one is still born a Brahman or a harijan (outcaste). In many parts of Europe, one can still be born into aristocratic status, though it means less than it used to. All over the world, children are born members of particular families, ethnic and religious categories (which they may or may not repudiate later in life). These identities are difficult to escape, not least because they are fundamental to being brought up as a particular kind of person. However, the specific occupational connotations of ascribed status may now be historical. Even in rural India, the traditional link between sub-caste or jati and a particular job, is breaking down as both individuals and whole sub-castes manipulate discrepancies between their existing wealth and education and their traditional ranking in the caste system. It is necessary first to examine the structural relationships which arise from ascribed roles, in order to understand how and how far individuals may distance themselves from such pre-determined social relationships.

Cultural Models and Socialisation

In chapter 1, we noted that structural-functional views have rested on understanding average social behaviour, which is constructed as a model by anthropologists and other social scientists from the regularities rather than the idiosyncracies of individual behaviour. Each structural relationship is modelled on a cultural ideal, and inculcated into new members of the society as they grow up, in the process known technically as `socialisation`.

Socialisation is a form of `praxis`, a marriage of theory and practice, a process of learning by doing. In most societies, little girls are still taught to model themselves on their mothers` behaviour from a very early age, while in many cultures small boys enjoyed and still enjoy a few years of relative freedom, supervised primarily by older boys, before confronting their society's model(s) of the adult male in their formal initiation rites or education.

In societies where social roles and statuses were ascribed mainly by sex, age and marital standing, what van Gennep (1909/1960) called 'rites of passage' marked important changes in ascribed status at critical points in the individual's life-cycle. Naming gave an individual a social identity. Initiation confirmed adult status. (Its absence left the individual forever a child, incapable of undertaking adult duties and responsibilities, including those of marriage and legitimate reproduction.) Further rites confirmed the status of parent, grandparent, and ancestor. Very often, as among the Gikuyu, one rite involved changes in the ascribed statuses of both child and parent. Until their first child was initiated, Gikuyu men could not become elders of the second grade and members of the 'council of peace'. Such linkages gave parents as well as children a vested interest in submitting to the initiation rites.

Both boys and girls might be initiated, but fewer societies initiated girls than boys. As more and more societies have been affected by new forms of religion and education, traditional forms of initiation have tended to lapse. Paradoxically, however, female initiation (marked, for example, by clitoridectomy and infibulation in many Muslim societies in Africa) has persisted where traditional forms of male initiation have been replaced. Perhaps this somewhat strange pattern may be explained by the fact that initiation rites for girls were always <u>primarily</u> a symbolic crowning of a life-long process of learning that occurred informally. In contrast, where boys were formally taught their adult roles in lengthy and secluded initiation schools, other schools have taken over this function and the symbolic importance of the older system has been so attenuated that circumcision, for example, may be done in hospital straight after birth. In the face of societal change, then, there has tended to be a greater degree of both practical and symbolic continuity in inducting women into adulthood than applies to men. 'Rites of passage' in many societies continue to define an important part of their cultural models of 'woman'. For individual women, their social identity remains incomplete without this symbolic transition. In turn, most of them will require their daughters to be 'complete' women.

Such are the ways in which the socialisation process is supposed to reproduce the agreed cultural models of specific, especially but not exclusively, ascribed roles and relationships. But if this model of socialisation worked perfectly, there would never have been any change in human society, and change, however slow, is manifestly an ongoing process in most systems. How do we explain this contradiction? The growth of deviance is obviously one answer, and relations of power among contradictory institutions may explain additional aspects. However, the decisions of individuals about the extent and form of their compliance with cultural models must provide the main key to an answer. As Malinowski (1926:15) first pointed out, `observance of the rules ... under normal circumstances, when followed and not defied, is at best partial, conditional and subject to evasions´.

In this respect, we need to note that the same culture may hold diverging models of particular roles and relationships. The expectations of youth behaviour by a peer group `hanging out´ on street corners, for example, may diverge dramatically from the expectations of the same youth by their parents. Both may again diverge from the expectations of teachers in formal educational institutions and of those in charge of the party youth wing. Individuals thus have to choose among different expectations, among divergent cultural models, at different times and in different situations. In complying with one model, they defy others. Contradictions and inconsistencies in models of behaviour are, therefore, inevitable, however effective - or ineffective - the socialisation process may be.

Furthermore, each `social personality´ is an aggregate of many distinct roles, and some of these may contradict one another, thereby creating an additional potential for conflict and change. The female cabinet minister, for example, may exercise authority in the workplace, but is probably well advised to act as a `woman´ in her home, if she wants her marriage to last. The university-educated, professional Muslim woman may not want her daughter to be infibulated, but may be powerless as a daughter herself against the authority of her own mother and mother-in-law. Jomo Kenyatta, as a Gikuyu nationalist confronting colonial authority in the 1930s, argued that female initiation underpinned the integrity of Gikuyu culture. Three decades later, as the President of independent Kenya, he argued in favour of its abolition.

Cultural models of ascribed behaviour, then, are not solely the product of the socialisation process. They are also generated, and changed, by relations of power at both national and individual levels. It is not uncommon, in the contemporary third world, for anthropologists to come across formal motions in powerful associations moving the abolition of particular customs: both Epstein (1968) and Cheater (1981) have recorded such debates. Many governments of developing countries have outlawed traditional customs and cultural models which they regard as inimical to human rights and the equality of the sexes before the law. That such customs continue to be practised clandestinely, does not invalidate the point that they are disputed within their own society of origin. The growth of dissent about the validity of cultural models, is the process of change. As Bailey (1969:53-4) notes, in the early phase of change, a few individuals, who are `branded by the traditionalists as self-interested and immoral´, deviate from the established order. But gradually the trickle becomes a tide and eventually `there are so many people marching to the new pace that they can no longer be called deviants. The new way of doing things, from at first being merely the effective way, now becomes the right way´. It is perhaps for this reason that ascriptive social relations are becoming less and less important in most societies. But the models on which they are based may also find new uses in voluntary social relations, as we have already seen in the ways in which idioms of kinship may govern work relations.

Age and Age-Grading

Like gender, age is a primordial mechanism for social differentiation, but relatively few societies have elevated it to a first principle in a system of formal age-grading. Where age did act as the major index of social differentiation, political functions were also differentiated among age grades, and responsibility for each function was diffused among all incumbents of the grade in question. All of these systems have now passed into history. However, the importance of the youth wing in the political organisation of the one-party state in Tanzania, perhaps reflects some degree of cultural continuity regarding age organisation, for many of those preliterate pastoral societies that based their government as well as their status ranking on socially-defined age, were found in East Africa. Among them were the Maasai, the Nandi, the Arusha and the Gikuyu. An interesting agricultural variant was found among the Nyakyusa, among whom entire villages were constituted by age-mates, their wives and their very young children. Even the older children set up villages which were separated from those of their parents.

All of these East African systems depended on male initiation and some, like the Gikuyu, also initiated girls. Initiation marked the individual man´s entry to political participation, as well as his entry to adulthood. After the initiation rites, which generally lasted some months, the age-set of young men (the age-mates who had been initiated together) was admitted as a unit to the warrior age-grade. Some societies, like the Nandi, ranked sub-divisions of the warrior grade according to the annual sequencing of initiation over four years. Others, like the Gikuyu, distinguished senior and junior divisions within the warrior grade on the basis of how many moons had elapsed since initiation (82 was the dividing point).

The warriors were responsible for defence and aggression, the latter primarily in the form of raiding cattle from ethnically-different neighbours. However, although they were responsible for the action, the decision to raid was not their's. Young men ascribed the role of warrior did not make the political decisions which were the prerogative and responsibility of the elders in these societies.

Warriors in most of these systems had their ascribed status changed to that of elders en masse, as they had become warriors together 15 to 20 years earlier. In many age-grading systems, this transfer of decision-making authority from the outgoing elder grade, depleted by death, to the middle-aged warriors, was marked by a national ritual of `handing over power´ from one named generation to its successor. The remaining elders, mostly frail old men, often took on important ritual functions after they surrendered their decision-making authority. On the same occasion, a new age-set of warriors was confirmed at the end of the initiation period. These militaristic rituals were an obvious focus for colonial prohibition, and few were held after the close of the nineteenth century. In their absence, the succession took place anyway.

We may understand these general principles better by examining a specific example of a society structured on the basis of age. The Nandi of Kenya opened a new initiation period roughly every 10-14 years. The time was set by the alternate flowering of the setiot bush, which under normal weather conditions flowers every seventh year. For the four years following, youths of widely varying chronological ages (from little boys to young adults) were accepted for initiation. Those initiated in any one of the four years comprised a sub-set of the warrior grade. These sub-sets were ranked in terms of seniority according to their order of initiation. When their period of seclusion and tuition was over, following their circumcision, the young men joined the warrior grade and were deployed in regiments in the 16 geographical divisions of Nandi territory. As adults, they had the right to engage in sexual activity with unmarried girls. Later, at their leisure, they would marry and have children. However, as warriors, they were forbidden the elders´ prerogative of drinking beer.

Each sub-set of warriors in each section of Nandi terri-

127

tory had a leader or `captain´, elected during the initiation period. The `captains´ liaised with one another when organising raids on the instruction of the Nandi ritual leader, the orkoiyot. Later, as elders, the former `captains´ were most likely to become `chairmen´ of the councils of elders in their different territorial sub-sections or `villages´, having demonstrated their leadership potential in their youth. So among the Nandi, there was a limited potential for individualised leadership in semi-formal political office, within the framework of ascription by age.

During peacetime, the administration of Nandi affairs rested with the elders. In each area, or `village´, the elders met in council to organise the details of planting and initiation, following directives issued by the orkoiyot for the 120,000 Nandi as a whole. The village council of elders was chaired by the poiyot for that area, a man of sound judgement and open hospitality. Succession to this post was by appointment and apprenticeship. An incumbent poiyot nominated his successor (called mistoat) as a type of deputy or understudy well before he died. At the `village´ level among the Nandi, it would seem that elders remained elders until they died. They did not, as among the Gikuyu, progress to a further grade of eldership, concerned with religious rather than administrative affairs, for these were the prerogative of the orkoiyot.

Ritual knowledge, among the Nandi, was the exclusive property of one lineage. The most senior living male member of this patrilineage took on the hereditary and ascribed position of the okoiyot, who made ritual decisions for the entire Nandi people. These ritual decisions included the confirmation of a new initiation period, the recognition of the most propitious time for planting crops, and whether or not to deploy the warriors against outsiders. In 1923, the orkoiyot apparently planned to deploy all Nandi warriors against the British colonisers. Yet the Nandi did not recognise their orkoiyot as a political head of state. Although he had the religious obligation to make these decisions, the organisation of Nandi government was, as Mair (1962, 1977) puts it, `diffused´ among the elder and warrior age-grades, not `centralised´ in the position of the orkoiyot. This particular position was, like other Nandi statuses, based on age, but defined in the idiom of ritual expertise based on kinship.

Concepts of Kinship

We have seen, in those systems where age was used to structure society, that chronological age was not necessarily the same as the social age defined by initiation. In the same way, there is a difference between shared blood, or consanguinity, and `social kinship´. Kinship has a biological basis, but most modes of reckoning kinship for social purposes, emphasise identical biological relationships differently. The Swazi, for example, treat marriage between cross-cousins (the children of a brother and of a sister) as permissible, where marriage between parallel cousins (the children of brothers, or the children of sisters) is regarded as incestuous. As Radcliffe-Brown (1950:4) put the point: `Kinship results from the recognition of a social relationship between parents and children, which is not the same thing as the physical rela- tion, and may or may not coincide with it´.

But why not? There are two main views as to why social kinship is not identical with consanguineal relations. The first has to do with the requirement that basic structural rules should be simple and easy to follow. Radcliffe-Brown (1950:43) expressed this idea in his dictum that `a continuing social structure requires the aggregation of individuals into distinct separated groups, each with its own solidarity, each person belonging to one group´. As we shall see later, systems that do not discriminate between different categories of kin, do not meet this requirement.

The second major explanation of the divergence between consanguinity and kinship is materialist and has been offerred by neo-marxists such as Meillassoux (1981). Social kinship, Meillassoux argued, is a means of equalising the discrepancies in household size that result from differential reproductive performance; it redistributes workers and consumers among the productive units in society, so that each unit has a roughly equal ratio between producers and consumers. Kuper (1950:96) prefigured this point long before Meillassoux, when she noted among the Swazi that `Calling a woman "mother" involves more than lip-service: the "mothers" cook food which all the children share and when the real mother is ill or away her child still has its share´. In this view, then, social kinship underpins what is seen as the egalitarian nature of pre-class societies.

We may assess the usefulness of these two views by examining those situations in which social and biological kinship diverge. Fostering describes a situation in which the `natural´ children of one set of parents are raised for a temporary and limited period by other adults. Among the Gonja of Northern Ghana, this fostering was often undertaken by relatives, whereas in Britain foster-parents have usually been unrelated to their charges and even of a different ethnic or racial category. Fostering in the African context certainly fitted Meillassoux´s point, and still does. Fostering may also be a means of supplying child labour in a domestic (rather than productive) context, as when urban families send their children to live with and assist their ageing parents in the countryside. In the `advanced capitalist economies´, however, child labour is rare and these arguments are less applicable.

Formal adoption carries the fostering situation into a changed legal context, by transferring parental responsibilities permanently and irrevocably from the natural to the adoptive parents. In many African societies, adoption was and still is rare. Shona people, for example, believe that an adoptee whose origins are unknown (such as abandoned children committed to state homes) may carry ngozi (the aggrieved and therefore dangerous spirit of a deceased person) into the family of adoption. However, among the Gikuyu adoption was sufficiently acceptable to be a recognised means of obtaining a male heir on whom an estate of production could be settled. The Chinese were somewhat more specific in their adoptive practices for this purpose. Adopting a son-in-law was common among the heirless, even though it went against the patrilineal grain; adopting an unknown stranger was much less frequent. The adoption of daughters, in contrast, seems to have been comparatively rare. Again, as in the case of fostering, materialist views seem to explain the general phenomenon of adoption quite well, including cases which result from divorce and the parent with custody taking the children into a new marital union. However, such views do not explain why boys are adopted rather than girls.

When we turn to more specific examples of the distinction between social and biological paternity, materialist explanations become still less satisfactory. A technique for type-matching genetic material is now available for establishing specific paternity (and maternity): British immigration officials used it for the first time in 1985. Prior to this technological breakthrough, the allocation of paternity in any society could only be a matter of faith or arbitration. In matrilineal systems that permitted a woman to marry two or more husbands simultaneously, in that form of marriage known technically as polyandry, the social paternity of the woman´s children was often arbitrarily assigned, on a roster system, among the husbands concerned. After all, determining the biological paternity of the children was clearly impossible and essentially irrelevant to the issue of who was socially and legally responsible for them.

Polyandry is by no means the only circumstance under which it is necessary to be able to distinguish genitor (the biological father) from pater (the social father). Leaving aside the ubiquitous, pan-cultural phenomenon of extra-marital relationships which may yield children, there are a number of

130

marital devices in strongly patrilineal societies which cannot be understood without bearing this distinction in mind. For example, in Shona society, the wife of an impotent or sterile man could, in great secrecy, be impregnated by one of his brothers. There is also the biblical tradition of leviratic inheritance and its more exotic cousin, `ghost marriage´. In the levirate, a man `raises seed´ with his bereaved sister-in-law on behalf of his deceased brother. He does not enter into a new marriage with the widow, and the children resulting from this activity are regarded by the society as those of his deceased brother. (We should distinguish the levirate, in which biological and social paternity are separated, from widow inheritance - found, for example, among the Shona - where inheriting a widow does entail a new marriage, the children of which belong socially as well as biologically to the inheriting, not the deceased, brother.) `Ghost marriage´ is simply a premature version of the levirate. When a man dies (for example, in a Nuer feud) before marrying, it is the duty of a close kinsman, preferably a full brother, to marry on his behalf and raise children to his name. Often the bloodwealth demanded to avenge his death will be used as bridewealth to marry `his´ wife. (Which is why bloodwealth and bridewealth payments are often set at similar levels.) Finally, in those societies (often strongly patrilineal) where a woman may invest bridewealth in marrying another, and become pater to her wife's offspring, their approved genitor is obviously a man.

If we ask why these marital devices are necessary, a materialist explanation seems somewhat lame. Why should it be necessary to ascribe <u>paternity</u> so evenly in a society? Here the answer lies in the ideological realm of patriliny. A man without sons does not become an ancestor. His name is forgotten. He might as well never have existed in the total social obliteration which follows his death. Clearly, no man wishes to face such a nihilistic future. And to this end of establishing the male memorial of sons, it may also be necessary to manipulate social motherhood, at least among that tenth of women who are naturally infertile.

In the same way as we have distinguished pater and genitor, in the sororate there is a difference between `mater´ and `genetrix´, as social and biological mothers respectively. In patrilineal societies, when a man pays bridewealth part of it establishes the rights of his patrilineage as well as himself to the children of his marriage. If his wife cannot produce children, it is the duty of her family to provide a substitute child-bearer in her place. Normally this substitute would be her younger full sister. After bearing a number of children who belong socially to the wife, the surrogate child-bearer returns home with her fecundity fully and honourably

131

demonstrated, to marry in her own right. She may even marry (as a junior wife) the brother-in-law with whom she has borne children for her sister. Here we must be careful not to confuse this `sororal polygyny´ with the sororate described above. After such a marriage, the children this woman bears will be her own: she will be both mater and genetrix. Again, while a materialist view rightly emphasises the production of future workers through the mechanism of the sororate, it ignores the way in which the prescribed status of `mother´ is achieved indirectly through the same institution. While the status of mother in patrilineal societies does not carry the same connotations of ancestral pedigree as that of father, it does protect a woman from ridicule and shame during her lifetime, and guarantees her limited recognition in the world of ancestral spirits.

Moreover, motherhood is frequently regarded as the ultimate fulfilment of womanhood. Marriage without children, so I have been told, is no better than legalised prostitution. Advances in medical science, such as in vitro fertilisation, have largely removed from western societies the technical necessity to juggle biological in order to achieve social motherhood, as occurs in the sororate. However, this technology, together with surrogate child-bearing and the creation of sperm banks, has created many legal problems in western societies. It is necessary, for example, for the biological parents to adopt their own `test-tube baby´ in countries like Britain and Australia, for the link between biological and social parentage is deemed to be broken by `unnatural´ fertilisation.

We may draw a parallel between biological as opposed to social kinship on the one hand, and `filiation´ as opposed to `descent´ on the other. Filiation refers to the (social) relationship between each parent and his or her child. In contrast, descent expresses only that parent-child relationship which structures the society in question. Descent is a legal or jural concept, which defines the rights and obligations of kinship, whereas filiation merely expresses a socially recognised link. In many, perhaps most, cases, only one of the two possible relations of filiation (with the father and with the mother) is selected for emphasis as descent.

Descent Systems and Complementary Filiation

As a jural concept, descent refers firstly to the rules by which kinship groups are composed. If a person takes his or her membership in a descent unit from the father in the first instance, and thereafter traces descent relationships only through men, the rule of descent is `agnatic´ or patrilineal. If, on the other hand, group membership is acquired from the mother, and descent links are traced through the mother´s female kin, the rule of descent is `matrilineal´. There are also some, relatively rare, examples of societies where an individual belongs simultaneously to both a patrilineage and a matrilineage. Such societies, found in parts of Nigeria and the Sudan in Africa, and on some Pacific islands like Yap, are called `double unilineal´ or `dual descent´ systems.

In addition to defining the rules by which individuals are ascribed to kin groups, `descent´ also defines the ascriptive rules by which property is inherited and people succeed to political office. Concerning these two issues, there is a wide range of different practices in patrilineal systems. The rules of inheritance range from conserving the property by leaving it to a single, normally male, heir (often the first-born son, in systems of `primogeniture´, but occasionally the last-born, in `ultimogeniture´); through partition among all sons; to Islamic systems in which all daughters also receive half-shares in their father´s property. The rules of succession to office are often simpler than those governing the inheritance of property because, unlike property, political office cannot be fragmented.

Concerning these issues of inheritance and succession, there is a very large difference between the range of patrilineal rules described above and matrilineal rules and practices. A child does not belong to its father´s descent group in matrilineal systems. Therefore it has no claims to his property. Instead, the claim to lineage property goes through the mother, to her male kin. As in patrilineal societies, there is wide range of rules of inheritance and succession. In the most common matrilineal rule, a man inherits property from and succeeds to political office through his maternal uncle, his mother´s brother. However, inheritance rules can also link brothers, and men and their mother´s mother´s brothers. Where women have rights to property (their rights to political office are much rarer), these rights are normally shared with all of their full siblings (of the same parents), or at least with all of their uterine siblings, with whom they share a common mother while having different fathers.

So far we have examined the ways in which descent rules ascribe relationships in society. However, there is also a relationship between a child and the parent from whom he or she does <u>not</u> trace descent, known as `complementary filiation´. In societies based on cognatic or bilateral descent, where all kin relationships count equally and lineages are

133

rare, the concept of complementary filiation is irrelevant. In lineage-based societies, however, complementary filiation provides an important residual security or insurance against the breakdown (for whatever reason) of descent relationships.

In patrilineal societies, for example, when bridewealth was not paid and rights in a woman´s children were not transferred to her husband´s lineage, their relationship to their mother provided the children with usufructuary access to the resources of her lineage, though they generally could not inherit such property. If a person was banished from his or her lineage as a result of witchcraft, matrilateral kin offerred a refuge. When a polygamist´s property was divided after his death, the matricentral `houses´ (based on different mothers) divided his property. The Swazi still say `a ruler is ruler by his mother´ (Kuper 1950:96). Although property and power were held by and transmitted among men, the rank of his mother within a polygamous marriage determined finally who among the many potential heirs would actually inherit.

Conversely, in matrilineal systems, the father represented an important source of income and property for his sons, as we have already seen among Ghanaian and Tolai cocoa farmers. Indeed, long before complementary filiation was conceptualised as such, Malinowski (1922) was the first to see that there is a deep conflict in matrilineal societies between a father´s emotional attachment to his own children, and rules of inheritance which debar his children from inheriting his property. Among Trobriand aristocrats involved in the kula, this conflict was often reflected in the father´s gift to his son of a kula valuable. Sponsoring his entry into the ceremonial exchange circuit, at that point in the young man´s life when he was supposed to leave his father and go to live avunculocally with his mother´s brother to whom he was heir and successor, was the father´s way of reinforcing material, ideological and emotional bonds with his son, notwithstanding their membership of different descent groups.

Having examined the basic concepts and definitions of kinship, now is the time to see how these rules constructed working descent systems, which in turn governed access to productive and ideological resources in society. Such systems have comprised descent units of varying size and inclusiveness. In the smallest family units, as well as in minimal, minor, major and maximal lineage segments, actual kin relationships may be demonstrated. At the most inclusive level of the clan, however, people may believe that they are kin, without being able to prove it.

134

Cognatic or Bilateral Descent

Let us begin with an example of cognatic descent, in which filiation to both parents is regarded as equal. Among a wide choice of possibilities, ranging from the Maori of New Zealand through the Lozi and Amhara of Africa to most European societies and their colonial offspring in the Americas, I have chosen the Lapps of Scandinavia, whose reindeer pastoralism we have already examined in chapter 2. We should note at the outset that the requirements of mobility and flexibility in herding cannot be used to explain the bilateral nature of Lappish kinship, for many other pastoralists are strongly patrilineal.

Pehrson (1964/1971:292) stated that `the Lapp conceives of himself as a point in a network of kinship relations and not as a member of any corporate entity greater than the sibling group`. This ideological assumption derives from the time when the reindeer used to be herded by migratory groups. As we saw in chapter 2, more recently the reindeer have been allowed to roam freely over local pasturelands, being mustered only in the spring and, more importantly, autumn. The migratory bands used to be internally differentiated by a rigid division between the generations of parents and children. Within each generation, however, there was equality and solidarity, reflected in the extension to cousins and in-laws (or affines) of the terms (in translation, brother and sister) which were applied to siblings. Marriages occurred between members of the same migratory band, and although Lappish notions of incest forbade marriage between third cousins or closer kin, sometimes such marriages did occur.

The terminology and other ideological features of Lappish kinship, have survived the transition from migratory herding to sedentary occupations. For example, sons and daughters continue to inherit wealth (in the past mainly reindeer) equally from both parents. And as in other European systems of kinship, there is no distinction between mother´s kin and father´s kin. In the kinship terminology known technically as `lineal´, Lapps have common terms for grandfather and grandmother, uncle and aunt, grandson and granddaughter, which are applied to kin on both sides. A newly-married couple is free to choose whether to live `virilocally´ with the husband´s or `uxorilocally´ with the wife´s kin, `bilocally´ with both, or `neolocally´ with neither, depending on which choice is the most convenient. In the past, `convenience´ was assessed in terms of available labour and pasturage as well as the wealth, status and dominance of the spouses´ respective families and sibling units within the migratory herding group.

Unilineal Descent

In contrast to the freedom of choice and bilateral symmetry of Lappish kinship, stands the Swazi example of patriliny. Here, provided bridewealth is paid, each child is ascribed the isibongo or clan praise name of its pater and belongs to his clan, even if he is known not to be the genitor. If bridewealth is not paid, however, children belong to their mother's clan. Members of a clan must marry into other clans, in the pattern called `clan exogamy'; and with the exception of members of the royal Dhlamini clan, people may not marry into clans that were, in the past, one clan. However, Swazi exogamy is sufficiently flexible to permit marriage into the clans of the mother and both maternal and paternal grandmothers, all of which are forbidden among neighbouring Nguni peoples such as the Zulu.

Kuper (1950:100) notes that `though a Swazi retains links with the families of both his parents, the emphasis on the paternal kin (kaboyise) and maternal kin (kabonina) is not identical'. The depth of knowledge of kin was greater in the patriline, though not normally exceeding eight generations among commoners. Because a married couple normally lived with the husband's extended family (the technical term for this pattern being `patrivirilocal'), fewer of the mother's relatives were known than patrikin (unless the mother was of royal descent). As among other patrilineal people, the knowledge of kin on the father's side (`patrilateral') and on the mother's side (`matrilateral'), among the urban Swazi, has probably become more equal than it used to be in the less mobile rural setting.

Keeping track of kin was relatively simple because the Swazi kinship terminology aggregated men and women by generation and by clan. Mage applied not only to one's own mother, her full- and half-sisters, her matrilateral parallel and cross cousins and co-wives, but also, by extension, to the mother's mothers' brothers' wives, and the wives of all `fathers'. One's own father, together with his full- and half-brothers, his sisters and his patrilateral parallel cousins, were all called babe. In contrast, all males of the mother's generation in her clan (that is, all the `mother's brothers') were called malume. Like the Lapps, the Swazi emphasised sibling unity in this terminology and also applied some kin terms to in-laws: malume, for example, covered both a mother's brother and his wife, while mage could apply to a father's brother's wife. This system of aggregating members of the parental generation of one's descent group and distinguishing them from non-descent kin, is called `bifurcate merging' kinship terminology. It is commonly found in systems of uni-

136

lineal descent, whether patrilineal or matrilineal. Rather confusingly, `lineal´ terminology (as we saw among the Lapps) is associated with cognatic descent!

As we might expect of a system including both bridewealth and a bifurcate merging terminology, the levirate, the sororate and ghost marriages occurred among the Swazi and polygyny was a cultural ideal. In theory a man had only one main heir to his property (notably livestock and rights to the bride-wealth cattle to be paid for unmarried daughters). This heir and successor was determined after the man's death, but was normally the eldest son of the highest-ranking wife. When he inherited, he moved up a generation, as it were, to replace his father, but did not inherit his father's wives, who went to genuine members of the father's generation. In polygamous marriages, however, each wife tried to prevent the property of her `house´ (including her daughters´ bridewealth potential) from being merged into her husband's `general estate´. (Wives themselves, like daughters, have no rights to inherit the male property of the patrilineage. However, they acquire livestock in their own right as gifts from their sons-in-law, or from a living father, and may bequeath these to their own sons.) Thus the `house-property complex´ among the Swazi to some extent contradicted the idea that a man should leave a single estate.

In many respects, matrilineal kinship is a mirror image of patriliny. A child is ascribed membership in its mother's descent group, from which it takes its name and within which it inherits, either from siblings or from a mother's brother. The pattern of residence after marriage is normally uxorilocal (with the wife's family), avunculocal (with the husband's mother's brother), or bilocal (when each spouse lives with his or her own family). Occasionally, however, a couple may move immediately or after some time to live with the man's family in the virilocal pattern, or may set up an independent, neo-local home. Virilocality in matrilineal societies tends to be associated with the payment of relatively high bridewealth and/or with the holding of political office.

In one respect, however, the `mirror image´ cracks. In both patrilineal and matrilineal systems, men control politi-cal authority and the allocation of productive resources, even though women in matrilineal societies may hold primary rights to land, especially where the residence pattern is uxorilocal. So although descent is traced through women in matrilineal systems, power still resides with men. Although inheritance may give women equal shares in the property of the matri-lineage, succession devolves from a man to his brother or to his sister's son. Such ascriptive succession may transform the inheritor's social identity even further than the Swazi system of shifting a man into his father´s generation. Indeed, it may transform an achieved status into an ascribed one. In what Richards (1950:224) has called `positional succession´,

> `Bemba succeed either to a position in a ruling dynasty or to a social status a commoner has acquired for himself by his individual efforts in the course of his lifetime. It is not the title of head of a clan or lineage that is inherited, but the <u>particular individual status</u> to which each man or woman has attained, and I found that the names of insignificant people were quickly forgotten, whereas those of eminent men or mothers of large families were remembered for some generations.´ (My emphasis)

Finally, there are a few societies that ascribe kinship status in both the patriline and the matriline simultaneously. Perhaps the most famous of a number of African examples is that of the Yako of the middle Cross River in South-Eastern Nigeria, who were somewhat less densely-settled cultivators than their Ibo neighbours. The land was owned by the patrilineages. However, within the patrivirilocal settlement pattern, the in-marrying wives were each allocated their own independent yam plot and were also responsible for growing the minor food crops. Permanent tree-crops (fruit and palms), in contrast, were owned, tended and inherited by men within the patriline.

The small local patrilineage (<u>eponama</u>), not more than five generations deep and comprising up to 30 adult men and their families, controlled rights to land for housing and farming. It was within the patrilineage that rights to arable land and permanent tree-crops were distributed and arbitrated in the event of dispute. However, the <u>yeponama</u> as land-allocating units were part of the larger patriclans (<u>yepun</u>) with distinct and bounded territories. Birth within the <u>kepun</u> territory normally established a child as a member of his or her father´s patriclan, though patriclan membership could also be acquired through adoption as an adult. Each patriclan had a central shrine to the patrilineal ancestors, presided over by a priest and peacemaker whose main obligation was to officiate at the annual new yam ritual. As the Yako used to say, `a man eats in his <u>kepun</u> [patriclan]´. The rights and obligations of patrilineal affiliation, then, centred on land, housing and co-operative agricultural work.

In contrast, the inheritance of movable property, together with bridewealth and bloodwealth payments, used to be the concern of the Yako matriclans (<u>yajima</u>). The matrilineal concern with the fertility of women and livestock explained this differentiation of property between patriclans and matriclans. However, Forde (1950) noted that by the 1930s matri-

138

lineal claims to such property were already being undermined, in much the same way as has happened in most purely matrilineal systems, by the devolution of wealth during his lifetime to a man's sons, and by fathers claiming bridewealth payments for their daughters.

In contrast to the concern of the patriclans with material production, Forde (1950:329) noted that matrilineal affiliation reflected `mystical ideas concerning the perpetuation and tranquillity of the Yako world´. The matrilineage, Forde argued, was united by the `mystical bonds of common fertility´ and endangered by the sins of anger and violence. In each Yako village, a matrilineal spirit dominated its religious affairs. Although dispersed, members of each matriclan gathered a couple of times a year for the ritual commemoration of this spirit. Matrilineal ties thus validated spiritually the patrilineal bonds around which production in local communities was organised. Sometimes, too, matrilineal links substituted materially for these patrilineal bonds, for a man in need could always appeal to his mother's brother for palm products and intercession with the head of his patrilineage concerning land or trees. Paradoxically, however, as Yako society confronted the twentieth century and its formerly balanced structure of dual descent slid into an increasingly individualistic patrilineal mode, what Forde saw as the traditionally weaker and more materialistic relations of production proved more resilient than the mystical bonds of matriliny. Perhaps the Yako exemplify the ascendancy of materialism over ideology, in contrast to previous examples!

Corporateness

One reason for the survival and extension of Yako patriliny may relate to the greater degree of corporateness exhibited traditionally by the patriclans as opposed to the matriclans. Radcliffe-Brown (1950:41) identified three criteria by which corporateness may be assessed: at least occasional collective action; formal leadership of a group by its accepted representative and spokesman; and the group's possession and control of property. To this list, it has been suggested that two additional criteria should be added. However, group action for defence and vengeance seems merely to be a special case of Radcliffe-Brown's first criterion of collective action; and to apply the criterion of exogamy would exclude many Islamic groupings that use marriage within the patrilineage as a means of consolidating control over lineage property that Quranic rules of partible inheritance tend to fragment.

Among the Yako, both the patriclans and the matriclans controlled property as groups, and were represented in their relations with similar units by heads or leaders. In addition, the matrilineage was exogamous. But the _eponama_ or patrilineage was involved in collective action, through co-residence and labour co-operation, much more frequently than the matrilineage oriented to ritual action. In the end, then, it is not surprising that this greater cohesiveness was translated into dominance. Even in the absence of new currencies and greater economic involvement in an external trading economy, the patrilineal principle might still have overridden dual descent. Traditionally, the Yako division of property, into immovable/patrilineal and movable/matrilineal categories, relied for its stability on the ideological dominance of the mystical. There seems to have been no reinforcement of the balance between the two descent principles in any other aspect of Yako life, for village politics were also dominated by the co-resident patrilineage, and the matriclans had no monopoly over other forms of material or non-material property, such as knowledge or skills, or even a specific religious cult of a regional nature linking all the Yako villages.

A `Lineage Mode of Production´?

In analysing societies structured on unilineal principles, anthropologists such as Meillassoux have been tempted into characterising them as having a `lineage mode of production´, in which hoe cultivation is combined with lineage control over access to the land and over the organisation of both labour and consumption. The deployment of women in marriage is also controlled by the lineage elder(s). These economic activities are `dominated´ by the superstructural features of the descent ideology and the lineage control of political organisation. However, supposedly in accordance with Marx´s own views, the economic base in theory remains `determinant in the last instance´, even though this `last instance´ never actually occurs.

This concept of a `lineage mode of production´ has permitted some neo-marxists to retain their belief in the pristine equality of ascriptive social relations in pre-class societies. However, this view has been criticised by other marxists who have argued that those who control such systems, notably the lineage elders, may indeed be regarded as a `class´ in the classic marxist sense of owner-controllers of the means of production.

Affinity and the Circulation of Women

So far I have treated kinship, family and household as if they were each autonomous concepts. But of course they all rely on marriage for their very existence, and the main purpose of marriage, as Radcliffe-Brown (1950) pointed out, is to re-arrange the social structure (as a network of social relations) at periodic intervals. Marriage has the effect of circulating women around the relatively fixed units of men and may, therefore, be regarded as prescriptive, if not ascriptive. There is no logical reason, as Levi-Strauss (1969) indicated, why we should not regard the men as being circulated around the women, except that empirically it is a somewhat misleading view, for most women actually move their residence after marriage, whereas men do not.

What is `marriage´? Provisionally we may define this institution as a socially-recognised and therefore legitimate sexual union, geared primarily toward the reproduction of society through the birth of children. Bronowski (1973:406) grasped the essence of the marriage institution when he noted that `we are uncommonly careful in the choice, not of whom we take to bed, but by whom we are to beget children´. Bronowski regarded this societal regulation of human reproduction as an important reason for the rapid cultural and technological development of <u>homo</u> <u>sapiens</u>. With some notable exceptions, in most societies the majority of children are born within the framework of marriages that satisfy the institutional rules for societal recognition. It is necessary to use such a broad definition precisely because there are so many different types of marriage, most of which we have already encountered in different contexts.

We may start by distinguishing monogamy from polygamy. Monogamous systems permit men and women alike only one spouse at a time, though often in series, along the Hollywood model, following death or divorce. Polygamy permits multiple spouses simultaneously. Polygamy is sub-divided technically into polygyny (where a man has many wives) and polyandry (where a wife is permitted numerous husbands). Examples of polygynous marriage include: sororal polygyny (where the wives are sisters), the levirate, ghost marriage and widow inheritance. Polyandry also comes in different forms, including the adelphic or fraternal variety (where the husbands are brothers) and the `village wife´ institution of the Lele, outlined in chapter 5. In both polygynous and polyandrous marriages, of course, the wives and husbands respectively may also be unrelated to one another.

Marriage Rules

We may classify the rules governing marriage initially into two categories. First there are the negative rules which define those whom, in a given society, one may not marry. They in turn come in two varieties: prohibitions against incest; and rules of exogamy.

Incest prohibitions - which vary in their specific targets from one society to the next - forbid <u>sexual</u> <u>intercourse</u> and, therefore, marriage. In most societies, incest prohibitions forbid sexual relations between specified <u>individuals</u>, such as parents and their children, and siblings (children of the same parents). But father-daughter and brother-sister incest are by no means uncommon, and in the case of ancient Egyptian royalty, the ruler was required to marry his full sister. And although the spectre of genetic abnormality is often invoked to explain incest prohibitions, animal breeders use inbreeding to select and reinforce desirable genetic qualities. The reasons for human prohibitions against incest are in fact social and political, concerned with forging relationships between different breeding units within and between societies. As Levi-Strauss (1969:481) noted, `the prohibition of incest is less a rule prohibiting marriage with the mother, sister or daughter, than a rule obliging the mother, sister or daughter to be given to others. It is the supreme rule of the gift...´. We see the arbitrary social nature of the incest prohibition even more clearly when we turn to the second subdivision of negative marriage rules, namely the rules of exogamy.

Rules of exogamy may be regarded as an extension of incest prohibitions, since they define <u>categories</u> of people who are <u>unmarriageable</u>. Sexual relations may not be specifically prohibited, though the penalty for illicit intercourse with an unmarriageable person is severe (in the Trobriands, for example, the penalty for publication of an incestuous liaison was ritual suicide). Like incest prohibitions, the rules of exogamy are social and arbitrary. In most Nguni societies in Southern Africa, one may not marry any member of the clans of one´s four grandparents. The Swazi, however, as we have already noted, permit marriage into three of these four clans. A more telling example of the arbitrary nature of negative marriage rules is seen in the view of the Lovedu of South Africa who, like many other patrilineal societies, distinguish among different types of cousin. A father´s brother´s child is prohibited, whereas a mother´s brother´s child is marriageable. Biologically and genetically they are equally close relatives, but socially the former is defined as a member of one´s own patriclan, whereas the latter is not.

This example leads us into the positive marriage rules, which include `preferential´ marriage and endogamy. The Lovedu not only define the mother´s brother´s daughter as marriageable. They _prefer_ such a marriage to other possibilities because, they say, it helps to `knit together´ and recreate ties of descent among kin who, with the passage of the generations in a patrilineal system, are growing apart. At the societal level, if adhered to widely, this particular marriage preference creates repeated `backward linkages´ with the mother´s clan. Strongly cohesive marriage links are duplicated in each generation. Preferential rules of sister exchange may .create similarly cohesive, ongoing relations between specific descent groups. However, the structural details of these preferential marriage systems do not, in my opinion, belong in introductory texts, particularly since the systems themselves have largely passed into history.

In some societies, the preference for certain types of marriage may lead to marriage within the local descent group. Muslims, for example, prefer that a man marry his (real) father´s (real) brother´s (real) daughter. Quranic inheritance divides a man´s property equally among his sons and gives half-shares to all of his daughters. This preferential marriage has the effect of reconsolidating part of the original family estate in the third descending generation, as grandchildren inherit fragmented shares from both of their parents.

The example of preferential marriage to the father´s brother´s daughter in a patrilineal system is also an example of marriage within the lineage, or lineage endogamy. But endogamy, or marriage within a specified category or group, is not often focussed on descent groups. The two classic examples are sub-caste endogamy in India and racial endogamy in South Africa. Endogamous marriage within the sub-caste, or _jati_, was perfectly compatible with exogamy from the perspective of the local descent group. Likewise, during the three decades of the mid-twentieth century in which it was illegal in South Africa to marry across the rigidly-defined racial barriers, it was perfectly feasible to observe other rules of exogamy based on lineal descent. Endogamous groupings, then, tend to be sufficiently populous to encompass the simultaneous observance of different rules of exogamy.

In noting what the various marriage rules achieve, we have already implied one function of marriage world-wide, namely to create relations of alliance between otherwise unrelated and frequently hostile social or national groups. In chapter 2, we saw that such alliances may permit access to important material resources under crisis conditions. The many other functions of marriage can be reduced to three major categories, including the legalisation of parenthood; the establishment of family units for the benefit of the children (in respect of their upbringing as well as their rights to use and inherit property); and the establishment between the spouses of rights to each other's sexuality (in widely varying degrees of exclusiveness and permanence), as well as services, labour and property. We should also note Engels' (1884/1948) view, that monogamous marriage in capitalist economies serves to subsidise the wages of employed male workers, by appropriating the unpaid labour of their wives in a system of 'domestic slavery'. Although Engels thought that earlier forms of marriage lacked this exploitative quality, we saw in chapter 5 that marriage as an institution in many societies legitimates the male appropriation of the value of women's labour.

Marriage Payments

Marriages are not only defined but also contracted in many different ways, and are everywhere usually costly, though the costs are distributed differently in different societies. The costs of publicly celebrating a wedding must be distinguished from those payments which, in many societies, used to constitute the legal validity of the marriage itself. Marriage payments come in three main forms: dowry, bridewealth, and labour service by the groom for his father-in-law. Dowry and groom service are generally 'enabling payments', the social validity of such unions being established by civil or religious procedures. Bridewealth payments, in contrast, used to legitimate marriage itself, although in much of contemporary Africa this older function has been usurped by churches and states.

Dowry is still found widely in Europe and Asia. It has always enabled rather than legitimised marriage, for state and religious organisations actually validate marriage on these continents. Dowry takes many forms, the most common of which are an endowment of property upon the bride by her family (which may be used by the husband for the duration of the marriage, but must be returned in the event that the marriage ends); or a settlement on the bridegroom by the bride's family. Minor variations include a settlement (usually of little value) on the bride by the bridegroom. Generally, then, dowry involves a property settlement on the bride or the marrying couple, normally from her family. This property enables a young woman to marry a man of higher status than herself, in the pattern known as 'hypergamy', in which material wealth may be traded off against social and religious status. Conversely, the absence of dowry may render a girl unmarriageable. An inadequate dowry, as recent events in the

144

Indian sub-continent have shown, may lead to physical abuse
and even murder of the bride by her husband's family.

As Boserup (1970) and Goody (1976) have noted, dowry is
found in agricultural economies based on a plough technology,
in which women do relatively little, if any, farm work. The
`dower´ confers some degree of financial security on the home-
bound woman in the event of her marriage dissolving, while
assisting the newly-married couple to establish an independent
subsistence and home. In contrast, bridewealth is found in
systems of hoe agriculture where most of the productive labour
comes from women, notably in Africa and Melanesia. Bridewealth
may, therefore, be regarded primarily as an indemnity payment.
Perhaps the clearest indication of its status as an indemnity
is seen in the practice of `marrying the grave´ (in Shona,
kuroora guva), whereby a man who has caused the death of a
marriageable girl is required to pay a post mortem bridewealth
to her father.

Bridewealth, traditionally in the form of capital goods
such as livestock but today more frequently in cash, is paid
by the bridegroom (with or without the assistance of his
lineal kin) to the father of the bride, who may or may not
distribute parts of it to his lineal kin. In patrilineal
societies, bridewealth transfers `genetricial´ rights (to the
woman´s reproductive capacity) as well as `uxorial´ rights (to
her labour and sexual services), to the husband as a member of
a corporate patrilineage. Bridewealth is, therefore, expensive, since men pay for the privilege of having their children
belong to their patrilineage. In contrast, in matrilineal
systems, where genetricial rights are never transferred and
the children always belong to their mother´s matrilineage,
bridewealth payments are often nominal. However, as Richards
(1950) has pointed out, matrilineal bridewealth payments may
rise when they permit a man to remove his wife from her kin
group to a new home or to live with his kin.

Bridewealth has been the subject of much controversy,
beginning with its name. Feminists and marxist anthropologists
who stress its status as an indemnity payment, prefer the term
`brideprice´. Those `integrationists´ who have argued that
this marriage payment functioned primarily to draw kin groups
into closer social relationships, prefer the more neutral term
`bridewealth´ to avoid any connotations of wife purchase.
Although my theoretical inclinations place me in the first
category, my professional socialisation and my third-world
identity lead me to use the term `bridewealth´ as the less
offensive of the two.

Bridewealth undoubtedly did contribute to the internal

cohesion of those societies in which it was found. However, it no longer functions as a `societal fund´ through which capital goods circulate among local descent groups which exchange wives. Formerly women circulated in one direction and capital goods went the opposite way (a little like the two types of kula valuables), in systems of `circulating connubium´ and indirect exchange in which both women and goods were individually identifiable. (We are not considering here those systems in which sisters were exchanged directly.) As each parcel of bridewealth goods was distributed in a given transaction, the onward movement of the livestock through other bridewealth deals made it difficult to reclaim them, in the event of one marriage failing and requiring a (partial) refund. Thus the bridewealth did indeed contribute to marital stability, and considerable pressure was exerted to prevent a marriage from failing, simply because of the practical difficulties of repayment.

Even within a single elementary family or matricentral `house´, such circulation might be manifested in the special link between siblings whereby a girl´s bridewealth stock were used to acquire a wife for the particular brother to whom she was `cattle-linked´. This link gave the sister enhanced authority over her brother´s wife, a marriage claim over his daughters, and executive authority over his estate. But this system of indirect exchange, leading to the integration of those lineages participating in the circulation of capital goods through marriage, worked only so long as the capital goods were individually identifiable and reclaimable. When anonymous currency notes replaced livestock, they were themselves much more easily replaced, even by wives who had reached the end of their marital tether and could buy themselves out through their access to employment or productive resources. Indeed, sometimes educated women in professional employment contributed to their own bridewealth in the first place, as monetisation combined with their own education to inflate their guardians´ bridewealth demands beyond a level affordable by young suitors whom they wished to marry.

Such collaboration by women in marriage payments that confirmed their social subordination to men, have been regarded by marxist feminists as a classic example of false consciousness and mystification. However, without bridewealth a marriage was not culturally valid in these societies, law and religion notwithstanding. Moreover, the status ranking of the individual woman was to some extent set by the amount paid for her bridewealth. No bridewealth entailed no status and much scandal. And in the case of cattle-linked siblings, a woman´s bridewealth indirectly gave her substantial leverage over her brother´s marriage and property. Such attractions

146

have power (and vice versa), even if they also mystify other
relations of power. Hence it is not surprising that, even
though modern states have taken over its functions of legiti-
mising marriage and children, attempts to abolish bridewealth
have met with firm cultural resistance from women as well as
men. Attempts to control its inflation have been more popular.
However, the issue of bridewealth is critical to understanding
contemporary conflicts within marriage, particularly conflicts
over the ownership of and entitlement to property.

Affinity and the Protection of Property

One effect of bridewealth inflation throughout Africa has
been to delay marriage, in many cases permanently. There are
growing numbers of what the Shona call <u>mapoto</u> unions, `shack-
ing up´ relationships in which `pots´ are shared but no
formalisation of marriage occurs by the payment of bridewealth
or by civil or religious procedures. In the context of urban,
industrial, or even self- employment, of course, a man can no
longer earn his wife by working for his father-in-law if he
cannot afford to pay bridewealth in goods or cash. `Groom
service´ remains a possible substitute for bridewealth only
among poor peasants. In African cities, instead, female-headed
or `matrifocal´ households are becoming common as the forms of
marriage change. The failure of men to pay bridewealth, by
virtue of their poverty, has contributed to the growth of
women´s economic independence and decision-making authority
within these households. Poor women have been `liberated´ by
default, where no transfer of property has legitimised their
pseudo-marital relationships.

However, the failure to pay bridewealth is not the only
factor that has changed access to property within, and the
forms of, marriage in Africa. The introduction of Christian
and Muslim religions has redefined marital relations, and so
has the introduction of the modern state and its legal bureaucracy. Its religious and statutory or civil forms have had an
important impact on older cultural concepts of marriage, as
Christine Oppong´s (1981) work on the matrilineal Akan peoples
of Southern Ghana has shown.

Traditionally Akan marriage depended on the prior celebration of a girl´s puberty ritual and the passage of bridewealth in the form of `drinks´ (<u>tiri nsa</u>). Children, whether
or not their mother had been formally married, belonged to her
matrilineage. Marriage conferred on the husband exclusive
rights to his wife´s sexuality, even though, in the potential
of every marriage to become polygynous, the reverse was not
true. Bridewealth also entitled a man to the domestic services

of his wife, while his wife could expect some material support for herself and their children. Most marriages linked people in a restricted local area (and cross-cousin marriage was preferred for this reason), so both husbands and wives could work the land of their respective matrilineages during the day but share a house at night. As a result, the marriage contract did not create a new, joint, productive and economic unit as it does in the west. Rights and obligations concerning property were unaffected by marriage and remained the exclusive concern of the matrilineage. When a person died, then, the primary heir was the mother if still living. If she was dead, the eldest full sibling of the deceased acted as trustee over property, in the interests of the whole sibling group and the children of its female members. Only if the mother and all of the deceased's siblings were themselves already dead, did this trusteeship descend a generation to a sister's child.

Christian influence on the Gold Coast, as Ghana was known prior to its Independence in 1957, dates back to the Catholic Portuguese traders of the sixteenth century. By the middle of the nineteenth century, both Catholic and Protestant churches were active well into the interior of Ghana. Part of the attraction of Christian belief lay in its close association with formal literacy and education, but Christianity in itself had two major impacts on the concept of marriage. Firstly, by emphasising monogamy and the relationship between the individual spouses, Christian marriages undermined the primary bond of each spouse to his or her matrilineage. Secondly, the churches also attempted to change customary law with respect to the inheritance of property, in order to strengthen the conjugal family based on Christian marriage. In the coastal fort towns, where Christian converts recognised English law, wives who had been married in church took their husbands' surnames. After his death, with their children they claimed half the movable property in his estate. In other areas, the proportion of the estate claimed by the wife and children varied.

In 1884, the Marriage Ordinance passed by the colonial government gave legislative approval to these changes in customary law affecting monogamous, Christian marriages. The Marriage Ordinance restricted the claims of his matrilineage to one-third of a man's estate, allotting two-ninths to his widow and four-ninths to his children. Oppong (1981:45) notes that this latter portion had to be shared among all of a man's children, including those of extra-marital unions where his paternity had been publicly acknowledged. By the 1960s, when Oppong did her fieldwork, less than one in twenty Akan marriages was contracted under the provisions of the Ordinance. However, the Confederacy Council of Akan chiefs had approved similar changes to customary law in 1948, which had not been ratified by the colonial Governor and therefore had no statutory effect. Attempts by educated Akan Christians to create marriages enclosing their property within the confines of the monogamous, conjugal family, therefore continued to be disputed by matrikin in terms of their customary rights to use and inherit the property of any of their number. What Oppong (1981:9) called `a plurality of legal norms and sanctions, based upon customary law, Christian church law and statutory law´, provided fertile ground for such disputes over property within marriage.

The most dramatic instances of these conflicts were seen when the matrikin stripped the widow and her children of all of the deceased´s property. Although Oppong interpreted this phenomenon as a consequence specifically of matrilineal custom affecting marriage, it is also a major problem in traditionally patrilineal societies, such as the Shona. This problem arises not merely because there is conflict between customary and Christian/statutory inheritance laws. More fundamentally, it results from the concept of lineage corporateness and the transfer between men of rights over women´s labour in bridewealth payments. Particularly where bridewealth is high, its transfer may give the payee a feeling of entitlement to the labour product of his wife. By extension, customary lineage corporateness transfers this entitlement to his lineal kin. A wife´s work, in this view, does not entitle her to the property which it generates.

Zimbabwe, like a number of other African states, has sought to control the division of matrimonial assets (whether by death or divorce), irrespective of the type of marriage or the cultural background of the persons concerned, in order to effect an equitable distribution of property. In this area, there is an important conflict between socialist ideology and traditional customs. Already the Matrimonial Causes Act of 1985 has been denounced by men as an incentive to unscrupulous women to use marriage as a means of `getting rich quick´, while the Succession Bill is coming under similar fire from those who see their customary rights jeopardised by such statutory redefinition and control.

The Concept of `The Family´

We might describe this conflict, between his lineal kin and a man´s wife and children, as centring on the control of his assets by the `family of orientation´ into which the man himself was born, and the challenge to this control that is posed by his own `family of procreation´ established by mar-

149

riage. In Radcliffe-Brown's terms, we might also see this conflict as one between two unified sibling groups belonging to two proximate or adjacent generations, between which relations are normally competitive and strained. In matrilineal systems, this conflict is exacerbated by the fact that a man's children have no descent link with his family of orientation. In patrilineal societies, this conflict causes mothers and their children anguish, because it drives a wedge between them on the basis of their membership of different descent groups. The children themselves may be forcefully appropriated as patrilineal property.

Clearly, then, there are a number of different `family' types. In distinguishing them, we should begin by noting that a family is formed on the basis of the marital link between the spouses to whom the children are filiated. A `family' may, therefore, be spatially dispersed. In contrast, a `household' is a collection of people living and eating together, whether or not they are linked by marriage. A marriage relationship, then, distinguishes a family unit from a mere household of co-resident people, among whom there may exist other types of relationship, such as those of consanguinity or descent.

Firstly we must separate the `nuclear' or `conjugal' or `elementary' family from the `compound' or `composite' type. The elementary family is a monogamous, two-generation structure, comprising a married couple and their natural and/or adoptive children. Occasionally a widowed parent is added to make up three generations, but such additions are usually temporary.

In contrast, compound families come in two sub-types. `Joint' families are composed of a number of elementary units, related collaterally (that is, in the Indian sub-continent where this type is a cultural ideal, the heads of these constituent units are usually brothers). All the component elementary units of the joint family share a common kitchen and eat together. As in the elementary family, temporary parental extensions may occur, especially through widowhood, but normally the joint family breaks up when the last surviving brother of the original unit dies.

While joint families are effectively aggregates of elementary units, extended families, as the second sub-type of the `compound' category, are rather different. In the first place, extended families incorporate a significant proportion of polygynous marriages. Secondly, they are extended lineally, rather than collaterally. They are often coterminous with minimal lineages or local descent groups, having a depth of up to five generations and rarely less than three. In both

150

matrilineal and patrilineal versions, extended families have numerous units for food preparation, almost as many as there are wives in the family. For the purpose of eating food, extended families break up into consumption units based on age, sex and matricentral `house´ affiliation. Some anthropologists, such as Murdock (1960), have regarded these `houses´ as elementary families in their own right. However, their perspective has been criticised as an example of western ethnocentrism by Fox (1967) and others, who have argued instead that the most fundamental unit of human society is not .the elementary family, but the mother-child dyad which forms the core of the `house´.

In the very broadest characterisation, the elementary family has been regarded as European, the extended family as African, and the joint family as Asian, bearing in mind that in each case there are exceptions to these geographical correlations. Some of these exceptions, which in the earlier literature have been described as `families´ (for example the matrifocal households in Africa and the Caribbean, or the historical household unit among the Nayar of the Kshatriya caste in South-West India), strictly speaking should not be described as `families´ because there exists no marital link between any of the people who live together.

At the centre of the arguments about what comprises a family is the question of what the family does in society: its `function(s)´. In the `functionalist´ view, the elementary `family´ is concerned to maintain itself economically as a producing and/or consuming unit, in order to regulate sexual relationships among its members, produce legitimate children, and socialise them. However, unless we add a fifth function, namely the legal regulation of property, to this list of functions, it is clear that these four, singly or in combination, can be performed by organisations other than the family based on marriage. Notably they can be done by matricentral `houses´ in polygynous marriages, by many different kinds of household not based on marriage, by `single parenting´, fostering, and a whole range of alternative institutions.

The legal regulation of entitlement to property is a crucial element of family relationships. If property is indeed theft, then families are the organisational godfathers behind it. Within the matricentral `house´, the elementary family, and the larger lineage, are controlled most forms of property in most societies. The forms of property controlled by descent groups or families include: natural resources (eg. hunting grounds) and natural products (eg. pastures); arable and residential land; housing; livestock (including the specific forms of bridewealth and bloodwealth entitlements); knowledge (including both craft and ritual skills); political authority (in non-elective systems of hereditary succession); rank and social identity in systems of caste and positional succession; services (both labour and ritual), especially in systems of clientship; money; and people (directly as slaves and descendants, indirectly as genetricial and uxorial rights in wives and as rights of guardianship over children).

The ascriptive rights over people that are controlled within families are of particular interest. Not only do these rights have material implications, for example through the appropriation of others´ labour. They also have a fundamental ideological significance, best exemplified in what anthropologists have called notions of `honour´ and `shame´ in Mediterranean and Middle Eastern societies.

`Honour´ has been associated, by male anthropologists, primarily with men´s ability to control the sexual behaviour of their wives and female kin, particularly sisters and daughters, within the framework of elementary families. Shame has been associated both with the licentious behaviour of the women themselves and with the men´s failure to control this. Yet Wikan (1984) has shown that the matter is not so simple. Honour is not an attribute of men alone, nor is shame associated purely with promiscuous female sexuality or a male failure to control it. Instead, honour, reflected in the respect of the self as well as of others, is a composite of the whole person, while shame attaches to specific behaviours of both men and women. In Oman, for example, a wider female generosity may excuse sexual lapses of a fairly flagrant nature, which may be hidden from the man whose public respect and honour they threaten. Both men and women may collude in this deception of honour, for to reveal `shame´ would force a man to act in ways that family and personal honour demand, but that every other consideration cries out against. Though some men may be prepared to kill their wives, sisters and daughters for acting in such a way as to impugn their family honour as well as their personal masculinity, in most Mediterranean societies it would appear that there is a large gap between the ideal of upholding honour and what people actually do. In their comic story <u>Asterix in Corsica</u>, Goscinny and Uderzo (1979:31-2) have immaculately parodied the ideal of family honour.

A Roman legionary tells a young, unmarried Corsican woman he has a warrant to search their house. Her brother tells her to get inside, and turns to the legionary. `You spoke to my sister.´
`I did?...I didn´t realise...´
(Springing handknife) `I don´t like people speaking to my sister.´

152

`But...but I´m not interested in your sister. I only
wanted to...´
`You don´t like my sister?´
`Yes, yes, of course I like your sister...´
`OH SO YOU LIKE MY SISTER, DO YOU? HOLD ME BACK OR I´LL
MURDER HIM...HIM AND THE REST OF THEM!´

`Machismo´ is, of course, a corollary of this concept of
honour. Both contrast markedly with Northern European cultural
ideals of behavioural restraint and, in particular, with the
idea that male `honour´ involves chivalrous, almost non-sexual
behaviour toward <u>unrelated</u> women, rather than control of the
sexual behaviour of female members of one´s family. Honour in
Northern Europe thus tended to be achieved. Honour in the
Mediterranean is still definitively ascribed, notwithstanding
what Herzfeld (1980:342) has called `the nominal equality of
[male] access to moral resources´, arising from families´
attempts to act in the way publicly expected of them. Even the
stigma of (female) shame has been eroded in Northern Europe,
as first divorce and later illegitimacy became more prevalent,
more acceptable, and finally demanded as a feminist right. The
family as an institution has begun to lose both its `honour´
and its social sanctity, as `single parenting´ has become
relatively common in many different situations in many different societies, not only those of Western Europe.

Let us examine one of the more extreme examples first.
The Caribbean has a history that drew people from matrilineal
African societies into slavery on the sugar plantations. But a
matrilineal background which was destroyed by slavery, and
past prohibitions on slaves marrying, do not explain why, a
century and a half after slavery ceased, legal marriage and
family patterns in Caribbean societies diverge so markedly
from those of other countries. While historical factors may
have some relevance, contemporary poverty is more important in
explaining why less than half of all sexual unions approximate
marriage, and why up to three infants of every four born are
illegitimate.

Labour migration among the men, low educational levels
among the working class, and limited work opportunities (save
in plantation agriculture) for the unskilled, combine to
explain why the poor cannot afford the substantial expenses of
a `proper´, legal marriage. There is also a `double standard´
of working-class values which applauds the premarital sexual
activity of young boys and men, while denying basic sex education to young girls. The honour of virginity is demanded of
young women getting married, while seducing virgins scores
very high points among men. The rate of `spoilage´ among
virgins is, not surprisingly, high. Hence we see a pattern,

153

for example in Jamaica. Here, in the 1950s, legal marriages comprised a quarter of all sexual unions and tended to be restricted to professionals, landowners, and the elderly. The young, poor, poorly educated and unskilled made do with non-resident liaisons and co-resident `shacking up´, in a cycle that repeated itself among their illegitimate children.

The instability of such unions (lasting an average of less than four years in Jamaica in the 1950s) led to the reinforcement of the mother-child bond in the absence or irregular presence of a man acting as pater. Households headed by women, in which they are the central focus of internal relationships and make all the major decisions concerning their children effectively single-handed, have been called `matrifocal´. As we saw earlier, in chapter 4, matrifocal households are no longer confined to the Caribbean, but are becoming increasingly common among the urban poor of Africa, under similar conditions and for similar reasons. Legal marriage apparently remains the ideal to which the urban, and perhaps increasingly also the rural, poor of the third world vainly aspire. However, the reality of their marital and family relationships is very different from this ideal of honour and respectability. Single parenting under these circumstances is a necessity, which is ideologically deplored, even by those who practise it.

Role Ascription and Unbalanced Exchange

Yet there are also circumstances in which single parenting may be respectable, socially condoned, and assisted financially by the modern state. (Indeed, most welfare systems make some provision for assisting unmarried mothers, irrespective of whether their motherhood is socially approved.) War widows, for example, may see themselves as having made a voluntary sacrifice to the defence of their society, and as a consequence entitled not merely to its respect, but also to its assistance. The state itself, like Israel, may acknowledge both this entitlement and the impossibility of repaying its sacrificial debt. At the same time, however, as Shamgar-Handelman (1981) has shown, this acknowledgement of entitlement and responsibility may in itself stigmatise those who claim their rights through bureaucratic procedures.

Israel has fought many wars in the course of its forty-year existence. Only after 1967, however, did the state make explicit its debt to war widows as a specific social category and stop treating them as undifferentiated `indigents´. In handling their financial entitlements through the Ministry of Defence, the state made plain that war widows were not its `welfare` clients. However, the professional social workers who handled their claims managed to reduce them to a similar status to that of welfare clients. The social workers wanted the widows to behave `as proper clients` so that they themselves could act out their professional role. The widows, pursuing their entitlement, refused to act as welfare clients. Some refused even to pursue their legitimate claims, preferring to forego what the state said it owed them, rather than impair their own dignity and self-image.

The ambiguity of the single mother's position, even in the super-honourable status of war widow, was reflected in two ways. Firstly, her ascribed status of `war widow` was temporary. As soon as she remarried, her sacrifice was effectively deemed not to have existed, although the bereavement of parents and children entitled them to permanent state assistance. Secondly, the process of overcoming her bereavement and moving back into social and sexual relationships with men, tended to be defined, by the social workers representing the Israeli state, as entailing emotional and even psychological `problems` which affected the way in which they were prepared to deliver the assistance to which the war widow was entitled. The war widow as single parent, then, found herself in a `catch 22` situation. By demanding what everyone agreed was her entitlement, she put the bureaucracy `in a position where it could not function`, precisely because Israeli society agreed that it was impossible actually to repay her altruism.

We might compare this incapacity of a male-dominated bureaucracy to repay wifely sacrifice, with the `cycle of reciprocal dependence` in Jamaica, which nominally obliges sons to support their elderly mothers in return for the mothers' sacrifices in their own upbringing. In practice, however, this obligation usually devolves on daughters, while elderly ex-migrant men, who have lost contact with their matrifocal home, eke out their declining days in state-supported penury. In each of these differing cases, it would appear that the ways in which men supposedly repay their debts to women, for what the men themselves describe as women's `sacrifices` within family institutions, often do not work. The exchange does not balance. Perhaps, in ascriptive roles of a familial nature, a balance was never envisaged. Perhaps the ideology of marriage and the family is merely a special instance of the general ideology of sacrifice (discussed briefly in chapter 5), in which the economics of the exchange also look similar. If so, there nonetheless exist other ascriptive exchanges, of a similarly unbalanced nature, which are also validated ideologically.

In Hindu Asia, the ascription of social roles within the

family is far less important than ascription through the Hindu religion itself. Caste is a religious construct, based on the concept and cycle of reincarnation. Deviation from ascribed roles on earth is believed to lengthen the cycle of suffering, by resulting in reincarnation in a lower form. Compliance, in contrast, hastens the soul's liberation from this cycle, by rebirth in a higher form, closer to ultimate incorporation into the universal soul. The `twice-born´ Brahman, Kshatriya and Vaishya castes therefore have a guarantee that they are on the right track, whereas the Sudras recognise the length of their future in part from the relatively polluting occupations to which they are currently ascribed. Since the thoroughly polluted outcastes have no future in this system, it is hardly surprising that they have provided the most fertile ground for conversion to Islam or Christianity. Yet even Muslims and Christians are tied into the relations of interdependence among villagers, in a division of labour that is ascribed by Hindu cosmology.

The occupational interdependence of castes and sub-castes in village India is reflected, at the family level, in the jajmani system. The praja is tied into a relationship of permanent clientship with his employing jajman, performing ritual or other services, or supplying regularly required goods, in return for regular, fixed payments in grain, and obligatory gifts on special ritual occasions. Some clients also receive parcels of land to cultivate in their own right, in addition to those which they work on a sharecropping basis for their jajman landlord. Jajmani links families in long-term, personalised, hereditary and unequal relations of patronage and clientship. Dumont (1972:144) has noted that this system guarantees landowners the services of specialists, and in turn also `indirectly guarantees the subsistence of the specialists, by giving them limited but real rights over the products of the land and the affluence of their masters´.

But the real force of jajmani does not lie in these material exchanges. Its etymological derivation, from the Sanskrit yajamana (meaning `he who has a sacrifice performed´), gives jajmani the unmistakeable connotation of religious obligation. The provision of services by the once-born to the twice-born is not merely a matter of unequally-valued reciprocity. The entire system of unequal exchanges between unequals is validated by the concept of hierarchy based on degrees of ritual purity. Caste, like motherhood, is an ideel reality, which structures the inequality of material exchanges on the basis of roles and statuses in society that are ascribed by the Hindu religion.

Yet neither caste identity nor motherhood is immutable.

156

As we have seen, biological motherhood does not necessarily
entail social motherhood. Young Jamaican women who turn over
the rearing of their illegitimate children to their own
mothers can quite easily abandon the role of social mother, at
least for some years. Similarly, Bailey (1960) has detailed
one of many instances of collective caste-climbing among a
polluted sub-caste of Sudra distillers. In a society that sees
alcohol as polluting, they made made enough money from their
traditional occupation to buy land and hire (at a premium) the
ritual services of renegade Brahmans. Later, in the ritually-
purifying process of `sanskritisation´, the ex-distillers
turned vegetarian and accepted food only from Brahmans, claiming Kshatriya status. Even in the role ascriptions that are
fundamental to the reproduction of a given social structure,
then, there is some leeway for manipulation and achievement.

CHAPTER SEVEN

VOLUNTARY SOCIAL RELATIONS

In chapter 6, we saw that there was some potential for the manipulation of ascribed roles and statuses, without altering the nature of ascriptive systems themselves. Moreover, ascriptive systems may allow a measure of achievement, notably in the area of political leadership. However, there is a fundamental difference between societies that are structured by ascriptive relationships and those based on achieved positions. `Meritocracies´ tend to be more open and to permit easier mobility among social positions than those based on caste, age or unilineal descent, even though `class´ status tends toward ascription in the initial instance and may be reinforced through socialisation and education.

There are a number of processes that contribute toward breaking down the bases on which ascriptive systems work. Among the more important of these processes are industrialisation, urbanisation, religious conversion and what some have called `peasantisation´, meaning the regular production of an agricultural and/or pastoral surplus for commercial marketing rather than subsistence purposes. In requiring new skills and fostering new lifestyles, these processes permit of new achievements - new forms and greater degrees of wealth; new and different opportunities for leadership; alternative forms of rank, status and prestige; and new ways of achieving social honour and respectability. Social scientists often gloss these processes and their outcomes as `social change´. We should be clear, however, that two issues require analytical separation here. On the one hand there is the institutional transformation that displaces, if not replaces, the traditional locus of ascription; and on the other we have the ways in which individuals adapt their behaviour to these new institutional possibilities.

It is in the context of such new institutions, often introduced from outside, that individuals and social categories, like the distillers, manipulate their ascribed relationships, with a view either to reinforcing `custom´ in new contexts, or to replacing it. In either case, we witness the growth of voluntary social relationships in new institutional settings. Voluntary relations are thus `institutionalised´, in the sense of being governed by agreed rules, but not all voluntary relations are `bureaucratised´, in the sense of being organised into formal associations. Where voluntary associations emerge, they `replicate´ the larger bureaucratic structure, copying its main organisational features. They, too, have formal constitutions, elective leadership, specified objectives, and identifiable sub-groupings. However, whether or not voluntary social relationships are bureaucratised in this way, individual choice in these relationships is freer than in ascriptive systems. But whether voluntary social relations actually change the basic statuses ascribed by another order, is open to question. As usual, we may understand these analytical points better by examining specific examples.

Transformational Gender?

We have seen that in very many societies, women's roles and social positions were ascribed within the framework of kinship, marriage and the family. Many African women have, in the past century, sought to escape such constraints by migrating to the prospects of the new towns established during the colonial period as administrative, commercial and manufacturing centres. As we saw in chapter 4, they rarely find formal employment in these centres, but do manage to subsist among the bright lights, by providing services traditionally associated with marriage to effectively single men, often within pseudo-marital relationships.

In the urban context, women not only identify themselves with others in a similar position. They also form associations to pursue their common interests: market women's unions, rotating credit associations, women's social clubs, women's institutes, mothers' unions within the churches, dancing groups and so on. These associations are important in helping women to adjust, both socially and financially, to the exigencies and demands of urban work and living. Some of these organisations also provide welfare services in the fields of education, child-bearing, and death. In their offices, they all offer new opportunities for achieving positions of leadership and its associated prestige, often - but not always - denied women in traditional societies.

We might, therefore, expect women's voluntary associations to act as a focus for new structural relationships that would free women from their traditional disabilities. Yet the vast majority of these associations have also stressed the importance of marriage, and have brought pressure to bear on members acting in such a way as to bring this institution into disrepute. Those women regularly involved in domestic altercations, as Little (1973) noted, have been expelled from these new associations. Notions of honour and respect customarily associated with women's ascribed statuses, have thus been upheld by urban women collectively pursuing their economic independence of men within or outside of marriage. Women have not, apparently, recognised this contradiction in their new voluntary relationships with others in similar circumstances.

Nor has there been complete solidarity among women collectively pursuing their right to self-determination. What we might call `class´ divisions have been reflected in the tendency of educated and professional women to form their own, exclusive groupings and to shun association with less refined `aunties´ (as they are called in South Africa) of rural or working class origin. The Catholic church in South Africa, for example, created a special `mothers´ union´ for state registered nurses, because they would not attend meetings of the St. Anne´s sorority. Similarly, protestant nurses joined the Young Women´s Christian Association in preference to attending the mothers´ unions of their particular denominations. Yet such elite organisations, as Cheater (1974) has noted of the professional association of black nurses in South Africa, have also been used by their members as pressure groups in the political arena, to change the conditions of access of non-elites to state educational and welfare facilities.

Within the mothers´ unions themselves, mature women have bewailed their failure to control the sexual behaviour of their adolescent daughters. In an attempt to exert institutionalised control over the younger generation, existing members admitted their daughters initially only to probationary status in these organisations. Both traditional and new distinctions of age, class and marital status, then, penetrated these female religious organisations, whose ideology (of equality before God) ostensibly provided a charter to overcome women´s ascriptive identities.

Yet rural women´s associations, having a specifically domestic orientation, such as the Zimbabwean women´s homecraft clubs and women´s institutes, have on occasion been used as an organisational base from which to change the ideology of ascription by challenging male domination. Cheater (1984) has described how the leaders of such groups in a freehold farming area challenged the men´s `right´ to make decisions about prizes in the women´s section of the local agricultural show. Having withdrawn their catering labour from male deployment, they then pushed the issue further, to extract concessionary changes regarding their participation in decisions about the organisation of the show itself, stating explicitly that they would not accept ridicule simply because, as women, they were assumed to be incompetent in this area. Hoist on their own petard of refusing to undertake `women´s work´ (cooking and making tea), especially in public, the men had no alternative but to accept the women´s demands. Paradoxically, however, few

160

women have penetrated newer institutions, such as the Ward and Village Development Committees, which were designed to involve both men and women in decision-making for their local areas. These are explicitly political bodies. Politics, both covert and overt, in most of Africa appears to be a field normally ascribed, by gender, to men.

Cohen (1981) has traced the political and ideological continuities of male secret societies in Sierra Leone, as part of his wider concern to understand the class solidarity of Creole male elites. The `provincials´ had always been linked by their membership of the traditional male secret society, Poro. But during the colonial period, Creole civil servants and professionals were fragmented into numerous, disparate voluntary associations, each pursuing similar elite identity. Being a privileged ethnic minority, to organise themselves formally into a political party was to ensure their continued exclusion from power. Particularly after Independence, `what [the Creoles] lacked above all else was a system for the regular articulation of corporate organisational functions, for deliberation, decision making, and the exercise of authority to ensure compliance and implementation´ (Cohen 1981:95-6). In two critical periods of political threat to Creole ascendancy, pre- and post-independence, there was an upsurge in their affiliation to masonic lodges. By 1970 the 17 lodges in Sierra Leone had nearly 2,000 members, the vast majority of whom were Creole.

Cohen (1981:122) has been quick to deny any intention to impute `conscious and calculated political design´ to this involvement of Creole men in freemasonry. As a system of ritual values in its own right, freemasonry had its own attractions. But the organisation of the lodges, precisely through the system of ritual secrecy, created a network of intimate and exclusive bonds among men of different occupations and bureaucratic seniority. Masonic integration created `a unified system of legitimation for a unified authority structure´ and a single view of what should be done. Freemasonry, then, like the Poro organisation, formed part of the `informal structure´ of (class) politics in Sierra Leone. Ritual secrecy and the exclusion of women, in both cases, contributed to male solidarity. Not only did these voluntary associations `replicate´ the bureaucracy of ·politics. More fundamentally, they defined both politics and the class structure of Sierra Leone as the proper concern of men, in which women were to be involved only indirectly, through their attachment to men. Again, as in all-female voluntary associations, the structure of male secret societies, both old and new, has not surprisingly reinforced rather than transcended the ascription of status by gender.

161

Transformational Ethnicity?

If new, single-sex associations, dealing with new interests, have not transformed gender relations in the structure
of contemporary African societies, what has happened to
ethnicity as it has become bureaucratically organised? In
chapter 4, we saw how Africa´s new mines and cities were, in
some cases, organised along `tribal´ lines by their white
managements, thus creating `urban tribalism´. In West Africa,
however, long the home of indigenous urban settlements, such
`tribalism´ was created by Africans themselves. Little (1957,
1973) has documented the growth of `tribal unions´ in West
African cities in the first half of this century, which met
the social, financial and welfare needs of immigrants seeking
work. They also provided death benefits, which, in Southern
Africa, were the <u>raison d´etre</u> specifically of `burial socie-
ties´, often organised on ethnic lines. In addition, the
tribal unions generated money for rural development back home,
and sponsored the education of their young men.

In West Africa, individual `tribal´ organisations were
amalgamated into larger confederations, such as the Ibo State
Union. These very large units wielded political influence
(particularly under the British colonial policy of indirect
rule) and were taxed as formal organisations. They provided
important opportunities for leadership and the acquisition of
administrative experience in large organisations. David Parkin
(1969) has described a similar `segmentary´ organisation of
certain tribal unions in East Africa, working upwards from the
level of clan organisations, through the location or sub-tribe
associations, to the apical union.

Responsibilities tended to differ among these different
levels. The East African unions themselves were concerned with
large projects like education, community halls and organisational services (for example, in organising dances, or soccer
in what amounted to leagues based on clans or sub-tribes).
Their constituent units (especially at the clan level) assisted individuals with their social or financial problems (in
litigation, returning home, settling disputes and the like).
Specifically, the clan associations sent home single women
found `roaming´ the cities, and Parkin (1969:165) noted that
all the men agreed about `the desirability of continued con-
trol over their womenfolk, however much they might differ in
their ideas as to how this might be done´. In their concern
with primary, face-to-face relations among closely related
people from the same home area, the clan associations sometimes found themselves in dispute with one another, within
their sub-tribe or location grouping, over what Parkin (1969:
156) called `clan nepotism´. (Ironically, it is this type of

162

particularistic behaviour that has been called `tribalism´ by observers foreign to Africa. To have Africans accusing one another of such behaviour within `tribal´ unions may, therefore, strike such observers as a little odd.)

The constitutions of East African tribal unions were written in both their home language and English. Some made specific provision for the affiliation of `foreign´ neighbours who supported the tribal customs in question, thus recognising that ethnic identity could be achieved, rather than merely ascribed by descent rules. Some, like the Luo, specified that their womenfolk could be members in their own right, and even tried to establish female branches and involve women in association offices. Yet Parkin (1969:167-8) noted that such integration `in many ways strengthen[ed] male authority by seeming to lend female support´ to `a special urban ethnic moral system´, dominated by men, which emphasised male brotherhood and female virtue in a system of customary propriety. Again, like associational gender, and notwithstanding its new interests and institutional forms, ethnicity seems to have been essentially conservative of those structural relationships underpinning social identity among the urban poor.

But yet again, if we look at altered ethnicity in the countryside, we sometimes get a different picture. Let us return once more to Darfur, in the Sudan, and examine ethnicity among the wealthy Fur, who have accumulated capital in the form of cattle. While a Fur man owned only a few livestock, he was happy enough to entrust them to the care of a nomadic Baggara herdsman exploiting the pasturelands lying below the arable massif which the Fur inhabited. As his capital increased, however, he was more likely to want to supervise the cattle himself. For a while he might move to the lower parts of Fur territory to diminish the risk of disease to his cattle while still being able to cultivate millet, though gaining poor yields in these marginal areas. But this strategy exposed him to poor ecological conditions for both cultivation and herding: he got the worst of both worlds. So, particularly when his herd exceeded a dozen head and provided sufficient dairy products for both consumption and trade, the Fur accumulator was likely to become a nomadic herder himself. To do this, he joined a Baggara herding unit and breached the cultural boundary of language and lifestyle that separated the two ethnic categories. He became a Baggara, though his Fur origins were remembered, and if he failed as a pastoralist he might well return to farming in his home village.

Haaland (1969) emphasised that becoming a Baggara under such circumstances was an ideological adjustment to changed material conditions, not a choice of cultural models as such.

The productive independence of husband and wife among the cultivating Fur, had to give way to their co-operation as a pastoral household, in which each depended on the other for certain services necessitated by the demands of the livestock. While one spouse physically moved the cattle in search of pasture and water, (s)he could not be processing milk into butter or cheese. While the other tended the children and prepared both food and commodities for marketing, (s)he could not be herding the livestock. Interdependence and a joint purse logically went together. Speaking Arabic was necessary to communicate with the neighbours. Raising the children as Baggara was a natural corollary of living in a Baggara community. There was nothing sacrosanct, under these circumstances, about `being´ Fur. In contrast to the urban circumstances of poor migrants, original identity in this context was a positive liability. The re-organisation of ethnicity reflected and was an adaptation to changed environmental conditions, both physical and social. Primordial identity yielded, ultimately, to the demands of capital accumulation.

We should be careful, then, not to over-emphasise the significance of urbanisation as such in the process of cultural transformation. Ethnicity, as Barth (1969:10) suggested, may certainly involve `categories of ascription and identification by the actors themselves´. But, as Parkin (1974:119) has noted, this articulation of their ethnic distinctiveness is most likely to occur among people locked into political conflict and competition over scarce moral or material resources. Such competition characterises the burgeoning cities of the third world, in which the demand for employment, housing and respectability far outstrips their supply. Common identity may allow claims on resources. Ethnic boundaries may provide a means of excluding the claims of others. Yet we should recall here the point made in chapter 4: that when political conflicts (for example in trades unions) are explicitly alleged to reflect `tribal´ divisions, they often do not!

Transformational Recreation?

Gender and ethnicity have a very basic structural importance in most societies. In comparison, what people do with their spare time may appear to be somewhat trivial. Nonetheless, sport and recreation do have an input into cultural and class identity. I was raised in a colonial system which firmly associated rugby, tennis, hockey and squash with the white bourgeoisie, and allocated football to the black underclass. Today I live in a system that is having perhaps more difficulty in breaking these associations of the colonial sporting past, than in achieving integration in other parts of the social system.

Many African workers in the past had precious little time or financial resources to devote to recreation as such. Formal non-working time was often devoted to other aspects of subsistence and social assurance, such as tribal welfare associations, burial societies and religious observance. Where recreation was funded by employers, it often centred on `traditional´ cultural activities, such as tribal dancing on the Zambian and South African mines. But soccer caught on early, perhaps because it was often the only sport taught at school, perhaps because it was cheap. Today Africa is a soccer-mad continent, and football is big business through the gate-money it generates. Control of the sport is often ultimately vested in a government ministry, and national associations are affiliates of the International Football Association. Within each country, there is at least one highly bureaucratised league system. As we have seen earlier, even tribal unions may participate in the organisation of league soccer, while both private companies and multinational corporations sponsor both teams and trophies.

Soccer is a highly competitive game, from club to international levels. It provides a very important arena for would-be administrators to make their political mark, as well as for players to establish their personal reputations. Yet the game is, fundamentally, a team game. Even the individual stars are part of the team, and it is the team which wins or loses. `Gamesmanship´ is an integral part of the team nature of football, and in Africa, the techniques of `psyching´ an opposing team show some continuity with both military and cultural traditions, as well as exploiting new possibilities. Putting up a team from a highland savannah area in an equatorial coastal hotel lacking air conditioning, requires familiarity with a new technology. Allowing the opposition to find protective medicine around the goal-mouth is a somewhat older technique, or at least rests on somewhat older beliefs. Both work. Indeed, to judge from the popular press, witchcraft remains an integral part of African soccer, as Scotch (1970) showed in some detail for South Africa over a generation ago.

Like most other contexts in which witchcraft operates, the outcome of competitive soccer is uncertain. Nor is it clear why some teams attract and retain good players and `click´ as a team. How a team wins may be seen in action replays. Why a team wins is a different question. Gluckman (1944) has shown that that the `why´ question contains the core of beliefs in witchcraft. Because the question `why´ is essentially unanswerable in terms of natural causation, and because `coincidence´ is an unsatisfactory answer to those personally involved, `why?´ lends itself to explanation in terms of the supernatural. So it is only logical that witchcraft should run onto the soccer field along with the players. But in the case of Zulu football, the game provided regular employment for izinyanga (traditional `doctors´) as well as some players. The inyanga´s ritual responsibilities included slaughtering a goat before the opening and after the close of the league season; doctoring individual players to protect them against the spells of the opposition´s `doctor´ and to make their gear `slippery´ on the field; and secluding the players on the night before the `battle´, as well as feeding them purificatory emetics on the morning of the confrontation itself. All of these rituals of hostility derived from Zulu military practice in the time of Shaka. If they failed to achieve their purpose, the team `doctor´, rather than the players, faced replacement.

Scotch (1970) interpreted the Zulu soccer material as reflecting the adaptation of old beliefs and ritual practices to the competitive tensions of new, urban lifestyles. But there exists a similar insertion of cultural traditions into new recreational activities in rural Papua-New Guinea, such as gambling and the singsing bisnis which has displaced the old pig festivals. It would seem, then, that new forms of competitive recreation are by no means purely urban phenomena.

Despite inadequate transport facilities and long walks to headload cash crops to the nearest road, New Guinea farmers now produce significant amounts of coffee and cocoa, which have brought substantial amounts of cash into remote village communities on a regular basis. Much of this cash has been invested in bisnis, notably small trading stores and transport vehicles, as the new route to big-man status. But a large proportion has also gone into recreational activities that themselves affect the prospects of bisnis success. MacLean (1984) has argued that gambling is a mechanism for distributing this cash within village communities, which detracts from its accumulation by those who earn or invest it.

Among the Maring of the Jimi Valley, MacLean found three distinct types of gambling, which correlated with individual and corporate activity. Mbeni was a card game in which skill had some place in the final outcome, and was played only as a confrontation between individuals for relatively low cash stakes. Sandu was a traditional dice game, also individualised, but based purely on chance and played for somewhat higher stakes. Laki, a card game of chance, involved very high stakes indeed and often incorporated teams (kampani) in which the wealthy contestants shared clan membership. Laki could,

166

therefore, express the old, pre-pacification clan hostilities in a new idiom.

Laki games often continued for days at a time, since winners at one point were obliged to give their opponents the chance to recoup their losses, and losers felt obliged to pursue the cash they had lost. After all, such loss might total a year's coffee earnings or store profits. Winning such sums was, of course, the main attraction of gambling among the Maring themselves, in order to set up bisnis, but MacLean argued that this `emic´ explanation for gambling behaviour was inaccurate. While such sums might be lost as a unit, as winnings they were fragmented and dispersed among the kampani members and their supporters. Gambling thus had the effect of evening out access to cash in the Jimi valley. Investment profits did not form the basis for capital accumulation, but were instead drawn into the circulatory system, partly in return for increments to the political and social prestige of the already wealthy gamblers.

One of the many public settings in which gambling occurred was the singsing, itself regarded as a bisnis opportunity for making individualised profits that were not to be shared by clansmen. (The early use of singsing bisnis profits to pay taxes and bridewealth for clansmen seemed to contradict this theoretical distinction.) Commercial singsing festivals in the Eastern Highlands of New Guinea date from the mid-1970s, and are generally held after the coffee harvest and receipt of payment. They are in many ways similar to the traditional festivals at which big-men slaughtered pigs and distributed gifts, in return for social prestige and political leadership. Boyd (1985:333) described singsing gatherings as `highly animated festivities of dancing, singing, drinking, eating and exchange´ among people who pay for admission as well as for what they consume. These festivals also support courtship, some degree of promiscuity, gambling, and physical confrontations between clans and villages, not only in the dance arena but also outside it. For the food- and alcohol-vendors, they represent an opportunity to make money within the village, and for the sponsor, an opportunity to accumulate capital as well as to enhance his reputation for generous gift-giving. For those who attend in their finery, the singsing offers the opportunity to let their hair down in a big way. Everyone whose opinions Boyd sought, including government officials, regarded singing bisnis as good for rural development as well as excellent entertainment. One sponsor noted that `The pig festivals are gone and now all we think about is money´.

New forms of recreation, then, also have their continuities with the past, and help to reinforce existing divisions within society. New, voluntary, recreational relationships may thus be no more revolutionary, despite their element of achievement, than the ascribed relationships of the past. Very often, ostensibly transformative voluntary social relations actually recreate the assumptions of former ascription, particularly where they themselves concern gender and ethnicity. But when we turn to the area of personal friendship, the discontinuities are perhaps more marked than in the areas examined so far.

Old and New Forms of Friendship

`You can choose your friends´, the English say, `but not your relatives´, thus distinguishing voluntary from ascribed relationships. But in many societies, friendship is not completely voluntary. `Bond friendship´ has often been confused with kinship (as `pseudo-kinship´ or `ritual kinship´ or `blood brotherhood´), precisely because of its contractual, ascriptive and sometimes hereditary nature. In what have been called `joking relationships´ between tribal categories in Central Africa, individuals may not take offence at licenced insults directed against them. Whether such relationships qualify as `friendship´ is open to question, but they are unquestionably ascribed, not voluntary. Finally, originally voluntary friendships may be changed by the imposition on them of additional, more formalised expectations, for example of god-parenthood. In none of these cases is the friendship entirely voluntary.

There are other cases, too, where friendship has taken on the linguistic idiom of kinship, as Blacking (1978) has shown among black schoolgirls in South Africa in the 1950s and 1960s. (A similar system also operated among African students training to become state registered nurses.) When a first-former entered a strange boarding school, she was to some extent protected from the `fagging´ and other demands of older girls by being allocated as `daughter´ or `wife´ to a particular senior, often of a different ethnic group to her own. Some of these institutionalised friendships between `play mothers´ and `play daughters´ lapsed rather quickly, but many extended into adult life and survived geographical separation. In addition, individual girls also entered into `free´ or `spontaneous´ friendships based on personal choice rather than institutionalised allocation, and these normally lasted well into adult life.

Friendships begun at boarding school are important all over contemporary Africa. `Old boy´ and `old girl´ networks and associations perpetuate links forged in youth. Like similar networks in the UK (and perhaps based specifically on the British boarding school model), such associations and friendships in Africa feed into the ongoing process of class formation. In the UK, the class aspect of public school education has survived (and has possibly been strengthened by) the reorganisation of state schooling. Cohen (1974:xix) has remarked that British public schools `socialise, or rather train, their pupils in specific patterns of symbolic behaviour [and] create a web of enduring friendship and comradeship´. In Africa, Jacobson (1968:129) has noted that `attendance at the same school does not necessarily mean that men will be friends later on, but this experience is for many elite Aricans one of the first situations during their careers, away from home and on the move, in which they establish friendships which are renewed at different points in their lives´.

Geographical mobility and friendship tend to reinforce one another among transient bureaucrats of many different ethnic identities working for government and private companies alike. In situations where the work hierarchy determines their on-job interactions, highly educated and well-paid elites generally structure their leisure-time interaction with others of similar sex, age and occupational rank, in order to confirm their own status. Friendship choices, as Jacobson found in the Ugandan town of Mbale, express these distinctions of status even within the elite stratum. Friends are status equals. Off-duty socialising with friends thus marks the boundary of voluntary interaction with class equals in `effective´ (as opposed to `extended´) social networks. However, by the mid-1960s Jacobson had found no evidence that Ugandan elites used their class boundaries, defined by friendship, in the way of London stockbrokers, `to articulate a corporate organisation that is partly formal and partly informal, in order to compete within the wider social system for a greater share of the national income´ (Cohen 1974:xxi). Emergent classes in Africa of the 1960s might therefore be comprehended more accurately as Weberian `status groups´ than as Marxist `classes´.

However, in independent African states, some marxists have argued that the `national elite´, bounded in part by its friendship choices, has become through its control of state power a `comprador bourgeoisie´. In this argument, altered relations of power have altered the class identity of elites.

Old and New Relations of Power

Politics in most of the third world has become less as-cribed in hereditary monarchies and more `voluntary´, through party political organisation, than previously. In rural areas, the pressure for this change came mainly from returned labour migrants, young men who had come into contact with alternative political ideas and who were no longer satisfied that their labour, marriages and lives should be arbitrarily controlled by older men. Ideas of democratisation and participation appealed to them, and they formed organisations designed to give them more power. First came `proto-political´ organisations, like the Melanesian `cargo cults´ and African `native welfare societies´, followed by trades unions and, finally, political parties overtly challenging the colonial order.

Democratisation, in the form of universal suffrage, has been achieved in most countries of the third world, as part of the process of shedding their former colonial status. However, some elements of ascription have subsequently crept back into politics. Some, but by no means necessarily all, choice has been removed in one-party systems. Voluntary choice has been more severely curtailed in systems of indirect election and sometimes direct appointment, for example to upper houses in bicameral legislative systems. But the area in which re-ascription has become most marked is the party structure itself, especially in Africa. Mature men have bounded themselves into a restrictive decision-making category within the party organisation by creating separate `women´s leagues´ and `youth wings´ (the latter often headed by men distinctly older than their constitutions normally permit to acquire membership!). These bodies probably account for between two-thirds and three-quarters of the total party membership, but they are usually represented on the central executive of the party by a small minority of its total members. Their separate constitutions, in turn, legitimate this under-representation by restricting their fields of competence to those matters specifically affecting women or youth as social categories in the wider society. Hence if one is female, or under thirty years old, one´s `voluntary´ participation in national politics is not even potentially identical with that of men over thirty (or whatever the cut-off age for `youth´ is defined to be).

These ascriptive aspects of gender and sex in party politics might justify regarding political relations as only `semi-voluntary´, for they are new impositions relating to relations of power in the present, rather than continuities from the cultural past. New institutions, then, do not necessarily imply purely voluntary relations among those involved, any more than traditionally ascribed relationships disallowed elements of achievement and voluntarism. Nothing is what it appears to be at first sight. Many structural realities in society are by definition concealed below its surface.

Mystification and Transformation

Perhaps the most elegant example of mystification (which is, in the marxist view, primarily but not exclusively the preserve of religion), comes from the Giriama living in the Southern Kenyan coastal belt inland from Mombasa. Living as they do in the Swahili sphere of influence, the Giriama for centuries resisted conversion to Islam. However, by the time Parkin did his fieldwork among them in 1966-7, a small minority (about 6 per cent) of Giriama had voluntarily become Muslims. Among this minority, who retained their Giriama identity and some traditional customs, were the first-generation, `therapeutic´ converts, who claimed to be possessed by peripheral Islamic spirits. They validated similar claims among other converts.

Being Muslim erected a `partial social barrier´ between the converts and the majority of the Giriama, for it imposed dietary prohibitions on their consumption of alcohol, pork, and all other meat that was not slaughtered by Muslim butchers. Normal, everyday commensality between kin and neighbours was, therefore, replaced by occasional lavish feasting, especially at Muslim funerals. This example inflated the general cost of funerals (and bridewealth, for different reasons), which drove the older and less wealthy Giriama to mortgage and sell their productive assets, notably land and palm-trees, to maintain their prestige in this gerontocratic society. The buyers of these assets tended to be the younger, wealthy Muslims, whose religious identity safeguarded their property from the normal patterns of redistribution, based on the customary obligations of feasting.

Parkin traced the origin of this polarisation between the young, wealth-accumulating Muslims and the older pagans, to 1944, when, under war-time conditions, the rising copra prices caused the demise of the palm-wine trade to the coast and a change in the payment for land and palm transactions from livestock to cash. As in other colonised societies, cash among the Giriama was at that time largely in the hands of young labour migrants, and this change gave them an edge in the property market. They began to accumulate land and trees in increasing quantities. But at the same time that they bought up the elders´ property, they also needed the elders to ratify these transactions in the traditional system, at least until the Kenyan state provided alternative land registers. It was at this point, apparently, that the young accumulators changed their religion. They had no choice: the Islamic spirits which possessed them demanded their conversion as the price of leaving them in peace and good health.

171

Interestingly, at no point was the conflict over productive resources presented by any of the Giriama as an economic or `class´ conflict. The conflict and competition over land and trees was conceptualised and articulated in the customary idiom of intergenerational tension. Thus Giriama custom was never explicitly challenged by those finding ways around it. Structural relations in the changing economy were mystified by a combination of custom and religion. Parkin (1972:75) has suggested that such `mystification of inequality´, based on achieved wealth and voluntary conversion to a different religion, may be associated with the early stages of agricultural accumulation, when `ambiguity in loyalties and group membership actually facilitates an emerging economic differentiation which has not yet given birth to a system of stratified corporate groups´.

The Giriama entrepreneurs were not the only people possessed by Islamic spirits, demanding a certain type of behaviour from them. Other marginalised Giriama, including women, and foreigners threatened with the loss of their land, were similarly afflicted. Lewis (1966, 1971) has argued that possession by spirits making abnormal demands is widespread among poor, deprived and marginalised people of both sexes, but women are particularly prone to such possession over a very wide range of societies. He has interpreted such possession as a strategy, albeit mystified, to redress inequality through spirit-sanctioned redistribution. More specifically, Lewis has argued that possession is the only strategy readily available to women in the `sex-war´ by which they are normally subordinated to men.

Wilson (1967) has argued, in contrast, that such possession mystifies intra- rather than inter-sex antagonism. Personally I find the weight of Lewis´ evidence more persuasive, which Wilson would not find surprising, since he attributes Lewis´ argument to muddle-headed western ethnocentrism among the protagonists of women´s liberation! Where a sex-based division of labour does not permit competition between men and women, Wilson argues, there can be no reason for conflict between them, since properly-socialised men and women accept these fundamental cultural values. We have already seen, in chapter 3, how such idealist and integrationist views on the division of labour have been countered by materialist approaches. And much of this chapter has shown how older forms of subordination and inequality are re-created `voluntarily´ in new institutions. This re-creation occurs as part of the micro-politics of organising voluntary associations, for all social relationships have a political dimension.

CHAPTER EIGHT

THE POLITICAL DIMENSION

Social anthropologists have made significant contributions to understanding two areas of political behaviour. In the first place, they have managed to re-create the precolonial political operations of certain African societies, in particular those that had no state organisation as such. Secondly, they have pioneered the analysis of micro-political behaviour, especially in the area of leadership, at all levels of formal political organisation, from family to national cabinet. They have shown how `log-rolling´ or `horse-trading´ (in the jargon of political science) actually works, among leaders and between leaders and their followers. In this chapter, we shall examine both of these contributions.

The fieldwork tradition in African political anthropology began in the late 1920s with Evans-Pritchard´s work in the Sudan, barely a generation after the British had suppressed the Mahdist revolt and established their colonial control of that territory. The precolonial situation was then still prominently in the minds of Evans-Pritchard´s Nuer and Azande research subjects. A generation later, such precolonial practices had been substantially modified, for example by the imposition of tax-collecting chiefs and headmen on societies, like the Lugbara, which previously had had no rulers of any description. However, political traditions (or their absence) had by then become part of the precolonial past, avidly remembered and recited to all who cared to listen. It is largely from oral tradition, then, not from direct observation, that our comprehension of how politics was embedded in lineage organisation, or age-grading, has been reconstructed. And this comprehension is itself a tribute to what can be known from oral tradition, notwithstanding Malinowski´s view of its role merely as a charter for contemporary political relationships.

Uncentralised, Diffused and Centralised Power

As anthropologists analysed political behaviour in the absence of overt political offices in many African societies of the past, they set up a dichotomy of `centralised´ (`type A´) and `uncentralised´ or `acephalous´ (`type B´) polities (Fortes and Evans-Pritchard 1940). However, this dichotomy accommodated intermediate types (such as petty chiefdoms) rather poorly. Mair (1962) therefore suggested, somewhat later, a tripartite classification into societies with `minimal government´ (such as family bands among hunters and gatherers);

those with governmental functions `diffused´ among and embedded within <u>social</u> categories (such as age grades or lineages); and those having a state organisation. Rather than dealing in such discrete categories, I would suggest that the international and historical range of political organisation is best understood along a continuum, stretching from family bands to modern bureaucratic states. That way we can find a place for every variety and, more importantly, avoid endless disputes about taxonomies.

What is at issue in taxonomic disputes, however, is how `politics´ is to be defined, and this is important. We cannot, as anthropologists, define politics as pertaining to the apparatus of government, because many systems exhibited both political behaviour and unusual forms of `political´ organisation, while not having any political offices. In the absence of governmental offices, it is senseless to seek an institutional `separation of powers´ among non-existent legislatures, judiciaries and administrations. Yet everywhere, even in the absence of `laws´, we do find a set of shared behavioural conventions, called `custom´, existing within a recognised territory, as well as agreed procedures for settling disputes arising from breaches of this customary `rule of law´. Judicial <u>functions</u> exist in the absence of judicial offices, and are concerned with the maintenance of social order. There also exists everywhere an accepted authority structure embedded in certain social roles (such as father, lineage head, ritual expert and so on). Leadership, in other words, is possible even when it does not inhere in specifically political office. So we can recognise political behaviour, firstly, in institutionalised relations of power; wherever these exist; and, secondly, in its concern for social order within specified boundaries, however this is maintained. As the following examples show, however, it is exceedingly difficult, in many but not all African societies of the past, to find a state that was the executive of the ruling class, as Marx conceived the political structure of industrial capitalism.

Lineage Segmentation as Political Organisation: The Nuer

Numbering nearly a quarter of a million people in the 1930s, most Nuer of the Southern Sudan still live as transhumant pastoralists, herding cattle and cultivating sorghum in the floodplain of the White Nile. Belligerent and warlike, the Nuer seem to have been expansionist in the past, and there has been some argument as to whether they and their neighbours, the Dinka, are not actually the same people under different ethnic designations. While they raided one another before colonial pacification, for the past twenty-five years the Nuer

174

and Dinka and other `nilotic´ neighbours have contributed men and support to the Sudanese People´s Liberation Army, fighting to secede from the northern, Arab domination of the Sudan and more recently (since 1983) the nominal imposition of Shari`a´ law on the whole country, particularly the Christian south. Not only have they been drawn into a modern army using both guerilla and conventional war tactics, the Nuer have also been Christianised, educated, and drawn into non-agricultural jobs as their territory has been affected by `development´ of various kinds.

Traditionally the patrilineal Nuer (calling themselves `Nath´: `we, the people´) were divided into some 20 different `tribes´, each sub-divided into clans. Each tribe had a dominant or `aristocratic´ clan whose members (dil) claimed special prestige from living in their clan territory (which they lost if they moved out of it), but no other privileges. In turn, the clans were segmented into lineages of varying depth, from the largest (maximal) units in which members were able to trace their descent from a common ancestor, to the smallest (minimal) units not exceeding five generations in depth. Each local descent group, or minimal patrilineage, formed the agnatic core of a village. Neighbouring villages, comprising a minor lineage, shared a bounded territory which Evans-Pritchard (1940) called the `tertiary tribal section´, the smallest separate territorial unit in the Nuer system. The tertiary sections were aggregated into secondary sections, dominated by a major lineage. In turn, the secondary sections were grouped into primary sections, controlled by maximal lineages or small clans. The primary sections were the largest sub-divisions of the tribal territory as a whole. Within the tribal territory, disputes were supposed to be settled by compensation. Beyond this territory, with unrelated neighbours, open warfare erupted, which, against the Dinka but not other Nuer tribes, often culminated in the acquisition of livestock, women, children, and even land by the victors.

The disputes that gave rise to feuding (and occasionally warfare) often started in the dry season (between December and April) at the cattle camps. As the flood waters receded, Nuer moved individually from their permanent villages on the inter-fluvial ridges, to the permanent watering-holes in the dessicating plain. As more and more people sought to water more and more cattle at these camps, treading on another´s toes could, quite literally, spark off a fight, a homicide and a feud among members of the same tribe. Feuds started in cattle camps among distantly related Nuer normally living well apart, might smoulder on for years. In Nuer ideology, a feud never ended, though it might be interrupted temporarily by the payment of cattle as compensatory bloodwealth. Such temporary settlement of feuds was negotiated by the earth priest, who afforded the killer refuge in his homestead until the agnates of the deceased, seeking his life, dispersed home. Earth priests came from lineages monopolising special ritual powers. As successful negotiators, they could achieve, off this ascriptive position, considerable prominence as informal leaders, but they had no access to any instruments of force to make feuding disputants comply with their recommendations. The best they could do was threaten to curse the recalcitrants by the earth, to cause the fertility of their land, cattle and women to dry up, which normally resulted in co-operation and the acceptance of compensation.

Feuding created gross inconvenience when it polarised close agnates, affines and neighbours living in the same tertiary tribal section. Feuding at this level was, therefore, most easily settled by compensation, not least because there were built-in structural limits on the feud itself. These limits inhered in the relationships through which support was sought. Basically, the old Arab proverb applied: `I against my brother; my brother and I against my cousin; my cousin, my brother and I against all outsiders´. In other words, agnatic proximity structured the support which feuding antagonists could muster. The more closely related they were, the smaller was the number of potential supporters, before they reached a common ancestor who united them with their antagonists. The more distant the relationship, the greater was the number of supporters who could be mobilised, before an ancestor many generations back defined the limits of recruitment. Evans-Pritchard (1940), therefore, in his structural analysis of this political behaviour, regarded it as part of and embedded within the genealogical relationships of patrilineal descent. At the same time, however, he emphasised that agnatic closeness also increased the intensity of the `structural opposition´ between lineage segments.

To understand Nuer politics fully, a supplementary analysis of informal leadership is also necessary. In addition to the earth priests as mediators in feuds, the village `bulls´ or big-men, and the prophets possessed by sky-spirits (the sons of the High God, Kwoth), were important in Nuer politics. The prophets, in particular, organised armed resistance to both Arab and British colonisers, managing to unite men from different Nuer tribes into armies numbering up to 300 men. Not surprisingly, by the time Evans-Pritchard reached Nuerland in 1930, the prophets were maintaining a very low profile, some having been imprisoned for their military entrepreneurship. It is conceivable that, had their unificatory activities not been interrupted, these prophets might have created some form of divine kingship among the Nuer. Similarly, at the village

176

level, the `bulls' (especially where they were simultaneously
earth priests and aristocrats) might have become headmen or
even petty chiefs. They provided advice, guidance and assistance on both productive and judicial matters. Through their
charismatic personalities and fighting prowess, these `bulls'
attracted non-agnates to their villages. Their lack of political office, then did not deprive the Nuer of informal leaders
with political functions.

Age-Grades as Political Organisation: The Gikuyu

Although initiation marked a Nuer man's transition to
adult status, there were no age-grades in Nuer society. In
contrast, the patrilineal Gikuyu arranged their society not on
the basis of segmentary lineages, but into age-grades which
accommodated political functions. By the age of twenty, Gikuyu
youth (male and female) had been initiated, after which the
young men entered the junior warrior sub-grade and became part
of its `council' (the njama ya anake a mumo). They fell under
the military and social discipline of the senior warrior sub-
grade, and its `council of war' (njama ya ita), headed by the
war priest (mondo mogo wa ita) who was presumably an elder.
Some six years after initiation, a junior warrior moved up
automatically to senior status, having served his military
apprenticeship in the ranks, so to speak. The warrior age-
grades, both `officers' and `men', were charged with defence
and raiding, under the control of the decision-making elders.
The warriors were organised at village, district and national
(or tribal) levels, with elected leaders and spokesmen at each
level.

The Gikuyu transition from warrior to elder status was
achieved individually by marriage, after which a man was required to join the council of the lowest of three sub-grades
of elderhood, the kiama gia kamatimo. In this capacity he
again became an apprentice, this time in judicial and administrative matters. Having spent fifteen or so years learning,
as an observer, how to maintain and restore social order, when
his first-born child was initiated, the junior elder was promoted into the `council of peace' (kiama gia mataathi). Here
he took part in the judicial process of resolving disputes
(concerning land, stock, trade and marriage) brought before
the village council. Finally, when all of his children had
been initiated and all of his wives had passed the menopause,
he could enter the third and highest grade of elderhood and
become a member of the ritual council (kiama gia maturanguru),
which sat in the centre of the decision-making village council, flanked by the senior and junior elders. Accession into a
more senior age-grade was, at all levels, accompanied by oaths

swearing the newcomer not to reveal the secrets of that level of political responsibility to those junior to him.

In the precolonial past, individual mobility through the Gikuyu age-grades had been confirmed categorically, at the national ritual whereby authority was devolved from the retiring to the incoming generation of (senior and junior) elders. This ritual was last held in the 1890s, before its proscription by the British and the disruption of the traditional Gikuyu social order by white settlement on their land. Subsequently, the colonial government introduced chiefly office and selected incumbents on the basis of their leadership qualities demonstrated previously in their capacity as senior elders. After the second world war, elements of traditional politics, notably oathing, were revived and incorporated into the anticolonial, Gikuyu-dominated Mau Mau movement. The Gikuyu were split into those opposing colonial rule, and `loyalists', including chiefs, who were employed by it. This split, rather than any traditional status within the defunct age-grading system, provided the fuel for conflict within the Gikuyu-dominated Kenya African National Union, both before and after Independence in 1963. Notwithstanding Kenyatta's (1938) treatise, against the backdrop of colonisation, on the logic and desirability of Gikuyu tradition, politics in independent Kenya, as a centralised state dominated politically by the Gikuyu, apparently owes little to such models. Precolonial models of (male) democracy seem to have little attraction for those who attained state authority off the base of party organisation and universal suffrage.

Petty Chiefship among the Shona

Although some measure of unification had been achieved earlier under Rozwi rulers, by the time of the nineteenth-century incursions into their territory by the Ndebele and white invaders, the Shona were fragmented into hundreds of petty chiefdoms, each controlling a bounded territory (nyika). In most cases, two or more ruling families rotated the chiefship around themselves in a complex system that regularly sloughed off the families of elder sons from the chiefship roster. A man could become chief only if his father had held the position, but he could not succeed his father directly, since the office had to move to another family on the death of an incumbent chief. By the time it returned, the older sons were senile or already deceased, and even the younger sons were well advanced in years. The average chief's tenure was fairly short, interregna were frequent, and disputes between potential successors were often extended.

178

This system was disliked by colonial officials seeking to use traditional leaders in new forms of `indirect rule´, in which the chiefs came to occupy an invidious, conflict-ridden `intercalary´ position as the highest-ranking representatives of their people in the traditional system, and the lowest-ranking representatives of the new administrative system. The settler administrators regarded the chiefs as hide-bound old men, and usurped from the spirit mediums (who were ostensibly in contact with the chiefly ancestors as well as public opinion in validating a successor), the ultimate right to approve a new chief. While not overturning the rules of succession, district commissioners tended to select the younger and better educated from among the claimants, rather than those with the strongest genealogical entitlement to the position. Competition for and validation of the chiefship became increasingly influenced by external political institutions, as Weinrich (1971) has shown. The chiefs were paid small salaries by the state for their judicial and tax-collecting responsibilities. In the last two decades of colonial rule, they also enjoyed an increment to their rights to allocate land, and found themselves increasingly threatened by the political nationalism of their juniors. With some notable exceptions, the chiefs were widely denounced as collaborators with colonial rule and some were killed during the liberation war.

After independence, the chiefdoms were no longer regarded as independent administrative units, but were aggregated into new district councils, to which representatives were elected. The chiefs themselves were frequently elected to the district councils, on whose less-inclusive colonial predecessors they had held ex officio positions. The chiefship was retained as a symbol of traditional values, but the chiefs themselves were stripped of all their administrative and judicial functions, while retaining their salaries and perquisites. Their subordinates in the precolonial and colonial administrative systems, the sub-chiefs (or ward heads) and the village headmen, lost even their tax-collecting functions after independence. Their administrative responsibilities were assumed by district councils, and their judicial functions by community courts. However, village and ward headmen were often elected to the village and ward development committees, which were established in an attempt to give local people more say than they had had previously in what happened to their particular area, in terms especially of land-use planning for development. The Zimbabwean technique, of phasing out traditional political authority, has thus incorporated the incumbents of old offices into a new system under the control of an elected majority, and undermined the offices themselves, while not formally abolishing them. What the final outcome will be of this strategy of political modernisation, in comparison with other African states' direct confrontations with and abolition of traditional offices, remains to be seen.

The Abolition of Monarchy: Rwanda

While many precolonial African states had monarchies, few - notably Morocco, Swaziland and Lesotho - have retained them into the late twentieth century. In a minority of cases, such as Buganda and Barotseland, elected politicians have abolished monarchies. More often, however, monarchs have been overthrown in military coups d'etat, as in Egypt, Libya and Ethiopia. The monarchy in Rwanda, however, collapsed in popular revolt even before the country regained its independence.

Virtually at the end of the `scramble for Africa´, in 1899, Rwanda was colonised by Germany. In 1925, in the dismemberment of German overseas territories following the Treaty of Versailles, it was mandated by the League of Nations to Belgium, which had occupied the country in 1916. The first electoral experiment (in the form of indirect elections to the sub-chiefs´ advisory council) was held in 1956. In 1962, following a constitutional referendum supervised by the United Nations, Rwanda became independent as a democratic republic.

Rwanda is a mountainous equatorial state of considerable agricultural fertility (and some ecological degradation) but few mineral resources, supporting a high population density (averaging over 400 people per arable square kilometre) in an area of just over 26,000 square kilometres. Lying on the western fringe of the Great Lakes area, in the traditional heartland of state formation in Central Africa, the Rwandan monarchy sat atop a traditional caste structure, in which status was ascribed by birth and protected by a strong distaste for intermarriage. Maquet (1961) argued that the pastoral, nilo-hamitic Tutsi, comprising only one-sixth of the total population but exercising political dominance, probably infiltrated the country peacefully rather than conquering it, but acknowledged that such infiltration was a form of conquest and that Tutsi military traditions and organisation were compatible with their own assertion of conquest. In the south, the Tutsi had established firm hegemony over the negroid Hutu, who comprised 80 per cent of the total Rwandan population; and in the north, the early German colonial administration helped the Tutsi to extend their control over traditionally independent Hutu chiefs. The pygmoid Twa were both numerically and politically insignificant in Rwandan society.

Precolonial Rwandan government was highly centralised, under the Tutsi king (mwami). To the equal-ranking army, land

and cattle chiefships he appointed his own loyal Tutsi supporters, or confirmed the nominations of suitable successors by dying incumbents. The hill chiefs were appointed by the land and cattle chiefs, on a similar basis. The highest level to which a trustworthy Hutu client could rise in this administration, was that of hill chief, if both of the Tutsi land and cattle chiefs controlling that area agreed on his suitability. In turn, the hill chiefs selected men to head the smaller administrative divisions known as neighbourhoods, though this selection was limited by considerations of patriliny (because the neighbourhoods were the home of local descent groups), and was also subject to interference by army chiefs. Below this neighbourhood level, heads of families were not really part of the state administration.

There were few effective controls over the right of individuals to make these appointments in accordance with their own personal interests. The queen mother acted as an aide to the king, rather than as a check on his authority. Only the council of great chiefs or _biru_, the hereditary heads of the 13 clans in Rwanda, could not be deposed by the monarch. Three of these chiefs were actually in a position to manipulate the succession to the monarchy, though whether they ever did so was, by definition, impossible to tell, because by that time the king who knew what he had told them was always dead, and there was no other witness. All levels of the precolonial Rwandan system, then, tended toward the despotic, although the actions of political subordinates could be reversed by disapproving patrons on whom their own authority depended.

Tutsi control of this administration rested on their ownership of cattle and their monopoly of military power, both of which enabled them to set up the all-pervasive system of clientage (_ubuhake_). Cattle, as highly prestigious capital goods, were owned by Tutsi but herded by Hutu. Occasionally a herdsmen would receive animals in payment for his services, but these were always male, in order to ensure that the Hutu acquisition of (limited) wealth remained entirely dependent on the goodwill of their Tutsi patrons, not on natural reproduction. In the several, independently-commanded armies, each directly responsible to the king, Tutsi warriors ensured that military tactics and technology did not filter down to the knowledge of Hutu ancillaries. Each army chief, as a client of the king, had considerable authority in non-military matters, being able, for example, to dismiss the neighbourhood chiefs (the leaders of local patrilineages), and to arbitrate in disputes over cattle (normally the prerogative of the cattle chiefs) in which his soldiers were involved.

Clientship pervaded all precolonial political relationships in Rwanda, and was the primary means of integrating a highly differentiated and inegalitarian system of administration, in which the king was the ultimate patron (shebuja). (Other integrating devices included common Tutsi and Hutu membership of the 13 clans and of the Ryangombe cult.) The tax-collecting efficiency of this administration permitted each client, as an official, to `taste´ the `revenue´ (produce) on its way upwards. It also allowed the Tutsi as a caste to live a life of leisure, while the Hutu herded their cattle and produced the staple grains (which unprestigious food the Tutsi consumed in private, while pretending not to eat grain at all). This appropriation of surplus was achieved by channelling the taxation of dairy production through the Tutsi cattle chiefs, and that of grain through the Tutsi land chiefs, while `buying off´ the occasional Hutu hill chief with his administrative cut, which depended on his continued collaboration in the system.

Maquet did his original fieldwork in Rwanda in 1949-51, with subsequent shorter trips in the later 1950s. From this experience he attempted to reconstruct the precolonial system, which was still accessible through the memories of the older generation. Having ignored completely the experience of colonisation in Rwanda, he concluded that `the premise of inequality´, as a `paternalistic blend of protection and profit´ (Maquet 1961:162-3), was then still accepted by Tutsi and Hutu alike. This conclusion seemed to be confirmed as late as 1956 by the results of the first indirect elections, which returned Tutsi candidates to the sub-chiefs´ advisory council.

Three years later, however, Rwanda erupted into inter-ethnic violence in which thousands were killed, mainly Tutsi. In 1961, the king fled into exile in Kenya and many Tutsi sought refuge in neighbouring states. Between independence in 1962, and 1964, invasions by Tutsi exiles provoked Hutu reprisals against those Tutsi who had remained in Rwanda, many thousands more of whom were killed. The 1962 and subsequent elections confirmed the transfer of power to the Hutu majority and `the premise of inequality´ succumbed to a republican democracy. As Maquet (1970:214) later admitted,
> `This situation of inequality was resented by Hutu to an extent that most observers did not perceive. The suddenness and the violence of the Hutu reaction to that situation when they were convinced that they had the opportunity to change it indicate that they were perfectly aware of their exploited condition, and that they endured it only because they did not think that they were strong enough to change it.´

Rwanda was, perhaps, one of the few precolonial political systems in Africa to approximate Marx´s view of the state.

State Formation

In the case study of Rwanda, perhaps without noticing it we have crossed the definitional boundary between `political behaviour´, with which we started, and `state organisation´, to which we must now give explicit consideration. Let us begin with the marxist perspective, in which the state is not external to and imposed upon society, except in cases of conquest. In Engels´ (1884/1948:166) evolutionist view, based on L.H. Morgan´s work, the state `is a product of society at a certain stage of development ... a power seemingly standing above society´, in its ability to arbitrate conflict and maintain order among the citizens inhabiting a specified territory. `The state, then, has not existed from all eternity. There have been societies that did without it, that had no idea of the state and state power. At a certain stage of economic development, which was necessarily bound up with the split of society into classes, the state became a necessity owing to this split´ (op. cit.:170). The state as a `public power´, then, maintaining itself by taxing its citizens, is, as a rule, the state of the most powerful, economically dominant class, which, through the medium of the state, becomes also the politically dominant class´ (op. cit.:168).

The state distances power from the control of the people, by basing itself on territory and citizenship. It stands in contrast to the segmentary and confederal model of Morgan´s (1877) kin-based `gentile society´, from which, in the marxist view, it emerges when economic differentiation has reached a certain point. Such economic differentiation occurs through an increasingly complex division of labour, which first separates pastoralists from farmers, then craftsmen from farmers, and finally merchants from the rest of society, in the process of civilisation. `Civil society´, as the obverse of the state, therefore cannot countenance the treatment of certain of its citizens differently from others, for example on the basis of their religion (as Marx argued in On The Jewish Question). Their equality before the state and its law (especially its law of property) is precisely the mechanism that underpins the differentiation of citizens into classes. As Engels (1884/1948:113) put it: `All revolutions until now [including those that established states] have been revolutions for the protection of one kind of property against another kind of property´.

For the most part, this view of the state has been resoundingly ignored by social anthropologists, even those who, like Evans-Pritchard, have grappled - equally speculatively - with the problem of how states may arise. It has been consigned, along with Morgan, to the archives of quaint, but long-outdated, conjecture. In a book entitled From Tribe to Nation in Africa, for example, there is no mention of state formation, even though its sub-title is Studies in Incorporation Processes. Yet the issues that Engels raised, of the change in emphasis from kinship to territory, and the means by which unrelated strangers are incorporated as citizens, are precisely the concern of this book.

Three processes, in addition to citizenship and a common language, are critical to the formation and extension of state power: conquest; colonisation; and incorporation. The first is straightforward and requires no elaboration. The second and third are more complex, multi-facetted processes which may be elucidated by specific examples.

Among the better-known figures from African political history is the early nineteenth-century Zulu king, Shaka, who is remembered as the man who united some 200 formerly autonomous petty chiefdoms into a state with a formidable army. In one sense, Shaka was a conqueror, particularly in the early years of his reign; in another, he was a coloniser, taking advantage of conditions that favoured, if not necessitated, expansion. It is possible that, given the increases in both people and, more particularly, cattle, in that part of Zululand from which Shaka came, the colonisation of other territory would have occurred even without Shaka's particular military genius. The initial colonisation of the territory of subjugated neighbours may have been an ecological necessity for survival. However, the later mfecane, which spun other colonising Zulu military fragments (such as the Ngoni, Ndebele and Shangane) into Central Africa, under commanders fleeing Shaka's wrath, was a purely politico-military phenomenon.

Incorporation is perhaps less simple than colonisation, not least in its motivation. Incorporation was a feature of many precolonial African states, such as Bornu in what is today Northern Nigeria. Incorporation remains important in the creation of nationality, within the artificial boundaries of contemporary African states. Cohen (1970) has isolated three conceptually distinct aspects of incorporation in Bornu: the ways in which the kingdom itself was integrated; its relationships with tributary states beyond Bornu's borders; and the integration of Bornu into modern Nigeria.

The Muslim Bornu kingdom dates from the fifteenth century, when it succeeded Kanem. Its northern and eastern borders were clearly demarcated by rivers, but in the south and west territorial control was more easily disputed. In this area, agricultural peoples were incorporated into the Bornu state through territorial fiefdoms, and pastoralists by ethnic fief-

184

doms. In each case, their political link to the state went through their own apical leader to a Kanuri noble at the Bornu court (often through the noble's local representative in the area concerned). In addition, settled cultivators tended to adopt Kanuri culture, whereas the mobile pastoralists retained their own language and cultural autonomy. Cohen noted that the distinction between territorial and ethnic fiefdoms was not immutable, for settled groups might disperse and change their linkage from a territoral to an ethnic basis, while nomadic groups might settle, at least temporarily, and change their linkage in the opposite direction. Moreover, Muslim agriculturalists and pastoralists alike were more likely to retain their cultural identity, than non-Muslims of either productive persuasion. Becoming Kanuri and converting to Islam, as the cultural and religious complements to political incorporation within the kingdom, also involved intermarriage as another facet of the total process of incorporation.

The fiefdom model, with modifications, was also applied in the creation of political alliances between Bornu and autonomous units beyond her borders, for example on the trans-Saharan trade routes which Bornu had an interest in controlling. Bornu conquered and colonised the town of Bilma, for example, in the sixteenth century. Thereafter Bilma paid tribute to Bornu, sometimes in slaves, and sought Kanuri assistance when attacked by other states. However, like other tributary states, Bilma retained its judicial autonomy, in contrast to the fully-incorporated fiefdoms within Bornu's territorial boundaries. Tributary status, then, implied a greater measure of political autonomy for client states, in which the links of clientship were reinforced by those of trade and marriage. Slavery also played an important role in such partial political incorporation, for some slaves, as unrelated non-Kanuri loyal to their masters, were important political aides, while others provided agricultural and domestic labour. According to the rules of patriliny, the descendants of non-Kanuri slave women were automatically freed and incorporated fully into (tributary) Kanuri society, even though the original status of their mothers might be remembered. Their status might in fact be lower than that of the slave descendants of male slaves, whose lineages were affiliated to those of their noble owners and patrons, and who held titled office at the tributary or Bornu courts.

The incorporation of Bornu `emirate' itself into the new state of Nigeria dismantled some of Bornu's own incorporative mechanisms. Slavery, for example, was abolished by the British, who also reoriented Bornu's trade links away from the Sahara, towards the southern coastal ports. Former tributary relationships were broken by the absorption of client states

185

into non-British colonial territories. Finally, the authority of the Kanuri monarchy was undermined by the creation of new administrative divisions (districts, regions and provincial states) and offices (in the civil service) by the colonial government. These new units effectively destroyed the old fiefdoms within Bornu's boundaries, although the expectations of political performance and administrative efficiency that were associated with the old order persisted. Finally, the provision of western education and job opportunities in other parts of Nigeria created a wider political frame of reference within which Kanuri ethnicity, identified with the emirate, was no longer dominant, but did provide a basis on which to compete for new resources within the larger political whole.

The Kanuri core of Bornu was incorporated as a unit into a new and larger political entity. Many other ethnic groups in Africa were split two or even three ways in the process of colonial incorporation. Somali, for example, are today found in Somalia, Ethiopia and Kenya; Lugbara in Uganda, Zaire and the Sudan; Tonga in Zimbabwe and Mocambique; Hausa in Nigeria and Niger; and Fulani all over West Africa. There should be little wonder that the Organisation of African Unity regards the national boundaries established during the `scramble for Africa´ as sacrosanct. Their total irrationality in the first instance has precluded any later application of rationality without a good deal of international upset, such as that following the Somalian invasion of the Ogaden desert in order to incorporate the Ethiopian Somali into their traditional ethnic homeland. Incorporation is, therefore, an issue of particular significance for those states created de novo by external colonisers, whose entirely artificial boundaries have converted their often fragmented ethnic components into political competitors within the larger `national´ framework. In these states, the problem of `state formation´ is precisely that of incorporating the `ethnic´ as the `civil´, of creating a citizenship that will supercede, not reinforce, less inclusive politico-cultural identities.

State Transformation

The precolonial African monarchies that have survived into the post-colonial present are, not accidentally, states in which colonial boundaries encompassed an ethnically homogeneous population, even if a minority found itself on the other side of these borders. Kingship could, therefore, form the focus around which the anti-colonial struggle was fought. In Swaziland under Sobhuza II, who reigned from 1921 to his death in 1982, `kingship has been the core of Swazi national identity´ (Kuper 1978:347). The problems of transforming such a state are encapsulated in the Swazi example, which forms an interesting contemporary counterpoint to the ancient Mediterranean city-states, on which Engels based his ideas about the transition from societies based on kinship to those based on citizenship.

The Swazi state emerged in the upheavals of the early nineteenth century which centralised many of the polities of South-East Africa, and takes its name from the fourth king, Mswati, in whose reign (1840-68) the age-regiments were formed along Zulu lines. The Swazi dual monarchy was somewhat unusual, though by no means unique in sub-Saharan Africa.

In the ideology of the dual monarchy, power was shared between the Ngwenyama (lion: king) and Ndlovukazi (she-elephant: queen mother). The patrilineal successor to the kingship was actually chosen on the basis of the rank of his mother. The king controlled the highest court of appeal, which meted out the death penalty for treason and witchcraft; but the queen mother's shrine hut was a sanctuary against the king, and her court ranked second in the land. The king controlled the allocation of land (over which, together with all cattle, he had an ultimate lien), but the queen mother could rebuke him publicly should he waste national wealth, and the rain magic to enable the land to bear had to be worked by both in harmony. She was custodian of the national sacra, but their power was ineffective without his co-operation.

In practice, however, the ideal of a dual monarchy seems often effectively to have given way to a single ruler. Queen mothers sometimes had long reigns as regents for their minor sons; and Sobhuza II, in 61 years as king, outlived his mother, her sister, and two of his wives selected as replacements to fill the office of queen mother.

There were also checks on Swazi monarchical powers other than the dual monarchy itself. Two advisory councils operated. The `inner council´ (liqoqo) comprised mainly the king's male agnates of the royal family. The national council (libandla lakaNgwane, named after the first king) was very much larger and included all chiefs, the leading court councillors, and district headmen. It was required to approve decisions referred to it by the inner council, before they were implemented. The monarchs did not attend council meetings personally, but received full reports on the proceedings.

District administration, under the chiefs and headmen, replicated the monarchy in miniature, together with its advisory councils. Kuper (1963:35) made very plain the segmentary, `gentile´ nature of district authority when she stated that

187

`Knowledge of the principles involved in government is acquired by every adult male as part of his domestic experience. In the homestead, the smallest local unit recognised in the political structure, the headman exercises towards the occupants rights and obligations comparable on a smaller scale to those of the chiefs.´

In addition to the councils, a leading commoner was appointed to the position of chief councillor (sometimes translated as `prime minister´) to the king. This check was ambiguous, however, for although he held administrative authority that was second only to that of the monarchs, and took the rap for things that went wrong, the chief councillor could never succeed to the kingship. The king could trust such a man, together with his matrilateral kin who were also excluded from the line of succession, further than many of his agnates who were his potential successors.

Indeed, distrust was institutionalised in the kingship in a number of ways. Each monarch acquired his own bond-friends (<u>tinsila</u>), who were commoners, as a kind of bodyguard designed to protect him especially from his agnates. The function of the ritual of kingship, the <u>incwala</u>, was explicitly to strengthen and protect the king `against rivals from within, and enemies from without´ (Kuper 1978:340-1). The king´s own regimental affiliation was perhaps intended to provide him with further commoner support than that of the chief councillor, who might collude with conspirators against the king even though he was not himself eligible to succeed. Marriage links provided still more direct links to unrelated clans, as well as dynastic alliances with other rulers in the region. The king controlled the regiments, while the commander-in-chief had to live at the king´s capital, over which he was described as `presiding´ (Kuper 1963:30).

Almost since its beginnings, the Swazi state has had political relations with neighbouring whites in South Africa. Having earlier entered into a number of concessions that alienated land to whites, in 1894 Swaziland became a `protected dependency´ of the South African Republic (now the Transvaal province). In 1902, following its victory in the Anglo-Boer War, Britain `inherited´ Swaziland and the following year placed its administration directly under the Governor' of the Transvaal. (The 1903 Order in Council established a `constitution´ that was to last until 1964.) In 1907, falling under the British High Commission for South Africa, Swaziland received its own resident commissioner. Dual administrative and judicial systems were instituted, under district commissioners and chiefs respectively, to apply to non-Swazi (mainly whites) and Swazi, though the chiefs sometimes advised the magistrates' courts. This colonial administration was instituted during Gwamile's 22-year regency, following Ngwenyama Bhunu's death in 1899. By the time the young Sobhuza II acceded to the Swazi kingship in 1921, the colonial system was firmly entrenched. One of its first actions after his accession was to remove from him the English title of `king' as `pretentious'. This action perhaps motivated all of Sobhuza's later attempts to restore to the kingship its rightful dignity.

For the first thirty-five years of Sobhuza's reign, the colonial administration called the political tune and permitted a racially-segregated society to develop. The `paramount chief' and the libandla (renamed the Swazi National Council) were consulted on administrative matters to a greater or lesser extent, depending on the individual resident commissioner. By 1960, however, the first political parties were formed by educated and professional Swazi, and the following year public facilities were desegregated. In 1963 the British formulated proposals for a formal constitution, based on a Legislative Council under the jurisdiction of a High Commissioner, to which members would be appointed as well as elected, in a suffrage that excluded all women except monogamous wives and the first-married wives of polygynists. In these proposals, by comparison with the High Commissioner's `potentially absolute' power, that of the ngwenyama was `negligible'. Sobhuza and his councillors suggested amendments to these proposals (including civil immunity for the king, in his private capacity, in law) which the High Commissioner was unwilling to accept. Although Sobhuza had earlier professed himself against western political models, he then insisted on a referendum to demonstrate his people's overwhelming support for these amendments.

In 1964, the constitution as originally envisaged came into being, with the royalist Imbokodvo party gaining 85 per cent of the popular vote in the elections to the Legislative Council. The king signalled his displeasure by not attending the official opening. `Some saw in the King's conspicuous absence from the opening of the Legco a symbolic protest against the imposed Constitution ... had this been the Ncwala all his people knew he would have "hidden" his illness, and "danced the Kingship"' (Kuper 1978:259). This tactic was used repeatedly by the royalists in the following nine years. However, the negotiations begun in 1965 about internal self-government, preparatory to full independence, yielded a new Constitution more acceptable to the Swazi authorities and, apparently, the OAU. The 1967 constitution, based on universal adult suffrage and the separation of powers (administrative, legislative and judicial), incorporated a bicameral legislature under the king as head of state. In the 1967 elections, the royalist vote sagged below 80 per cent of a smaller poll, for which fewer people than anticipated had bothered to register.

Independence in 1968 was, however, welcomed by everyone. `The end of an era´ was marked not only by the new flag and national anthem as the symbols of statehood, but also by the formation of a new traditional regiment of that name, to which Sobhuza also gave the emblem of the royal hawk. But opposition to royalist domination of the multi-party system was growing, albeit slowly, and by 1972 the royalist vote had fallen again, sufficient to permit three opposition candidates to take their seats in the Legislative Assembly.

The visible presence of `politicians´, as opposed to supporters of the Swazi monarchy, resulted in 1973 in the suspension of the constitution and direct rule by the king-in-council. Significantly, at least in Engels´ analytical framework, this political crisis was precipitated by the issue of citizenship in the new state. Of the three successful opposition candidates, one was a Swazi born in South Africa, who had lived and farmed in Swaziland for many years without formally offering his allegiance to the king in the khonta procedure. He was deemed a non-citizen, and his election declared null and void by the royalist deputy prime minister. His appeal against this decision was upheld by the Swaziland High Court; but later reversed by a new Chief Justice, whose decision was supported by the three South African judges called in to constitute the Swaziland Court of Appeal (which had replaced the British Privy Council as the highest appellate in the country). Although Sobhuza apparently took no personal part in these judicial manoeuvres, he had long been in favour of restricting immigration to his country. Although he was prepared to offer political asylum when necessary, `asylum was not citizenship´ (Kuper 1978:281), and he did not want non-citizens involving themselves in local politics. Sobhuza was right to see non-Swazi citizens as a threat to royalist control, for the district which elected the three opposition candidates in 1972 had an unusually high proportion of foreigners.

The suspension of the constitution arguably made little difference to the Swazi while Sobhuza lived. However, in 1982 his death unleashed a struggle for succession that was not mitigated by the operation of constitutional government. The royal family, which Sobhuza had regarded as a political corporation bound by the overriding ties of patriliny, split into bitterly-opposed factions which used every possible tactic to pursue the kingship, now the font of absolute control of a modern state. Unintentionally, perhaps, Sobhuza´s modernisation of the kingship, at his death, left it the despotic instrument which he had always denied that it was intended to be. To understand this paradox, we need to examine the late

190

king's ideological stance, in contrast to his tactics of leadership in fighting to end colonial subjugation.

`It is the tradition of all African kingdoms that their Kings are leaders as well as Kings', declared Sobhuza. `A King is not argued against, he is advised. But a King is King by the Council' (Kuper 1978:290, 313). In this view, a king is a kind of rubber stamp for decisions that have popular approval. Nonetheless, the challenge to his leadership, status and dignity posed by argumentative political parties, is a kind of lese majeste, for it draws him firmly into the hurly-burly of politics, rather than allowing him to practise statecraft, and in so doing impairs his dignity. (Dignity is one of the most fundamental cultural precepts of the Swazi.) Therefore Sobhuza was opposed to (undignified) western politics, arguing initially that the system of one man, one vote licensed a majority to incorporate a culturally-distinct minority; that political parties threatened national unity, and the kingship as an institution; that modern ballot procedures had some sinister cultural affinity, in their very secrecy, with witchcraft, sorcery and poisoning. Kuper (1978) makes clear on a number of occasions that Sobhuza did fear assassination, notwithstanding his (and her) presentation of himself as the essence of his peoples' wishes. His refusal to use his regiments to maintain order in the `capitalist' sector of the Swazi economy, or to break strikes (of which, along with trade unionism, he disapproved), reflected his awareness of the potential consequences of civil war for both the kingship and the king.

Yet, notwithstanding this ideological stance, Sobhuza was quick to use new institutional possibilities if they would strengthen his own claims to political leadership. Referenda could be used to express support for royalist proposals rejected by the colonial administration; universal suffrage could mobilise the support of the women; a royalist party could beat its opponents; provision could be made for reciprocal membership of royalist party and traditional council; opponents could be disqualified by new citizenship regulations. The king himself did not have to do the `dirty work'. His expressed viewpoint would be sufficient for royalists, whose own political fortunes were related to the kingship, to sort out the details and, of course, to take the blame if things went wrong.

The Swazi example sheds interesting light on the concept of `political modernisation', in which process traditional institutions are supposedly replaced by modern and bureaucratised forms of democracy. At the level of central state authority, the outcome of one hundred years of colonial history in Swaziland has been a monarchy which, although essentially un-

changed, now <u>incorporates</u> those elements of `political modern-
ity´ which strengthen it still further. The model is one of
syncretism, not modernisation. This model is common in Africa,
even where politicians have attempted to replace traditional
with new political institutions. As Skinner has rightly noted,
neither the organisational capacity nor the personnel may
exist to make the ideology of political modernity possible in
practice (Miller 1968).

Centre-Periphery Relations in Contemporary Africa

If we descend from the national to the local political
level, we can find examples of governmental attempts to abolish chiefship and headmanship, as well as policies to retain
them. In both cases, the outcome of bringing party organisation into explicit relations with traditional office has often
been unexpected.

Zambia and Tanzania are neighbouring Central African
states, both of which attained their political independence
from Britain in the early 1960s. Both have professed varieties
of socialism as guiding principles, but Tanzania has been the
more radical in attempting to implement socialist policies.
(Indeed, it has been said that Tanzania is so willing to
change that it has never given its experiments a fair timespan
before declaring them failures and introducing something different!) Zambia and Tanzania inherited similar dual administrations from their common colonial parent, as that already
described for Swaziland. `Native authorities´ or `administra-
tions´ were staffed by chiefs, headmen and their respective
councils, and had limited civil judicial authority. The chiefs
were directly responsible to the district commissioners or
officers, and thus mediated uneasily between the two separate
systems. In both countries, newly-formed nationalist parties
disputed the traditional authority that colonialism had but-
tressed in its own administrative interests. In Zambia, however, Kaunda´s United National Independence Party (UNIP) recognised that the functions of the `native authorities´ would
not easily be replaced, especially given the dearth of suitab-
ly-trained Zambian bureaucrats to man the district administration. In contrast, the Tanganyika African National Union was
responsible for the official abolition, in 1963, of all traditional political offices.

We are fortunate to have available information from areas
in both countries in which the traditional as well as the
colonial systems were similar, in order to compare the outcome
of these diverging approaches. Uyombe in North-Eastern Zambia
and Unyamwezi in Tanzania traditionally had petty chiefdoms in

which the village headmen were subordinate to (and sometimes appointed by) the chiefs. However, in Uyombe the chief himself was controlled by an additional institution, the royal clan council, which appointed the more important headmen. Both chiefs and headmen in each case had their own advisory councils. In addition, the Yombe chief selected his own personal advisors from among cognatic kin and trusted commoners outside the agnatic line of succession. This system of offices had in both cases been strengthened by official colonial recognition and remuneration for duties performed (notably collecting taxes). In both areas, the cleavage between educated and uneducated people, which had started two generations ago, was reflected, together with the generation gap, in divergent political attitudes and patterns of political support. The younger, educated men introduced party political organisation to their home areas, while the older, less educated people supported the chiefs and headmen. There the formal similarities between the two areas ended.

In 1963, Tanzania abolished all traditional political offices. Chiefs and headmen were stripped of their status, salaries and regalia. Their posts were replaced by those of `village executive officers´ chairing the village development committees. However, in Tabora district, within a few years of their formal demise, Miller (1968) found that some 90 per cent of former headmen and 30 per cent of former chiefs had been elected as village executive officers! They had the full support of the older and younger men who were uneducated, together with that of most (uneducated) women, and traditional healers and ritual specialists. Only a minority of younger, educated men and women, civil servants, and `village dissidents, agitators and rebels´ did not support them (Miller 1968:194). Furthermore, although this was illegal, most of these deposed traditional leaders continued to act as informal judges of local disputes concerning livestock, bridewealth and marriage.

In Uyombe, in contrast, party officials infiltrated the inherited `native authority´ in order to increase their local influence. In 1961, educated UNIP members set up a local constituency, divided into 11 branches, which offerred 66 new, but part-time and unremunerated, political offices in each of the men´s, women´s and youth organisations. The early legitimation of these branches was achieved by electing existing headmen as their chairmen, while some degree of operational efficiency was ensured through literate branch secretaries. The following year, the educated UNIP members manipulated their kin links with the royal clan to get a royal (who was also a party activist) elected as deputy chief. He in turn was responsible for converting the traditional chief´s council into an `area committee´ dominated by elected (party) members. The area committee comprised so many members that it was unworkable as a political committee, so a development committee, dominated by educated party activists, was set up as an executive agency for local projects. Into this committee´s control were channelled resources for development which emanated from the central government as grants and loans. Naturally there ensued an argument as to whether these resources should fall under the formal control of the party or the area committee, with uneducated party members, their eyes on their local constituencies, arguing for parochial party control.

This close relationship between party and local authority continued until Zambia gained her independence in 1964, when many of the educated party activists were promoted into urban vacancies in the civil service. Their party posts in Uyombe remained unfilled for five years after their departure; the deputy chief lost his educated supporters; and both party and local authority went into a decline that was related to the siphoning out of the countryside of the rural elite. Bond (1975) argued, therefore, that rapid `Zambianisation´ after independence had had the unintended consequence of strengthening traditional, uneducated forms of political leadership in the countryside and undermining UNIP local branches. UNIP had nothing against traditional leaders, but it had attempted to undermine their influence in favour of its own. The party strategy of infiltration had worked quite well, until it was overtaken by the more important agenda of `Zambianising´ the civil service.

Infiltration can, however, work both ways. In their post-independence concern to retain control over the deployment of developmental resources in their own hands, some Zimbabwean freeholders protected their (modern) local councils by assuming party membership and acquiescing in directives to fight council elections on party tickets. It seemed unlikely, however, that such symbolic identification would alter their allocation of resources in the interests of their particular sub-class of commercial farmers. Taking out membership of a party with whose policies they often disagreed, was perhaps a ploy to deflect attention from the underlying conflict of objectives between themselves and central government.

This particular example, from a wholly non-traditional society, perhaps contradicts Miller´s (1968) views that rural authority must be legitimised as `traditional´, in some syncretic form, if the co-operation of rural people is required; and that (only?) traditional authorities can mediate between central government and its rural citizens. Miller argued that, if no syncretic alliance between traditional and modern poli-

tical authorities is achieved, the resulting coercion of rural
people by state authority will lead to mutual hostility and
the failure of political modernisation. While he is undoubtedly right about political modernisation failing in Africa, this
argument overlooks three important points. Firstly, as we saw
earlier, syncretism itself endangers political modernisation.
Secondly, not all rural societies, even in Africa, are `tradi-
tional´. Thirdly, hostility between differing classes, represented by different political leaders, is an inherent feature
of economies in which agriculture provides the fiscal base for
the state, even while taxation and the terms of trade direct
`surplus value´ into urban rather than rural areas. But the
rural leaders in this conflict with the state need not be
traditional. Their power base may lie equally in new religious
groupings or other voluntary associations, as we shall see in
detail in later chapters.

The Politics of Leadership

For years political anthropology concentrated its attention on structures, organisations, offices - the institutional
trappings of political relations - and carefully shunned un-
provable conjecture about how political structures are actually generated in society. Into this concern with political
form, Barth introduced a totally new dimension. He argued, on
the basis of his study of the Pathans of the Swat valley in
Pakistan, that `persons find their place in the political
order through a series of choices, many of which are temporary
or revocable´ and that consequently `the authority system...
is built up and maintained through the exercise of a continual
series of individual choices´ (Barth 1959:2). He showed how
khans (land-owning chiefs) differed from saints (Muslim holy
men) in the strategies that they used to establish themselves
in the political (dis)order of the Swat valley. Swat valley
politics, in other words, were by no means static in any
`traditional´ mould, but resembled, in their methods and out-
come, western democracies.

The central task for political anthropology then, Barth
argued, must be the exploration and analysis of the multiple
ways in which individuals systematically manipulate their
relationships with others, in order to build themselves positions of authority. It is from these regular manoeuvres by
individuals that politically corporate groups (and perhaps
also the structural or institutionalised `frameworks´ which
constrain individual action) result. To appreciate this point,
we might think back to the Nuer prophets and earth priests,
and others in uncentralised polities, who carved out for themselves niches of informal political influence, even while

195

their societies denied them the possibility of recognised political office.

Bailey took up Barth's theoretical challenge and tried to identify `the fundamentally similar and comprehensible ways´ in which political behaviour is structured in all societies irrespective of their superficial differences of cultural idiom (1969:xi). Politicians of all types are in the game to win, so their prime concern must be with the effectiveness of their behavioural tactics in the matter of political survival. There exist <u>general</u> principles of political manoeuvre which underlie the formal rules of <u>particular</u> systems: these are the tactical rules of how to beat the opposition and come out on top oneself. Bailey refers to these tactics as the `pragmatic rules´ of politics. They are distinct from, and to some extent in opposition to, the `normative´ or ideological rules of how to play the game like a gentleman. To play politics using only the normative rules, says Bailey, guarantees that one will lose.

Like all ideological premisses, the normative rules of politics are vague and generalised statements of intent, which require to be interpreted and applied to specific cases. Even written constitutions (the epitome of normative rules) need interpretation. If politicians are required to be `honest´ and to `conform to the will of the people´, we must know, under specific circumstances, when a failure to reveal the truth will be classified as `protecting the public interest´ rather than as a `deliberate intention to mislead´; and just what `the will of the people´ comprises and how it is assessed.

To some extent, this clarification of the normative rules is itself part of the pragmatic tactics which successful politicians use. These tactics may operate within or beyond the ostensible normative limits. Cheating is eminently possible, and normally a matter for regret only if discovered and publicised. Then the normative rules are seen to have been transgressed and punitive action must be seen to be taken, if the credibility of the referee is to be upheld and the game is to continue. Pragmatic tactics may also include questioning the normative rules themselves. Republicans may call for the abolition of their existing monarchies, for example, or constitutions may be amended to fit changed circumstances.

Bailey regarded both normative and pragmatic rules as governing five areas of political behaviour, with the balance between them differing in each case. The definition of political goals or `spoils´ is primarily normative, for these are - with the exception of power itself - always respectable and highly valued, partly because they are scarce. But the desire

196

for power is rarely respectable. An ambivalent `prize´, power should not be alluded to openly even when pursued ruthlessly. Similarly, in the second area, the rules governing who is eligible to compete are largely normative. But as the earlier Swazi example showed, the definition of who was an eligible political contender may also be manipulated pragmatically, after the competition has been concluded. Pragmatic tactics dominate the third area of the methods by which leaders recruit political followers, and also the fourth sphere of political action, in which the leader must be able to communicate the strength of his team, both to its members and to its opponents. In the fifth and final area, of procedures controlling the political game, normative and pragmatic rules are normally well balanced. In the long run, the neutrality of political `umpires´ or `referees´ is in the interests of those who benefit normatively from their respectability. However, this neutrality may be subverted pragmatically to favour short-term interests. This area of control is, however, ambiguous. It is usually a judicial area, even in systems without the western `separation of powers´. But the judges usually owe their positions to politicians, so their neutrality may be insecurely founded. Here we again confront Barth´s problem: political institutions do not drop ready-made from heaven, but are made on earth from the actions of individuals pursuing political ends. Even the control procedures, therefore, have their defects.

Let us pursue Bailey´s ideas on leadership in a little more detail, for we have seen that, even in systems of ascriptive, hereditary succession, there is often room to achieve the office in question. The rulers of patrilineal systems often fear assassination by their agnates; and among many sons of a deceased ruler, only one will succeed.

Leadership is a process of making both policy and administrative decisions, particularly under conditions of uncertainty that have not been encountered before and where no well-tested rules apply. The political leader normally seeks to keep his team together through such decisions, as well as maintaining his team´s position in the wider political arena. If he makes astute decisions, they will enhance his political strength and credibility. Inept decisions that weaken his team´s position are likely to diminish the leader´s credit rating, among followers and opponents alike. This distinction, between strong and weak leadership, is separate from the formal recognition of political office. Informal leaders may have greater credibility than those who hold formal office: eminences grises and `retired elder statesmen´ exist even in centralised systems. Such people, like Nuer earth priests, may hold no formal political office, or legitimate authority, yet

197

their reputations and high credit ratings afford them power.

It is the leader's responsibility to hold his team together so that it may continue to compete for political goals. To do this, he must act as referee within his own team, to ensure that disputes do not impair its effectiveness. His techniques of adjudicating internal conflicts will range from low-cost mediation to high-cost arbitration. By mediating successfully among disputing factions, the leader will increase his own credit rating. But should he attempt to knock heads together and fail, he may face what Bailey called `a run on the political bank´.

Occasionally the leader will be faced with a conflict that cannot be contained within his team while he himself continues as leader; and there will always be challengers for his own position. So he must also be able to control his subordinates and followers. The leader's techniques for maintaining his own position may include the physical `elimination´ of insubordinates, but are more often variations on the principle of `divide and rule´. He may delegate limited responsibility to intermediate leaders and retain overall co-ordination and knowledge of the whole political enterprise in his own head. He may promote the subordinates of his subordinates to equality with their former bosses, and strengthen his `moral´ (as opposed to `transactional´) ties with them. He may publicly entrust potential rivals with difficult tasks. If they refuse such responsibilities, they will be seen as unworthy of leadership; if they fail, they will be discredited; if they succeed, the leader miscalculated and will face stronger challenges from those quarters in the future. The sensible leader will make of his subordinates clients who depend for their own positions on his personal favour. Rwandan army chiefs were the clients of their king; monarchs in patrilineal systems favoured their matrilateral kin and affines as trusted advisors, and commoners as administrators. For where a subordinate has his own political credit and resources, and the rules permit it, he can afford to challenge the existing leader. This is one reason why the leaders of poor third world countries, whose political credit rating among their own electorates may be low, should beware economic rescue by the buccaneers of capitalism, or even by friendly neighbours. `He who pays the piper, calls the tune´, is perhaps the most fundamental political homily of many such proverbs.

Underlying all of these pragmatic rules of leadership, Bailey has argued, is the fundamental distinction between two separate aspects of politics: the ideological and the material, or the moral and the transactional. `Hirelings´ in their masses follow a political leader for what `spoils´ they can get out of him, personally or institutionally. To the `moral core´ of his following, however, the leader is related not merely by shared ideals, but also by the `multiplex´ social links of kinship, friendship, affinity, association, class, religion and old school ties, among others. The stability, and to some extent the strength, of his leadership, depend on the ratio of the moral to the transactional ties among a leader´s following. All-moral teams (such as lineages) may last forever; but they are small and politically ineffective. All-transactional teams readily split into ephemeral factions pursuing the leader who offers most in the short term; but their votes count. Both types of relationships are, therefore, politically necessary for the person seeking to become and remain a political leader. It was, perhaps, Sobhuza II´s pragmatic tactics of leadership that preserved and strengthened the Swazi kingship in circumstances of change and uncertainty. Where traditional monarchs failed to match the political strategies of new leaders, their offices were abolished, in terms of a new set of normative rules governing the altered political game.

CHAPTER NINE

ISSUES OF LAW AND SOCIAL CONTROL

As we worked through other areas of social life in previous chapters, we came up against law at certain points: new marriage laws, new constitutions. And at many more points we encountered areas of conflict which had some relevance to the problems of establishing social order and maintaining social control. Society, as we have seen, comprises both rules and behaviour which deviates from these rules. In one sense, instead of defining `law´ as a set of binding rights and obligations, we might regard it as the relationship between these rules and actual behaviour, and how this relationship is managed. Here we are including within the definition of law not merely explicitly legal institutions, but also the broader field of the `customary´ resolution of conflict.

Differing Views of `Law´

Like religion, family organisation and technology, law fascinated nineteenth-century western evolutionists, who formulated a number of dichotomous categories to understand `primitive law´ in relation to their own. Maine (1861) recognised that all societies had some form of contract, but nonetheless postulated that there was a general historical progression from assessing a person´s rights and obligations in society on the basis of his of her ascriptive status in a `corporation´ based on kinship, to the individualisation of contractual responsibility. Durkheim (1893) regarded `repressive´ law, which punished infractions, as a corollary of integrating society by means of `mechanical solidarity´, in which humans as workers were (within the limits of age and sex) substitutes for one another. In contrast, Durkheim saw `restitutive law´, which sought to restore the social status quo ante among disputants, as part of the `organic solidarity´ based on a more specialised division of labour. Restitutive law was also identified with `civil´ or `private´ law, and the repressive variety with `criminal´ and `public´ law. The net result of these evolutionary dichotomies was the view that `primitives´ had a very different kind of law from that of `advanced´ societies, and were `enslaved´ by their habitual, automatic, unthinking obedience to such `custom´.

This view is manifestly incorrect. In societies based on face-to-face contact, the settlement of disputes more often seeks to restore social amity than to punish offenders. Moreover, as Malinowski (1926) pointed out, while it is in the long-term interest of individuals to co-operate with others, their pursuit of short-term interests often results in breach of the rules and conflict. What constrained people to abide by the rules, argued Malinowski, were the benefits of systematic reciprocity and the psychological as well as material rewards that such compliance normally brought. But if people thought they could do better by breaking the rules, they would; and the withdrawal of reciprocity, together with their public shaming, would soon bring them back into line. Malinowski´s functionalist views, then, in contrast to the dualism of the evolutionists, emphasised the universal aspects of legal behaviour, rather than the institutional differences among different cultural systems. Not all societies had courts and policemen, but they all had `law´ in both its public and private manifestations.

With this view, I think, both Marx and Engels would have concurred, even though they, too, were evolutionists. As we saw in the previous chapter, marxism regards law as a necessary adjunct of property and its protection. Beyond the postulated prehistoric era of `primitive communalism´, in which there existed no law because there was no property, marxism assumes a `universalised´ type of law. In this view, as soon as property emerged in its public or communal form in the `gentile corporation´, it was protected in `law´. As property became privatised and individualised, the law changed. By the time the capitalist mode of production established itself, the dominant feature of the law was its enactment and control by the property-owning class. Law, enacted by the legislature and enforced by the judiciary, thus became the `executive´ of the propertied, ruling class, through which differences between the classes were perpetuated. Law as part of the superstructure in capitalist societies thus `dominates´ the economic base, which should nonetheless remain `determinant in the last instance´.

A contemporary variant of this approach attempts to link the proliferation of the `rule base´ with the specific property requirements of different types of economic activity (eg. Roberts 1979). In this view, hunters and gatherers have `minimal´ law and government, because their notions of property are unelaborated. Pastoralists require legal protection for their ownership of livestock. Agriculturalists need still more rules of property to govern arable and residential land, the distribution of the product, and so on. With literacy comes the codification of these customary rules into written law, explicitly to maintain societal order, so as to protect property. The centralised state then comes into existence to administer law in the interests of property.

Perhaps the most important problem with this argument is that societies with multiple property rights do not necessarily have a centralised state organisation. We have already seen the complexity of Ibo land law, and its operation within the village group as the largest autonomous political unit, under the control of its council of titled men. Now is the time to pursue further Ibo ideas regarding property. Ibo society was organised around the legal distinction between freeborn (amadi) and slave (ohu), which probably predated Ibo involvement in the trans-Atlantic trade through the slave markets at Bende and Aro Chuku. Slave villages still formed a defensive perimeter for the central freeborn villages of the Nike group when Horton (1954) did his fieldwork there in the early 1950s, though slaves no longer worked the fields of the freeborn except as hired workers. In Ibo law, however, as opposed to colonial Nigerian law, ohu remained the property of the freeborn. As chattels, slaves and their children were inherited. Intermarriage between owner and chattel was strictly prohibited and sexual relations of any kind between freeborn men and slave women attracted ridicule and derision. The structure of Ibo society was upheld in the application of separate systems of law to slave and freeborn, and was seen most vividly in the reaction to homicide by a slave. If a slave killed another, he destroyed property, whose owner had to be compensated. As property himself, the killer was not responsible. The debt belonged to his owner. If a slave killed a freeborn person, his owner was required to hang himself, or a freeborn substitute, to expiate this offence against the tutelary goddess Anike. Again, even the life of the slave could not atone for his offence against the earth, since, as property, it had so little value. We might expect such complexities of both property and law to require centralised political adjudication and enforcement, but neither existed in the Ibo social order.

The Concept of Social Order

If we assume that the centralised political state evolved in order to administer an increasingly complex set of laws (Engels 1884/1948), then we can understand the interwoven concern of both law and politics to maintain order within specified territorial boundaries, using force if necessary. But in all societies, the vast majority of order, if we can put it that way, actually emerges from relationships that are strictly speaking neither political nor judicial. What for lack of a better term I shall call `institutionalised order´ results from being brought up to follow certain behaviour patterns (the process of socialisation); from formalised bureaucratic ritual (including diplomatic protocol); from the expectations of reciprocity in social relationships (`do as you would be done by'); from converging social interests; and from a system of positive social sanctions that reward approved behaviour through moral honours and long-term social security, and negative sanctions which punish `bad' behaviour in various ways that have little to do with the law. These `diffuse' negative sanctions, as Radcliffe-Brown (1952) called them, include public gossip and other forms of satire, beliefs in automatic supernatural retribution, and various forms of sublimated or deflected physical violence, such as competitive gift-giving, song-duels, nocturnal declamations, and gambling, which shame those who offend or injure others.

However, there are ambiguities in the very notion of `social order'. To start with, the more autocratic and rule-bound an order, the more likely it is to incorporate, as part of its `custom' or `tradition', approved temporary but regular reversals of itself. Armies are tightly-controlled orders; but at Christmas officers wait on their subordinates at table. Zulu women were excluded absolutely from male authority; but once a year they took it upon themselves to strip naked and beat up any man who was foolish enough to approach their spring ritual. `Rituals of rebellion', in Gluckman's (1956) phrase, act as safety valves to maintain ascriptive systems, precisely by inverting the normally-accepted order under controlled conditions.

Secondly, most ordered systems contain rules which conflict with one another. To abide by one set of rules or expectations will then automatically mean contradicting others, as we saw in chapter 6. Indeed, as Malinowski (1926:80) noted, even the most fundamental rules, like those of incest and exogamy, which deal with basic structural relationships, may be contradicted by `a well-established system of evasion'. To apply general rules to specific situations may also create conflicts with other potentially applicable norms. For example, if a man defends his family honour by murdering his promiscuous sister, he will have breached state order while applying that of the family.

Thirdly, the dividing line between `order' and `disorder' may be extremely fine. We see this perhaps most clearly in witchcraft accusations, which in Marwick's (1964/1970) view act as a `social strain gauge'. Beliefs in witchcraft are found mainly in sedentary societies, among people who are expected to live in amity and co-operation but cannot get away from one another when conflicts arise. The specific content of witch beliefs varies with cultural ideals, as Wilson (1951/ 1970) has shown. Pondo witches, in a society beset by rules of exogamy, invert the normal ideals of sexuality. In contrast,

Nyakyusa witches, in a society where sharing food indicates close social relations among age-mates, lust after milk and meat, the most prized foods. Likewise, the frequency of accusations reflects the culture-specific areas of social tension: among the Pondo, between mothers and daughters-in-law competing for the resources of the men who are simultaneously their sons and husbands; between co-resident Nyakyusa age-mates living in the same village or fellow-workers on mines; among polygynous co-wives competing for the affection and other resources of a common husband; between men and their wives, the in-marrying female strangers on whom exogamous patrilineages rely for their reproduction; between brothers competing for a non-partible inheritance; along the line of succession linking men and their sisters´ sons in matrilineal societies. These are the relationships on which the social order is founded. Yet when they turn rancorous, the order which they exemplify is totally inverted, to reflect the most heinous crime imaginable in that society.

A further aspect of the fine line dividing order from disorder (in the form of witchcraft) relates to the process of making an accusation. One does not accuse others lightly, for the very knowledge on which an accusation is based may implicate the accuser. If only witches move around at night, and I accuse someone of witchcraft, the basis for my accusation - that I saw her outside her house around 3 am - must raise the question of what I myself was up to. Divinatory oracles may, however, evaluate such accusations and relieve the accuser of such embarrassment. Where - as among the Azande - these oracles are controlled by powerful and high-status royals, their controllers may conveniently be freed of potential complicity, by their removal from the ´common´ field of witchcraft and allocation to the more specialised manipulation of material objects in the distinct field of sorcery. But in most African societies, it is the individual diviner, even more than the accuser, who risks identification as a witch, through his or her abuse of their familiarity with the world of witchcraft, against which they offer magical protection.

With respect to the specific variation concerning law and the political order which upholds it, this point is made best by the patrilineal Lugbara, of the Sudan-Uganda-Zaire border zone. Traditionally uncentralised, the Lugbara minimal patrilineages lived in small, dispersed hamlets under the gerontocratic headship of their senior agnates. These lineage elders were thought to be in direct contact with their ancestors, whom they would shortly join. Should his ancestors perceive an elder to be offended by disrespectful or disorderly behaviour among his juniors, even if he did not explicitly invoke their assistance, they were believed to send illness and other

204

misfortune to teach a lesson to the insubordinate. If, however, a group was continually plagued by such misfortune (perhaps because it had grown too large for its resource base), the explanation for this disorder changed. Instead of accepting his right to invoke supernatural assistance to redress his legitimate grievances, junior kinsmen accused the elder of exercising his power illegitimately, as witchcraft; and the group split.

The distinction between politico-cosmological order and disorder, between authority and its abuse, therefore became a matter of interpretation and micro-political persuasion, in which the support of the elderly women diviners (who certified the cause of misfortune) had to be detached from the lineage elder and directed towards his youthful political challengers. The dividing line between respected elder and vilified witch was conceptualised as the difference between order and disorder. Yet this difference was one of interpretation only: the behavior itself remained constant. I would therefore disagree with Beattie's (1964:181) suggestion that action, rather than ideas, maintains the social order. Both appear to be involved in the legitimation of political manoeuvre, on which, at any given moment in time, `order´ actually rests. Order, in other words, must be disputed so that it may be seen to exist.

The Resolution of Conflict

Conflict and dispute are endemic to human society. Yet they are by no means wholly negative in their social effects. Durkheim (1895/1938) reasoned that, if society had no concept of `crime´ or anti-social behaviour, it would be necessary to invent one, for it is against their breach that the rules are themselves upheld and restated. If they were never broken, no-one would know what the rules were! It is for this reason, too, that `trouble cases´ establish the law through the very difficulty of their resolution. The `function´ of conflict, then, appears to be to uphold order; always assuming that the conflict is not `revolutionary´, not itself designed to overthrow the existing order. But even revolutions have their continuities with the social order ex ante, and `continuing revolutions´ have had little political success in their attempts to prevent a stable order emerging.

In the area of conflict and its resolution, then, the interconnections between law and politics are structurally inescapable. We have already seen, in the previous chapter, that judicial decisions are a necessary part of leadership in order to hold a political team together. When we say that diffuse negative sanctions both maintain order and punish its breach, we are not so much trying to have our cake and eat it, as demonstrating the indivisibility of law and politics, of order and influence, at the micro-level of personal interaction. It is at this level that most disputes in all societies are resolved, within the organisational arrangements of other social institutions.

Within the authority structure of the family, for example, family gatherings or councils or moots may make initial decisions on conflicts over marriage payments, or illegitimate pregnancies, or domestic disputes. These decisions may in turn take the conflict into a judicial forum through litigation or the formal demand for redress. Within a university department, the chairman may spend more time than he wishes adjudicating fights among his academic and secretarial staff, and entertaining student complaints about both (and vice versa). Occasionally, the more lurid of these conflicts may reach legal firms and even the courts in the form of lawsuits for slander and defamation of character. But on the whole they do not. There is considerable pressure on the members of `communities´ of all kinds not to wash their dirty linen in public; to keep their conflicts with others, similarly placed to themselves, out of the public eye; and to discipline their own troublemakers. The public appearance of order, then, is organised in the first instance through ostensibly non-legal, non-political institutions. Only when these institutions fail to resolve the conflict may disputes break the surface of public order. Only then are these disputes channelled into formal institutions specifically designed to resolve disputes that have been publicised as such.

These institutions come in two forms: the social and the judicial. Social or customary dispute-resolving institutions include all of those mentioned earlier as providing `diffuse negative sanctions´ on behaviour: the slanderous song-duels, the sublimated forms of aggression, the verbal fights in the school playgrounds, the impossible challenges. (The latter we have encountered earlier, as a technique for controlling ambitious political subordinates.) These work on one of two principles. Either the energies of the disputants are deflected into non-violent competition, the outcome of which is normally and sensibly manoeuvred to look equal and share the honours. Or all the historical rancour of the relationship underlying the dispute is exaggerated in full public measure in a cathartic release of hostility, after which everyone not too badly alienated by the performance can resume normal relationships. At the extreme, if neither of these techniques works, disaffected individuals may remove themselves physically from what they define as an intolerable context of social conflict, by moving elsewhere or even by committing suicide. (As we have

206

seen, there are societies in which mobility does not exist as an option. Here conflict turns inwards before being re-externalised in witchcraft accusations, which often end in enforced mobility.)

Judicial institutions for resolving disputes are known as courts. (Semi-judicial or `a-legal´ institutions of the past, based on self-help, such as vendettas and feuds, are for obvious reasons suppressed by centralised polities: they constitute too great a threat to state control.) Where courts exist, in centralised polities, there is normally an appellate hierarchy moving from the local level to a court of final appeal. Civil appeals went, then, from headmen´s to chiefs´ courts in Swaziland, before being referred to the king´s court. In the UK, the appeal structure runs from assizes through magistrate´s benches to the Old Bailey and various appeal tribunals. The quarterly assizes, which visit small centres four times a year to hear accumulated local cases, are equivalent to a traditional African headman´s court. But there is a major difference between assize tribunals as part of the <u>judicial</u> structure of the British state, and Swazi headmen as part of their <u>political</u> structure, to which judicial functions were attached in a system that formally conflated, rather than separating, state powers.

We should not, however, be misled into assuming that the formal separation of the judiciary from the legislature means that law and politics are unrelated, or that `law´ is not `political´. Gluckman (1974:45) has recorded the case in which a British court, in the middle of the twentieth century, heard and rejected a charge of treason against striking dock-workers. The charge was laid under a fifteenth-century statute promulgated by Richard III, but deemed `incompatible with industrial civilisation´! In the problem of maintaining social order, the significance of law to political control was also seen all over Africa in the colonisers´ usurpation from traditional law-givers, on behalf of the new <u>state</u>, the right to adjudicate offences which they defined as threatening its political integrity and their ability to police it. The creation of new courts, whether by settler parliaments or metropolitan administrators, to parallel traditional adjudication, was politically motivated. Likewise, recognising and sometimes codifying `customary law´ and appointing and paying customary court officials was, in British colonies, fundamentally necessary to Lugard´s policy of `indirect rule´. European colonisers went instead for direct rule from the centre, which replaced existing institutions instead of creating dual systems.

Dual Systems of Statutory and Customary Law

From the beginning of the colonial period in Africa, `criminal´ cases have been reserved for adjudication by the legal system associated with the new state. Traditional courts have been permitted to handle only civil cases. In Swaziland, then, criminal offences were heard by a magistrate´s court before proceeding before a judge or bench of the high court, with a final decision (that could not be appealed further) being made by the British Privy Council (later replaced by the Swazi Appeal Court). Such dual judicial systems were characteristic of British colonies in Africa, and they have been retained in independent African states.

Statute law, administered by the new courts, governed the affairs of the colonial states and their non-African settlers. Customary law, applied within the traditional courts, arbitrated disputes among indigenous peoples. In theory the two were entirely separate. In practice, customary law was everywhere affected by the existence of statute law as a competitor, an alternative to itself. Statutes defined the limits of responsibility of customary law. In codifying custom, the statutory system not only rigidified but often created custom. While `the invention of tradition´ is hardly new, since without it cultures would never have changed, in the colonial context this phrase has a particular significance. It refers to the legal manipulation of `custom´ by colonial administrators. For example, in Southern Rhodesia the recorded payment of bride-wealth became compulsory if a `customary´ union was to be registered as a marriage; and enabling certificates for civil or religious marriages, in terms of the Native (later African) Marriages Act, were issued only when bridewealth had been certified as paid, by both the prospective husband and his father-in-law. These requirements undoubtedly stemmed from the historical reluctance of many Europeans to recognise any form of sexual union in Africa as equivalent to their `civilised´ and sanctified `marriage´ (Phillips and Morris, 1971:3). But they continue to apply in independent Zimbabwe, notwithstanding the introduction in 1982 of some contradictory clauses in the Age of Majority Act.

The manipulation of marriage custom was, however, a relatively minor example of the colonial creation of `customary´ law. A more important example, at least from a marxist perspective, pertained to land tenure. As we saw in chapter 3, all over Africa the colonial registration of individual rights to specific land parcels threatened the customary usufructuary access to this land of informal or secondary right-holders. Codifying the rights of allocating authorities also, in many instances, gave statutory form to procedures that in the past

208

had been somewhat amorphous. The Tribal Trust Land Act of 1967, for example, gave to chiefs an authority over land which they had never had previously, in an attempt to win their support for the illegal Rhodesian administration.

But perhaps the most telling example of the colonial manipulation of land law comes (yet again) from the settler-controlled legislature of Southern Rhodesia. In 1930 the Land Apportionment Act confined African land-holding generally to the `native reserves´, but also created a new category of freehold land specifically for blacks called the `native pur-chase areas´, which covered some 7 per cent of the country. Land was never customarily held in freehold, but since the turn of the century blacks (especially immigrants) had been buying and leasing farmland on a small scale under the provisions of statutes that made no reference to race. Later, in 1933, the Native Wills Act allowed Africans to dispose of their fixed and movable property by will, but specified that if they died intestate, customary inheritance procedures would apply. These two acts thus created racially distinct provisions for landholding and the devolution of property. They also brought customary landholding and inheritance provisions into potential conflict with statutes governing the same matters among the black population.

.The conflict centred on the status of land in customary law. In Shona and Ndebele custom, land was never owned. Those seeking to defend their claims to freehold land which the Native Wills Act forced into customary inheritance, therefore argued that customary law could not decide these cases. The inheritance of freehold land had to be decided by the statutory system. Those administering the legal system agreed that customary law was not competent to decide on land ownership, but insisted nonetheless that `customary law´ must handle these cases, because it was required to by the Native Wills Act. In a further legal twist, the Native Wills Act actually contradicted customary inheritance by specifying that the customary heir would succeed to the immovable property in an intestate estate in his individual capacity, where Shona custom required him to succeed as `head of house´ and trustee for the rights of the family as a whole and the bridewealth interests of minor sons in particular.

This conflict between statutory and `customary´ law dis-qualified legitimate heirs to property and refused individual Africans the right to choose between the competing legal systems. Some very intricate legal manoeuvring and attempted manipulation of the normal precedence of statutes ensured that the property rights of blacks would be confined to the sphere of `customary law´, except under the precise conditions specified by statute. A series of legal decisions reiterated the fundamental racial distinction between black and white land-holding and property ownership. At that time, property owner-ship was one qualification for both racially-separated voters´ rolls. As in most British colonies, a series of political agendas underlay the dual legal system in Southern Rhodesia.

Indeed, one marxist perspective on the dual legal struc-tures of British colonies, argues that statutory law was de-signed to underpin the capitalist sector of their dual econo-mies, while customary law was retained as a low-cost method of handling disputes not directly relevant to the capitalist mode of production. In this view, capitalism required the continued existence of precolonial peasant production, onto which it offloaded all of the costs of reproducing its own workforce. The recognition, codification and manipulation of `customary law´, therefore, enabled capital, through the colonial state, to control those societies subordinated to its economic power. The application of customary law to these subordinated frag-ments of a larger political system, ensured that they could not compete with capital for land or other productive resour-ces which were controlled by the statutory system. Areas of traditional jurisdiction, which threatened state control, were removed from the domain of customary law and transferred to statutory responsibility. In addition to arson and insurrec-tion, then, accusations of witchcraft and sorcery were also included in the list of offences punishable by statute.

At first sight this inclusion seems rather strange. The French, Portuguese, Belgian, British and Italian colonial administrators all agreed that witchcraft was a figment of the imagination. Why, then, did they all make it a crime to accuse someone of practising what they defined as non-existent? At one level this contradiction is resolved by acknowledging the colonisers´ recognition of the power of what they called `superstition´ over human behaviour and their desire to con-trol the actions of those who operated the divinatory oracles by which witches were detected and accused. But the issue of social control penetrates much deeper than this.

Wherever witchcraft (the power to harm others by super-natural means) is believed to exist, it operates within local communities, among people in everyday, face-to-face inter-action. As we have already seen, accusations of witchcraft reflect the structural tensions and conflicts of the relation-ships on which particular societies are constructed. While it was possible, in many African societies (such as the Shona), to `vote with one´s feet´ against the tyranny of a disliked chief, there was no justification for deserting one´s agnates (except, among women, through patrivirilocal marriage). Hating

210

kin was not only no excuse for anti-social behaviour, it was literally and conceptually unspeakable. Without legitimate vent, the rancour turned inwards and consolidated itself. When it manifested itself outwardly, it was interpreted as witchcraft, and then punished by the method everywhere applied to heresy, namely casting out from the local community, sometimes by public execution. These methods of dealing with witchcraft (including the associated methods of divining and confirming responsibility), threatened the authority of the state and its ability to maintain social order at the village level. So witchcraft, even though it didn't exist, had to become the judicial responsibility of the state.

The marxist view outlined above may perhaps be questioned, on the grounds that independent African states have retained dual systems of law instead of trying to rationalise them into a single system. One counter to this criticism notes that, socialist rhetoric notwithstanding, their dual economies have not altered. Therefore there is no reason why legal dualism should not continue, and every marxist reason why it should continue.

Law and Social Change

The proscription of witchcraft by legislation was one of the earliest attempts to change (other people's) society by using the law (in this case, by introducing parallel legal systems rather than by changing existing laws). For the most part, law has in the past tended to reflect social custom, not to create or alter it. The legal suppression of witchcraft was notably less successful in achieving its aims than the later and much more famous American attempt to desegregate all-white schools. Today `affirmative action` and `positive discrimination` are widely accepted as useful legal tools in attempting social change. At the very least they enable states to fine or jail their traditionalist citizens (which is conceptually possible perhaps only in countries with a fetish for modernity).

The premiss that society may be changed by legal action rests on the normal gap between rules and behaviour. If actions are at least vaguely oriented toward ideas of what is right and proper, then new ideas about social correctness should elicit roughly corresponding behaviour. Conversely, if in fact people's behaviour generates their attitudes, at least as much as their attitudes generate their behaviour, then changing their behaviour may lead to attitudinal change too, whether they like it or not. The law is an instrument of behavioural rather than attitudinal change, and is sometimes effective because of its coercive authority. Where this

211

coercion is not applied, or is easily evaded, the law may remain a dead letter, ignored in social practice. For example, where the law prescribes monogamy, but declines to pursue adulterers, turns a blind eye to extra-legal unions, and disallows divorce, the pursuit of monogamous marital rights in the courts by offended wives is not likely to yield them much satisfaction. The effective policing of the law usually requires the voluntary co-operation of ordinary people. If they define the law as contrary to their interests, this co-operation is unlikely to be forthcoming. And so we arrive back at the connection between law and social control, in the relationship of the law to social change.

This problem is no less acute in socialist states than in the west or in third world countries, although they have had longer experience of dealing with it. Relations of production may be `determinant´, but the prime instruments of revolutionary change for socialists, following their accession to state power, have been the (bourgeois) laws determining land tenure and marriage. The Chinese Marriage Law of 1950, for example, abolished the right to arrange marriage in the `arbitrary and compulsory feudal marriage system´; outlawed bigamy, concubinage, child betrothal, `interference with the remarriage of widows´, extortionate marriage payments, infanticide, and illegitimacy; specified minimum ages for marriage (20 for men and 18 for women); and conferred equal rights on both spouses to `status in the home´, to follow the occupation of their choice, to own and manage `family´ property, and to seek divorce.

In the three years following this legal reconstitution of Chinese marriage, these provisions were implemented with some success in 15 per cent of the country, but were a total failure in 25 per cent of areas. This failure was caused as much by the active ill-will of many male rural party cadres as by the resistance of the Chinese peasantry. The All-China Democratic Women´s Federation, with over 20 million members, experienced difficulty in distributing its pamphlets advising women of their rights before the law. Daughters were imprisoned in the home and tortured for pursuing their legal rights by resisting marriages arranged by their families. There were at least 10,000 suicides among young women trying to defy their families and a smaller but unknown number of deaths among women policing the law in rural areas. Finally, the state backed off and in 1953 started emphasising the importance of the family, rather than the rights of women, in constructing a new social order. Women did make small gains subsequently. Some joined the Chinese Communist Party (of whose membership only some 13 per cent is female) and became rural leaders organising other women. Urban women became workers, occupying most of the unmechanised manual jobs in factories and a small proportion of the more desirable posts. Population statistics indicate that female infanticide declined quite notably. But these achievements rested on the acquiescence of women in the traditions of patriliny and marriage, and their effective agreement not to confront these institutions with the new law. Indeed, in the 1980 update of the Marriage Law, many of the clauses governing practices considered to be defunct were dropped. Perhaps fortunately, infanticide was not among them.

From 1979, Han families were limited to one child apiece, a policy which resurrected many of the issues associated with the 1950 Marriage Law. Notably this new policy caused an upsurge in female infanticide, which stung both women and the state into action. `They can hardly believe that even after all the reforms of the past thirty years, female infants should be so discriminated against as to lose their lives´ (Croll 1984:31). Widespread contravention of the law against infanticide provided the Women´s Federation with a rationale for its organisational reinvigoration. Recently it has become very active in the area of women´s legal, educational and occupational rights, as well as family issues. Thirty-seven years and nearly two generations after liberation in 1949, new China´s social practice seems to have changed sufficiently to allow the state to pursue its original policies in the area of family law and women´s rights. How long it will take Cuba to be able to enforce its 1975 Family Code, requiring spouses to share the housework, is anyone´s guess!

> `Law and order arise out of the very processes which they govern. But they are not rigid, nor due to any inertia or permanent mould. They obtain on the contrary as the result of a constant struggle not merely of human passions against the law, but of legal principles with one another. The struggle, however, is not a free fight: it is subject to definite conditions, can take place only within certain limits and only on the condition that it remains under the surface of publicity...
> The true problem is not to study how human life submits to rules - it simply does not; the real problem is how the rules become adapted to life.´ (Malinowski 1926:122-3, 127.)

CHAPTER TEN

IDEOLOGY AND SOCIAL CONTROL

The sceptic might wonder why societies bother to create
rules of order when these are so frequently reworked in social
behaviour. As we have seen earlier, however, `why´ questions
are the explanatory preserve of witchcraft (and of religion
more generally, as well as psychology). Social anthropology
and cognate disciplines would prefer to examine how, rather
than why, the rules are socially constructed. Here `the rules´
refer broadly to norms and values, ideas about what is right
and proper, rather than to `laws´ which encapsulate only a
fraction of these `ideological´ issues in a practical rather
than a conceptual framework. We have already encountered numerous instances of the ways in which such ideas underpin social
behaviour. It is now time to consider ideology as a separate
issue in its own right; and perhaps to ask whether my earlier
interpretation of, say, jajmani relationships was actually
justified.

As diagram 1 (see page 14) indicated, orthodox marxist
approaches allocate to the superstructure all non-economic
components of society, including social relationships, legal
and political controls, and values, as part of the cultural
ideology which integrates that society. Godelier (1978), however, has asserted that this conceptual separation of base and
superstructure is, specifically for social anthropology and
perhaps more generally, wrong. Earlier, in trying to analyse
other aspects of social behaviour, we came up against ideological issues on numerous occasions, illustrating this point
that social institutions are not divided, by separate functions, into distinct levels in a conceptual hierarchy. They
are interconnected, and have multiple functions, many of which
are also undertaken by other institutions. Knowledge, for
example, which is expressed in language, underpins production.
It makes little sense, then, to relegate ethnoscience to the
apical superstructural level of `ideology´, when economic pro-
duction would be impossible without it. Much the same could be
said of kinship and affinity, or of the law of property, when
these define access to productive resources. Such superstructural relations are not, in Godelier´s view, generated in and
by the economy. Both in time and in their ideological value
to the society concerned, they are prior to economic relations. These `ideel realities´ are generated as fundamental
values in areas of what the marxists call the superstructure.
As organisational principles, they are vital to economy and
society alike. It is precisely through their simultaneous and
interrelated functioning, in both `base´ and `superstructure´

214

alike, that these ideel realities `reproduce´ society.

Ideel Realities: Fundamental Ideological Assumptions

Immobile people in rule-bound societies generally tend to
hold rigid views about the proper order of things. Their cultural ideologies depend on <u>relatively</u> immutable assumptions.
We shall begin by examining two such assumptions, based on
hierarchy and gender respectively, which exemplify Godelier´s
`ideel realities´. These `thought realities´ or `conceptual
basics´ (perhaps the closest English comes to being able to
grasp the original French idea) comprise `a complex body of
representations, ideas, patterns ... which ... are essential
for any material activity to be able to occur´ (Godelier 1978:
363). They infuse language (through which they are transmitted
down the generations), and the development of technological
knowledge.

Hierarchy

In Hindu India, according to Dumont (1970:104-5), the
concept of hierarchy provided the ideological principle `by
which the elements of a whole [were] ranked in relation to the
whole´. The ancient Vedas, or Hindu holy writings, distinguished four differentially-ranked <u>varnas</u>. In the order of
their diminishing status, these <u>varnas</u> comprise the priestly
Brahmans, ruling Kshatriyas and farming Vaishyas, all of whom
are categorised as `twice-born´, and the Sudra servants. While
the only religious obligation of the Sudras is to serve obedi-
ently, their twice-born superiors are enjoined to study, make
religious sacrifices, and donate charitable gifts to those who
have renounced the world to live on alms. Each of these four
major caste groupings is divided into hundreds of occupational
sub-castes, or <u>jatis</u>, the details of which vary from one part
of India to the next. The overall ranking system has emerged,
in Dumont´s view, as the aggregated outcome of the numerous
relationships between adjacent <u>jatis</u>. The higher-ranking <u>jati</u>
protects itself from pollution by the impurity of the sub-
caste immediately below it. The order in which <u>jatis</u> are ranked varies from one locality to the next, hence the overall
system appears somewhat confused, and even contradictory, when
specific districts are compared.

Dumont (1970:71) has argued that caste is, above all, a
`state of mind´. Throughout the system there exists an elabor-
ate code of pollution etiquette, defining the sub-castes from
which one may accept different types of food and drink, those
with whom one can share a common water source, and those whose

215

presence in the same space is an offence against one's ritual purity. In Dumont's (1970:74) view, then, the caste system is based on 'an absolute distinction between power and hierarchical status'. This disjunction codifies status on the basis of the dominance of ritual purity, while political power is not hierarchically codified and remains subordinated to religious status.

This disjunction between status and power, according to Dumont, rests on the more fundamental disjunction between pure and impure. The religious notions of purity and truth thus provide an 'immutable model' for the social relationships between sub-castes. Biological and organic activities and substances cause pollution. Those sub-castes which specialise in impure activities (such as washing menstrual garments) will, therefore, pollute all others with whom they come into contact. Such pollution may be removed by ritual bathing or by using the organic products of the sacred cow - blood, milk, urine, dung - to purify those contaminated by the biological products of other humans. Really gross pollution, however, for example among those responsible for funerary ritual, cannot be shaken off even by the expiation of sacrifice. As Dumont rightly observes, then, if some are to attain purity, then by definition as well as in practice, others must take impurity upon themselves. In this argument, the occupational specialisation of sub-castes is a consequence of their ritual interdependence. Their inequality is a function of their participation in the unitary ideological system. Caste hierarchy, as an ideology, requires that its individual elements be ranked as part of the whole, and not merely in relation to one another. (Similar arguments, ironically, have also been applied to - ostensibly less rigid - class systems.)

It follows from this view that the division of labour is itself an epiphenomenon or, as Dumont (1970:260) puts it, a 'non-ideological residuum' of the notion of hierarchy, based on purity. Hence we should not regard jajmani relations, for example, as a thin disguise for economic exploitation. Economic exploitation, as the possible core motivation for caste ranking, does not explain why Brahmans, as priests, rank above those who wield political and economic power, as rulers and landowners; or why Brahmans are hired to cook festive meals by members of lower-ranking jatis; or why those Brahmans who perform ritual services to bereaved households, or to upwardly-mobile, impure caste-climbers not entitled to such services, should be marginalised within their own varna. Nor does the thesis of economic exploitation explain why the claim of wealthy ex-distillers to twice-born ritual status, should be denied them by their fellow-landowners. Indeed, a materialist view of caste would have some difficulty in explaining, in the

216

first place, why less than half of all Hindus actually follow
their traditional caste occupations. Explanations for ideel
realities are perhaps better sought, at least initially, in
the realm of ideas than in the economy.

On the whole, social anthropology has accepted Dumont´s
exposition of why caste continues to operate as it does. But
there are some problems with his argument that their ritual
purity defines the superiority of the Brahmans in this system.
Parry (1980) has shown that the priestly duty to absorb sin
and spiritual impurity is perhaps more polluting than the
removal of organic wastes. The taint of death is so polluting
to the funeral priests in particular that, as Dumont himself
noted with respect to South India, they are effectively out-
casted in their exclusion from clean society. These Mahabrah-
man funeral priests are regarded as consubstantial with, as
actually being the deceased spirits (pret), whose funerary
rituals they perform. They are accordingly both impure and
inauspicious or `ill-omened´, and are `regarded with a mixture
of fear and contempt´ (Parry 1980:94). Furthermore, according
to Parry (1980:103-4), many other priestly Brahmans `admit
that they do not know the proper Sanskrit formulae nor the
correct ritual procedure´. Their acceptance of gifts (dan) for
their ritual services therefore increases their own sin, as
well as exposing them to the sins of the donors which are
thought to be embodied in such gifts.

The position of those at the apex of the caste hierarchy,
then, is ambiguous and riddled with contradictions. There are
insufficient hours in the day for any Brahman to fulfil his
spiritual obligations to the Vedic letter. The rewards for
their ritual services, which allow Brahmans to subsist (and
some to become wealthy), pollute them. Their ritual duties
themselves endanger the spiritual status and health of these
(imperfect) ritual specialists. Little wonder that many abandon their traditional responsibilities. `Moreover, if the
world were indeed composed of ascetic Brahmans who refused to
accept all offerings over and above their immediate subsistence needs, rituals would grind to a halt and the progressive
degeneration of the universe would be geatly accelerated´
(Parry 1980:105). Clearly, an explanation for the caste hierarchy and its control over social behaviour needs to go beyond
Dumont´s neat opposition of status, based on ritual purity, to
political power. This disjunction has helped our preliminary
understanding of caste, but the matter is more complex than
this disjunction allows.

Gender

When we look at gender as an ideological basis for allocating roles in production and society, we see that it too, like hierarchy, is more complicated than appears at first sight. We must start by distinguishing gender, as a technical concept, from sex. Human society divides into two sexes, male and female (though many languages allow for a third, neutered category). However, not all human males are socially `men´, nor are all females socially `women´. Nor are interstitial gender roles necessarily a matter for social shame. Arab society, in particular, incorporated eunuchs (emasculated ex-men) into powerful court positions. Transsexual men (homosexual prostitutes known as xanith in the gulf state of Oman) moved freely in the secluded world of Muslim women in purdah (Wikan 1977), since they were not defined as `men´. (Hormone therapy and modern surgery have permitted some of the western equivalents of Omani xanith to `become´ women, physically as well as socially, and ex-women to become men). Spirit mediums of both sexes have been honoured in many societies, even when they adopted the clothes and artefacts symbolically associated with the opposite sex.

`Gender´, then, as opposed to `sex´, refers to the processes by which differences between the sexes are constructed in society. These differences often, if not invariably, encompass important material dimensions, for example in the division of labour based on sex. However, they are in the first instance ideological. We see this ideological component in numerous myths of origin. From Eve in Genesis, through the Greek disaster of Pandora, to the Dinka lady who mortally offended her divinity (Nhialic) by hitting him in the eye with her pestle, the actions of women the world over have been held responsible for the breach of relations between men and their gods, and the consequent burdens of mortality and misfortune that men have to carry. The further social complications of the ideological construction of gender are seen perhaps most graphically in the case of Papua-New Guinea.

For most of this century, anthropologists have characterised societies throughout Melanesia as displaying marked antagonism between the sexes. The strength of this antagonism has been reported to vary from a low among the Trobrianders (whom Malinowski reported as denying males any role in the conception of children) to a high in the Eastern Highlands of New Guinea (where the male role in procreation is emphasised). Herdt and Poole (1982) noted that this idea of `sexual antagonism´ is an analytical gloss on a much more complex reality; and that the concept itself owes as much to the anthropological preoccupation with the western discourse on inter-sexual relations, as to Melanesian ethnographic reality. `Sexual antagonism´, as an analytical construct, emerged from the researches of male anthropologists among men in Melanesia, at a time when pacification and colonisation had threatened, if not destroyed, the warfare and competitive exchanges on which masculine identity was traditionally founded. The opposition of men and women, in this context, provided a convenient metaphor for Melanesians to talk about what was happening in their own societies. But this metaphor may have been a consequence of historical change in the colonial period, rather than a reflection of ancient tradition.

Antagonism between the sexes was reflected materially in residential arrangements. In most New Guinea societies, married couples did not live together. Men and women occupied different quarters within the densely-populated community long-houses. Women were also excluded from the ritual secrets and certain ritual activities of men. As elsewhere, women (especially wives) were associated with malevolent witchcraft. Finally, this antagonism also permeated the marital exchanges of goods and women between patrifiliated local descent groups. Sometimes, as among the Bimin-Kuskusmin (Weiner 1982), exogamous marriage created a tension between the roles of women as sisters, with ritual significance in the social reproduction of their patrigroups, and women as in-marrying, wifely strangers, on whom the physical reproduction of that group depended. The notion of sexual antagonism generally has revolved around the postulated differences between male and female with respect to their reproductive growth.

Simply put, most (men in) Melanesian societies seem to have regarded women as growing `naturally´, while men were thought to require ritual assistance to cultivate their own, less-easily achieved maturation. As Herdt and Poole (1982:23) put it: `Where cults and warfare emphasise male sex role dramatisation, men must "achieve" gender and social identity which, for women, are "natural"´. Hostility toward women may have contributed toward achieving such male identity. In some societies, however, women were regarded as necessary to `grow´ men. `Growing´ her husband was often the responsibility of a wife, for example, who had to manage her own menstrual and child-bearing rituals in such a way as to restore the depletion of her husband´s semen, skin and strength, which resulted from their normal marriage relations. Or female spirits, like the Paiela `ginger woman´, might `grow´ youths during their puberty rituals, in return for social recognition through the planting of a ginger garden (Biersack 1982).

Explicitly-stated male envy of this postulated female capacity for natural growth seems to explain some specifically

Melanesian ritual practices, including imitative menstruation and ritualised male homosexuality (in which semen was expended not on women, who grew without it, but on young boys and men who needed its assistance). Female homosexuality, in contrast, was (at least among the Bimin-Kuskusmin) associated with the most virulent form of witchcraft (Poole 1981). However, there were also paradoxes in these conceptions. The physiological capacities of women polluted men, as well as being envied by them. Ritualised male homosexuality was related to the emphasis on the male role in procreation, as well as to their own growth requirements. And many Melanesian men over the past few decades have favoured radical changes in the residential segregation of the sexes and the upbringing of children. Perhaps, in the end, the concept of sexual antagonism amounted to no more than different ideological formulations of each other by men and women in a unique historical situation. But this idea does indicate the great importance of ideological formulations in structuring social behaviour.

Ideology and Consciousness

We have been using the concept of ideology with what some might regard as gay abandon. But what exactly is `ideology´? To answer this question satisfactorily, we need to borrow from philosophy. Kolakowski (1979:119), for example, has defined ideology as comprising `the sum of conceptions which enables a social group (a social class, for example, but not only a class) to systematise the values in which the mystified consciousness and the activity of this group are expressed... The social function of ideology is to consolidate belief in the values which are essential to the fruitful activity of the group.´ This definition extends and systematises Godelier´s notion of `ideel realities´. As a set of consciously-held, systematised values which integrate the social group, ideology in this sense is also congruent with Malinowski´s view of `culture´. Both provide what a contemporary French sociologist, Alain Touraine, has called the `cultural model´ which a society holds of itself. Within such a `conscious model´ of social behaviour, Bailey (1971) has noted that the constituent values form a hierarchy, in which the most important values encompass and dominate those that are less inclusive and more easily changed.

But is the system of values unitary? Are there no alternative ideologies? As we shall see, such questions have rarely been addressed directly by anthropologists, who have assumed (with Durkheim) that a single ideology embraces all components of a single society. For to recognise equal and competitive ideologies within a single society, would be to imply that the society is not single after all. However, anthropologists´ interpretations of their evidence have often suggested, if not multiple ideologies, at least a notable divergence of ´peripheral´ from the dominating ´mainstream´ or ´central´ ideological values and beliefs. This perspective has resulted partly from the recent switch in anthropological focus, from studying ´culture´ or ´society´ to understanding the actions of individuals. However, ´ideology´ has also been dangerous ground for marxists, for related reasons.

There is a tension in Marx´s work, between his early but lasting view that the point of philosophy should be to change the world through human action, and his later assertion that men were forced into relations of production independently of their own will. This coercion depended in part on men´s acceptance of ideological constructions. ´It is not the consciousness of men that determines their existence, but their social existence that determines their consciousness´ (Marx 1859/ 1975:425). With this statement, Durkheim had no quarrel. From this tension between ideological coercion and social action, arose Marx´s problematic identification of ideology as ´false consciousness´, which by definition conceals and mystifies the relations of power between unequally-placed classes and, in its specifically religious guise, discourages action to change the existing relations of production by the promise of ´pie in the sky when you die´.

In the next chapter, we shall examine the problems of this view in detail. For present purposes, let us merely point to Mannheim´s later distinction between ideology as deception, standing somewhere between lies and errors; and ideology as reflecting the ´characteristics and composition of the total structure of the mind´ in specific societies (1936:49-50). In Mannheim´s (1936:54) words: ´We begin to treat our adversary´s views as ideologies only when we no longer consider them as calculated lies and when we sense in his total behaviour an unreliability which we regard as a function of the social situation in which he finds himself´.

Mannheim´s second option (of ideology as social unreliability) lay closer to Durkheim´s (1895/1938) conception of ´collective representations´ in society than to Marx´s premiss of deliberate deceit. What Durkheim called ´collective representations´ were the shared ideas and values generated by the ´collective consciousness´. Somewhat unexpectedly, this collective consciousness emanated from ´centres of secondary consciousness dispersed throughout the [individual] organism and unknown to the primary centre, while normally subordinate to it´ (Durkheim 1924/1965:22). Nonetheless, as social facts, collective representations were independent of and external to the individuals holding them, among whom they arose as a result of `association´. Unkind and unconvinced commentators have noted that, despite Durkheim's attempts to give sociology a non-psychological pedigree, his `collective consciousness´ sounds rather like mob action. But for Durkheim (1924:54), society was not `an epiphenomenon of individual life´. Society transcended individual consciousness, even though it was immanent in individual action. `The individual submits to society and this submission is the condition of his liberation´ (Durkheim 1924:72). Man's individual consciousness, in Durkheim's view, was therefore subordinated to the shared social values of the collective consciousness.

Still leaving aside the issue of power and its manipulation, we must nonetheless ask: where does the legitimacy of the collective consciousness come from? How is it generated? Durkheim's (1915) answers to these questions rested on an evolutionist approach. First he identified Australian totemism, based on a special relationship between natural species and descent groups, as the simplest or most elementary form of religious activity. Then he argued that the <u>intichiuma</u> rituals (designed to multiply the totem animal in question) generated a religious frame of mind among the participants, creating a special relationship among co-worshippers as well as between individual worshippers and their totems. (Drugs, as well as singing and dancing, may also achieve this heightened mental state.) Ritual activity, then, in Durkheim's veiw, produced religious belief through the `association´ of participants in this common expressive behaviour. Belief was a transformative refraction, not a simple reflection, of social behaviour.

Had Durkheim himself ever witnessed a ritual performance outside the standardised confines of the orthodox Judaeo-Christian tradition, rather than relying on anthropological descriptions in writing, he might have reached a different conclusion. The ongoing consultations and arguments during ritual performances about what should be done next, at each point in the proceedings, give a very different picture of reality from the sanitised analyses of ritual for publication. In Gilsenan's (1973:50) words: `anyone who has absorbed Victorian notions of reverent behaviour as being synonymous with whispers and quiet decorum soon has his assumptions disrespectfully shattered ... Huddled in a corner ... the anthropologist has time to reflect on the wreckage of his own fixed ideas about proper expressions of piety´. And had he not deliberately chosen a society with a unitary belief system, Durkheim would have had to confront the problems of competition for belief (and would thereby have spared himself some of the more obvious criticisms that his argument encountered). As it was, instead of facing the problems of ideology that Marx

222

had already encountered, Durkheim´s analysis led him to dicho-
tomise `sacred´ and `profane´ spheres of existence, and to
analyse religion, rather than the more inclusive analytical
category of ideology.

For Durkheim (1915:47), religion was `a unified system of
beliefs and practices related to sacred things ... which
unite, into one single moral community called a church, all
those who adhere to them´. Religion was also, as `the way of
thinking characteristic of collective existence ... a system
of symbols by means of which society becomes conscious of
`itself´. In arguing that religious beliefs projected social
organisation into the plane of the supernatural, Durkheim was
by no means the first observer to argue that religion is not
what it appears to be. Indeed, as Gilsenan (1973:63) noted,
`despite a distressing lack of knowledge of Durkheim and
Weber´, religious leaders in particular `show themselves very
aware of the functions and problems of ritual and organisa-
tion´. Moreover, the sceptical tradition stretches back to the
ancient Greek philosophers. The mystificatory nature of early
Christianity was specifically noted by Lucian of Samosata,
described by Engels (Marx-Engels 1975:277) as `the Voltaire of
classic antiquity´. However, Durkheim was perhaps the first to
stress the <u>social</u> (as opposed to the financial or political)
basis for religious mystification.

Religious Conceptualisation as the Projection of Society

The projection of human relationships into the postulated
plane of the supernatural is often very obvious. `God the
Father´ of Christianity; the numerous ancestral cults of
traditional Africa; the `all-powerful´ Allah of Islam - all
reflect easily identifiable models of socio-political control.
But for Durkheim, the process of deifying society was not
quite that simple. An element of mystification marked the
conceptual change from earthly `father´ to heavenly `Father´,
for collective representations were not simply the aggregate
of individual consciousnesses. Men created their religions
from the raw materials of their earthly experiences, but in so
doing these raw materials were themselves transformed. In
Durkheim´s view, religious concepts were not simply mirror
images of social relationships.

We could use numerous African examples to demonstrate
this point. I have chosen the Kalabari of South-Eastern
Nigeria to illustrate Durkheim´s argument, because their
ethnographer, Robin Horton, has argued (against Durkheim and
many others) that anthropology must accept religious belief at
its face value in order to understand fully what it does in

society. Horton's numerous papers became progressively more unsympathetic to `conspiracy´ theories of religion, which have argued that religious beliefs are not what they seem. Horton himself presented his arguments as `neo-intellectualist´ counters to Durkheimian approaches, which saw the content of beliefs as peripheral to their `real´ function of integrating society. However, in retrospect it seems more sensible to treat the two approaches as complementary rather than antagonistic.

Horton compared Kalabari religious thought with the process of building scientific theory. Kalabari religious thought could be characterised as timeless, magical, personalised, bound to specific happenings, disinclined to question and evaluate itself in any form of experimentation, primarily expressive, unable to discriminate among a number of converging causal possibilities, unwilling to admit ignorance or the possibility of coincidence, and ultimately self-protective and closed to alternative explanations. Nonetheless, Horton viewed the Kalabari construction of beliefs about the world and their place in it, as a form of conceptualisation or model-building, based on their experience of living in a mobile and flexible society. In Horton's (1967) view, the individual components of this belief system fitted together in much the same way that scientific theorising proceeds, from the specific to the general, from the less-inclusive to the more-inclusive explanation. In the end, however, the limitations of this model were reflected in the Kalabari conversion to Christianity, which seemed to offer a more inclusive explanatory framework for the new world of experience into which they were inexorably drawn.

The Ijo-speaking Kalabari live in the eastern mangrove swamps of the Niger delta. Traditionally fishermen, they increasingly turned to trade as their formerly autonomous towns and villages were incorporated into the administrative system of modern Nigeria. Each settlement was founded by a `hero´, a stranger who came from across the water, and who disappeared before death could overtake him or her. Within each settlement, cognatic lineages owned and allocated land. Lineage membership was determined by the amount of bridewealth paid at one's mother's marriage. A high bridewealth affiliated the children to their father's lineage, while a small payment tied them into their mother's kin group. Minor disputes were resolved within the lineage by its head and his council of adult male advisors. More serious matters went before the village assembly, in which representation was organised by age-grades rather than by lineages, although the village head came from the dominant lineage. Village government was organised by the village and lineage heads, rather than by the assembly, especially in those villages where the control of trade to the

224

coastal ports went hand-in-hand with village government.

Both trade and fishing, however, remained at the mercy of
the watery environment. The weather, the sea-tides and the
condition of the swamp waters all affected economic activity,
although fishing remained the riskier of the two occupations.
These environmental constraints on production were associated
with the polymorphous water spirits believed to inhabit particular waterways and mudflats. The water spirits (owuamapu)
were also associated with creativity, wealth, innovation and
deviance among the Kalabari individuals whom they possessed;
and it is possible that the mythical village founders were
once thought of as water people. Horton (1962:202) associated
the water spirits with `the forces of the extra-social´ in
Kalabari society. They might work in association with the
other two categories of `free´ spirit, the village heroes and
the ancestors, to strengthen village and lineage unity by providing good weather for a secure fishing harvest, new dances
and other useful inventions. Equally well, however, intra-
group quarrels over differential or poor catches and deviant
behaviour could indicate dissension between the water spirits
and the other spirits.

The village heroes (am´oru), unlike the water people,
once took on semi-permanent human form themselves. They, too,
were innovators, introducing new laws and customs, new institutions and even new economic activities (like trade) to the
villages in which they settled. `In return for worship they
strengthen[ed] the village and help[ed] it to survive in competition with its neighbours´ (Horton 1962:200). In particular, the village hero was thought to keep a watchful eye on
the village head, and to check any abuse of his authority, by
causing his death if necessary.

The third and final category of free spirits with whom
the Kalabari maintained personal contact, through the ritual
cycle, was that of the ancestors (duen). The ancestors were
concerned specifically with the continuity and strength of
their lineages, as important and identifiable sub-groupings in
Kalabari society. Deceased lineage heads were more important,
in punishing the breach of lineage rules, than ordinary ancestors, and they were thought to be particularly close to an
incumbent lineage head. The ancestors might strengthen their
descendants in competition with other lineages, and thus explain the rise to prominence in village affairs of a formerly
unimportant lineage. Conversely, lineages which were unsuccessful in such competition, might explain their failure by
reference to ancestral anger with the contemporary behaviour
of their descendants. In supporting their own descendants in
competition with other lineages, the ancestors might work

against the village heroes by sapping village unity. To some extent, however, the strength of the village was thought to depend on the strength of its constituent lineages, with ancestors and heroes working in collaboration with each other.

Horton interpreted the interrelationships among the water spirits, heroes and ancestors as forming a triangle of forces in Kalabari belief. Any two of the three categories at any given time might co-operate with or be antagonistic to each other, thus explaining in a regular and predictable fashion why things happened as they did in Kalabari social life. Although `every person, plant, animal and thing ha[d] its own particular spirit´ (teme) which made their existence possible, these `fixed´ spirits had less explanatory value for the Kalabari than the three categories of `free´ spirit, detached permanently from their material base. However, although Horton (1962:200) did not specify precisely how, it was actually through the fixed spirits that the free spirits were thought to influence the material world of the Kalabari.

We should note, too, that there were limits to what the Kalabari were prepared to accept from their free spirits. If a particular spirit got out of hand, its influence, together with its cult objects, could be destroyed by community action. Conversely, the Kalabari acknowledged that, like influential people, the free spirits acquired their power from their human followers. `The balance of cosmic forces´, as Sorum (1982:53) noted in a different context, was `dependent on human action´, among the Kalabari as among the Bedamini of Melanesia. As living people with their own fixed spirits, the Kalabari confronted their free spirits from a position of strength, rather than as helpless supplicants, even though the free spirits were, in theory, the more powerful.

Perhaps their independence of their free spirits arose in part from other aspects of Kalabari belief, relating to more abstract and remote levels of the spirit world with which ordinary people were not normally directly in contact. The concepts of creation and destiny in particular provided alternative explanations to those associated with the free spirits for what happened in the everyday world of the Kalabari. Individuals, like the world as a material whole, each had their own creator (tamuno), a refraction of the great female creator of the world (opu tamuno). Social groupings, notably villages and lineages, had no specific creators, but like individuals and the world, did have their destinies (so). Destinies, spoken for individuals at their creation, conceptualised the historical pattern of what happened to the individual or social unit over time.

226

The individual suffering misfortune might initially attribute it to a capricious water spirit. But if the misfortune was recurrent, the explanation would more likely be seen as resulting from a totally inauspicious destiny, which the individual's creator might be approached to replace with something easier to live with. (Given their water spirits and personal destiny to explain misfortune, it is obvious why the Kalabari had no use for witches in their cosmology.) With respect to the lineage, we might regard the Kalabari concept of destiny as incorporating the more limited idea of heredity. Horton (1962:206) equated the concept of destiny, at the village level, with the `national character´, `total culture´, and `way of living´ of that village, noting that its destiny was normally invoked before the village approached its heroes for assistance. At all levels of Kalabari social organisation, then, the behaviour of the free spirits was believed to explain isolated occurrences, while the more-inclusive concept of destiny was reserved to explain the recurrent patterning of related events.

There was certainly a close relationship between the everyday Kalabari world and the free spirits, in the association of the water spirits with the ecology, the village heroes with settlement in a mobile society, and the ancestors with their co-resident descendants. Even the more abstract concepts of creation and destiny were related to what actually happened in Kalabari social life. In this respect, the Kalabari system of beliefs and rituals was an impeccably Durkheimian exercise in model-building.

But built into this composite belief system, specifically in the notion of the water spirits, was also a capacity for innovation, change and even deviance in Kalabari society. Women possessed by water spirit `husbands´, for example, were partly released from their normal social roles of wife and mother, to form part of a healing cult. While refracting important social institutions in its constituent parts, then, the belief system as a whole went beyond simple refraction, to conceptualise limited alternatives to the existing social order. These alternatives were strictly controlled. They did not seek to replace so much as to maintain this unitary system, by providing safety-valves to release dangerous pressures on it. Yet Horton (1962:212) regarded the `structural hybridisation´ of Kalabari beliefs as explaining not only `the recurrent events of the delta world, but also ... non-recurrent social change through the transformation of the individual and the deviant into the normal and the institutionalised´.

Cosmological Unity and Societal Balance

Like all religions, Kalabari beliefs sought to explain the unpredictable irregularities of everyday life: misfortune, illness, death, unexpected success. Belief and ritual, forms of knowledge in their own right, also symbolised aspects of social life. The Kalabari seem to have had a fairly hard-nosed or `instrumental´ interest in the material outcome of their rituals, even those (like the ekine masquerades) which were primarily aesthetic art forms. Yet it was precisely this concern to obtain a satisfactory explanation for what happened in this world, on the basis of which the individual could take manipulative and redressive ritual action, that integrated Kalabari beliefs into a unitary system. Within this system, the various components achieved a working balance against one another and even against themselves. We saw this balance most clearly in the ways in which each category of free spirit could be held responsible for both munificence and disaster, alone or in collaboration with other spirits.

This cosmological balance depended on what anthropologists have called `converging causality´ and its obverse, the possibility of diverging or competitive explanations. Behind every initial answer to the question `why´, lay at least one alternative possibility, in the system of `secondary elaboration´ that protected the main categories of causation. So a poor fishing catch was first attributed to a disaffected water spirit. The third consecutive fishing failure might implicate disaffected ancestors as well. When a good catch became a matter for remark, the fisherman concerned would investigate his so. But at no stage did the Kalabari explanatory system based on religious belief question his fishing techniques.

Selecting one among the possible legitimate explanations, as in most traditional religions, was the responsibility of the diviner. Divination techniques, together with the competence of the individual diviner operating them, could be and were questioned. But only individual techniques or diviners were questioned, not the entire system of causation or the basic procedures by which causes were revealed. In the last analysis, where recurrently troublesome spirits threatened the stability of the total system, they could be removed by destroying their cult objects. The explanatory balance was thus restored.

This cosmological balance also depended on the inclusion in the system of ambiguous spirits who were either amoral, or who licensed and regularised behaviour that Kalabari society normally regarded as deviant. Horton (1963:96,97) noted that the male dancing society, ekine, celebrated peripheral, and

228

sometimes dangerous, water spirits, in ritual masquerades that adopted `no particular stance on behalf of the accepted moral code´, but instead revealed matters normally hidden. As Lewis (1971) has pointed out, the central morality of a particular society can be upheld only by explaining deviance from this morality in terms that do not contaminate the spirits upholding it. Ancestral spirits, like those of the Lugbara, may on occasion become righteously indignant about the behaviour of some of their descendants, and punish them. But should these spirits act ambiguously too often, they run the risk of moral reclassification, involving either themselves or their agents (such as the Lugbara elders accused of witchcraft).

Many societies, then, balance what Lewis (1966, 1971) has called central cults, which are manned by male spirits and male mediums and which uphold and refract mainstream social morality and political authority, against the cults of peripheral, usually dissatisfied, spirits. The peripheral spirits are also usually conceptualised as male, and frequently as those of foreigners. As we noted in chapter 7, however, and in contrast to the mediums of the central cults, these peripheral spirits normally possess women and deprived groups in a wide range of societies. They afford the socially disenfranchised a vehicle for limited protest about their condition, and occasional redress. To these peripheral spirits, witches and sorcerers, is attributed most of the blame for misfortune, particularly illness. Indeed, illness, especially if it becomes recurrent, may be interpreted as evidence that a spirit is seeking a human host and medium. Only after its acceptance will such a spirit cease disturbing the health of its chosen host, as we saw among the young Giriama entrepreneurs who were troubled by peripheral Islamic spirits.

Illness and its corollary, good health, materially affect the cosmological balance in societies where medical technology is underdeveloped. As Lewis (1971:82) put it, spirit pantheons, in this case of the Hausa bori, are `not merely a census of spiritual forces, but equally a medical dictionary´. The incidence of disease, and epidemiological patterns, sometimes reflect genetic as well as social adaptations to specific environments. In West Africa, for example, the distorted sickle shape of red blood cells, which causes a specific type of chronic anaemia, also confers an immunity against malaria. In other cases, marriage rules, especially in nomadic societies, which allow for easy divorce and frequent remarriage, may contribute to the spread of sexually transmitted diseases which cause sterility and a low rate of population growth. Indeed, among some peoples, like the Baggara and other nomads in the Sahelian region, it has been estimated that their net reproductive rates are negative, and that their social reproduction depends on in-migration from other ethnic groups (like the Fur). In all known human societies, at least 10 per cent of women of reproductive age are `naturally´ infertile (that is, as a consequence of factors other than disease); and few women are fortunate enough to have a perfectly balanced hormonal output and experience no problems with menstruation or child-bearing. Those of us who live in societies where the availability of modern curative medicine is taken for granted, and who avail ourselves of these facilities in maintaining our own balance of health, may find it difficult to appreciate the cosmological importance of `nature´ in defining and treating illness in societies lacking this technology. Given women's reproductive physiology, in conjunction with their widespread social subordination, it is hardly surprising that women in particular are so frequently possessed by peripheral spirits causing illness, and are so regularly inducted into healing cults centred on these spirits. Possession here becomes a means of controlling disruptive `nature´ and re-establishing `culture´ or social order.

Of particular note, in the relationship between illness and possession by spirits, is the question of psychological disturbance and its treatment. Lewis has noted both the etymological derivation of the commonest neurotic ailment, hysteria, from the Greek word for womb, and its association with the reproductive physiology of women (1971:95); and the widespread problem, for religious communities, `of distinguishing between madmen and mystics´ (1971:38). Regrettably, relatively little collaborative research has been done in this area between anthropologists and psychiatrists. It would seem that possession behaviour, including glossolalia (`speaking in tongues´) and locomotor disturbances, may be a means of controlling psycho-organic or psychosomatic disease. However, Lewis has emphasised that psychotic elements comprise a very minor part of all religions, which are, as Durkheim noted, primarily social phenomena. The psychiatric face of possession, therefore, should not be spotlighted while other, more important areas are shadowed.

Every religious ideology, then, offers answers to the `why´ questions, but with different degrees of success. Those closed ideologies, which balance various categories of spirit in refracting and explaining the small worlds of local communities, are at greatest risk of replacement when the local community loses its autonomy and becomes part of a larger, intrusive society. Lineage ancestors offer no resources for explaining or coping with unrelated city neighbours. The spirits of deceased chiefs have difficulty in coming to grips with parliamentary legislation. Even the spirits of tradition-al protest may not provide the most suitable mechanism for adjusting to the problems of urban unemployment. The cosmological balance is shattered by radical social change.

Cosmological Diffraction in Changing Worlds

When their social world has changed so dramatically as to render an existing cosmology inapplicable or redundant, people have rarely turned agnostic and abandoned religion. Instead, they have formulated new religious ideologies, often of a confrontational type; or (especially in the case of world religions) they have adjusted their doctrines to accommodate these changes; or they have converted to entirely different belief systems which are regarded as more appropriate to their changed circumstances.

New Religions

New religions are constantly in the process of formation. They generally follow the pattern identified by Weber (1947) in which a charismatic leader (like Gautama, Christ, Mohammed) recruits believers on the basis of a vision of the future revealed to him (very rarely her) by a deity. Following the death of this leader, the group may also dissolve in squabbles over the succession. But if the competition to succeed is resolved, the organisation of ritual in this `sect´ becomes more `routinised´ and an official `church´ hierarchy emerges as a bureaucracy. Not all new religions of protest survive, to become the bastions of later traditions, but a surprising number do, even within the organisational confines of the world religions. Fundamentalist splinter sects are common in all world religions. Even more common are the syncretic, `millenarian´ movements founded by men with new educational, work and religious experiences but debarred from participating in colonial power structures. Millenarian visions among such men have foreseen the elimination of death, misfortune and despair from this earth, and the inauguration of sinless utopias, sometimes based on traditional ideals of social behaviour.

Such millenarian religions have characterised the colonial experiences of North America (where they were referred to as `nativistic´ movements) and Melanesia (`cargo cults´), as well as Africa (`independent churches´). Their prototype, as Engels (Marx-Engels 1975) and others have noted, existed in the Roman colonisation of biblical Palestine, where the self-educated son of a carpenter, who experienced his vision in the montane wilderness, challenged the rabbinical hierarchy. The colonial power was, as usual, instrumental in his crucifixion, though politically wiser than many later colonial regimes in

231

refusing to take responsibility for his martyrdom. Following his death, the millenarian nature of the early Christian communities was reflected in their belief in the imminence of his `second coming´. But like many other believers subsequently, Christians had to come to terms with the indefinite postponement of their millenium; with their later fractionation into eastern, coptic and catholic orthodoxies; and with their still later splintering into Russian and Greek, Egyptian and Ethiopian, catholic, protestant and fundamentalist fragments, and finally neo-Christian offshoots. Concerning its basic truths, Christianity became competitive within itself. Islam, divided into the orthodox Sunna (way or path, in turn differentiated by two forms of religious law) and the mystical Sufi orders, followed suit, in adapting unitary religious beliefs to the specific social needs of local communities. Many if not all `central´ religious orders, then, started life as millenarian protests in periods of social disturbance, and have also spawned such offshoots after their establishment.

Burridge (1969:6) has stressed the significance of what he called the redemptive process (by which social obligations are discharged) in the emergence of new religions. Salvation from the world of sin constitutes the ultimate form of redemption, and was often the only competitive sphere of prestige remaining open to colonised people. Where they could not aspire to social status, or to political authority, they could work toward their own salvation and the restoration of their social dignity, not least by the symbolic reversal of the order which demeaned them. (Funerals, in bringing redemption into direct confrontation with secular political reality, provide the most dramatic opportunities for such protest.)

Lawrence (1964) studied this process of religious construction in Madang district, New Guinea. He argued that the `cargo movement´ in this area had progressed through five cosmological phases, in which the precise content of the `cargo beliefs´ had changed. Fundamental to all of them, however, was the perception that `cargo´ (western commodities) could be obtained exclusively by ritual procedures. These beliefs must be seen against the background of a colonial experience, beginning in 1871, which included seven different administrations (two German, four Australian and one Japanese) and both catholic and protestant missionary activity. In these cargo beliefs, `the relationships between human beings, cargo deity, and ancestors were so defined as to establish the natives´ inalienable rights to the cargo´ (Lawrence 1964:235). The precise ways in which the different cargo beliefs established these claims, reflected the changing relationships, both hostile and friendly, between New Guineans and their colonial masters, but `the natives´ rights to the cargo were always

vindicated through their original association with the relevant deity´ (Lawrence 1964:239).

In their first cargo belief, in the late nineteenth century, New Guineans tried to fit the colonising strangers,
sometimes as incarnations of traditional deities, into their
own framework of behavioural assumptions and expectations. The
German colonists, who alienated land and demanded labour for
very little return, were finally seen not to be assimilable.
However, their manifest political and military power over
local society was then attributed to their control of the
supernatural powers, which produced the goods which they owned
in such abundance and were so unwilling to share. The second
cargo belief thus centred on the acquisition of guns, following the failure of the Madang Rebellion in 1904. In the third
phase, the Madang people converted to Christianity in order to
gain access to God (the cargo deity of this phase) who really
controlled these goods. Missions proliferated. In the fourth
stage, some Melanesian converts synthesised elements of their
traditional beliefs and behaviour with this new experience,
while rejecting Christianity itself. This fourth stage coin-
cided with the second world war and the New Guineans´ collaboration with the Japanese occupation. The displacement of white
colonisers by Japanese soldiers revealed the fragility of
colonial political control and fuelled the fifth phase of
development of millenarian protest afer the war, when extravagant demobilisation promises were not kept, even though post-
war reconstruction goods of all kinds arrived in profusion.

In all five phases of the movement, numerous prophets
emerged to organise ritual activity, in anticipation of the
arrival of the expected `cargo´. This ritual activity took the
form of the construction of ports and harbours to offload the
cargo expected by ship or aeroplane, and disciplined singing
drills based on military models. Sometimes these prophets took
advantage of the reputations of their precursors in earlier
phases. Sometimes their imprisonment enhanced their appeal.
When the cargoes failed to arrive on schedule, a few managed
to adjust their religious message to overcome the dashing of
millenial expectations among their followers, but most were
repudiated as `false prophets´. The history of recurrent mil-
lenarian failure, however, did not prevent new prophets from
emerging.

How should we explain such millenarian activity? As a
normal outlet for the frustrated leadership ambitions of individual prophets, cynically manipulating their gullible followers? As proto-political protest against colonial domination
and dehumanisation? As a metaphor, like that of sexual antagonism (with which it flourished contemporaneously), to talk

about the demise of the old social order?

Undoubtedly each of these possibilities has some explanatory attraction. But none of them begins to address the problem of why such mundanities should be clothed in language and concepts relating to the supernatural. We are back, once more, to the problem of why ideological mystification so often chooses a religious idiom. Lawrence (1964) noted that two points were important here: the lack of an alternative explanatory idiom; and Melanesian ignorance of the process of industrial production. While these aspects are undoubtedly important, they do not exhaust the possibilities. For example, did the leaders of cargo cults perhaps regard the religious idiom as relatively safe in the colonial context, since most people regard the violation of any sacred order as sinful, rather than merely criminal? If indeed they reasoned along these lines, it was probably a mistake, for, as Burridge (1969:34) has noted, `a powerful regime is a powerful regime. It can choose to ignore a little harmless excitement, it can also choose to obliterate it.´

Burridge (1969:56) instead argued that `millenarian activities force a tolerant regime out of its hypocrisy, compel it to take notice. Either the administration is forced to join the game - albeit in an oppositional role - or it must abdicate.´ In other words, a religious idiom may be chosen to emphasise the importance of transcending, as opposed to maintaining, existing social boundaries in situations of societal change. `The We/They opposition inherent in a colonial situation must resolve itself into Us: a single and synthesised total community´. We are back to issues of social control and manipulation in a Durkheimian mould.

Religious Adjustment

The second type of religious response to radical societal change is adjustive rather than confrontational. Gilsenan (1973) has recorded the historical development of the Hamadiyya Shadhiliyya order in Egypt, which provides a useful example of such controlled adjustment. Egypt is largely an Islamic country, but in North Africa Muslim fundamentalism has long been regarded with grave suspicion. Following the 1981 assassination of President Anwar Sadat, in which fundamentalists were implicated, the state proscription of Sufi-type mystical activity completed its prior slow decline, notwithstanding the emergence of new sects in the early twentieth century.

Established in the late nineteenth century and formally recognised as a Sufi brotherhood in 1926, by the mid-1960s the

Hamadiyya Shadhiliyya order had some 16,000 adherents from all social classes. Although Gilsenan (1973:7) described the order as `the most highly organised and active group in Egypt´, its membership was in fact concentrated in the towns and cities of the Nile delta. Unlike other Sufi orders, the Hamadiyya Shadhiliyya maintained and expanded its religious influence during the transformation of Egyptian agrarian society by the processes of urbanisation, mass state education, and proletarianisation. Whereas in the countryside, after the fall of the monarchy, Sufi sheikhs lost their land to the peasant fellahin and their religious influence to the Sunni ulema (priests), the Hamadiyya Shadhiliyya order flourished in an urban environment which was never traditionally hospitable to Sufism.

The founding saint, Salama ibn Hassan Salama, was himself born, in 1867, in one of Cairo´s poorer areas. Like many charismatic religious leaders, he came from a poor but spiritually impeccable lineage, and saw to his own religious education. Diligent but apparently unambitious, he nonetheless rose in the social hierarchy to become a senior bureaucrat. Ascetic in his lifestyle and revered as holy by all who knew him, Salama devoted his main life´s work to establishing his order under the visionary command of Allah, and to the religious teaching necessary for proselytisation. He is remembered as a miracle-worker, whose religious learning often stumped the ulema. Following his death in 1939, he was succeeded as leader or sheikh by one of his sons.

Once established, Salama´s saintly charisma was routinised and codified in the organisation of the order, while being retained in the annual celebration of his mulid (saint´s day) by both male and female followers. (Women were, in contrast, strictly excluded from the normal ritual of the dhikr or prayer meeting.) During Gilsenan´s fieldwork in the mid-1960s, more than 80 tents celebrated Salama´s mulid in fine and very expensive style. This celebration played an important role in unifying the order, as well as marking the internal socio-economic differentiation among its members (muridin).

The sheikh himself, as religious and administrative head of the order, was assisted by his deputy and the members of the order´s central office. These officials had been promoted from earlier leadership of the local chapters or lodges of the order, the zawiya. They approximated `an unpaid managerial class´ (Gilsenan 1973:81) and protected the sheikh´s personal propriety and reputation by administering the financial and judicial affairs of the order. In the early days, the sheikh personally appointed his officials. More recently, in the bureaucratisation of the order, changed rules disqualified all hereditary succession to office, in order to emphasise the principles of unity and equality among all _muridin_ in the order.

The Hamadiyya Shadhiliyya, like other Sufi orders, was divided into local chapters, each headed by a _khalifa_, subordinate and responsible to the _sheikh_. All communication from the _sheikh_ to his followers went through the _khalifa_, through whom in turn the individual devotee (_murid_) took his oath of allegiance to the _sheikh_. The chapters, in accordance with the order's fundamental postulate of equality among _muridin_, resolved disputes and adjudicated religious lapses among their members. In illness, misfortune or personal difficulties, fellow-_muridin_ in the _zawiya_ were obliged to visit and assist a member. Should a member move elsewhere, he would be received into a new _zawiya_ with its ready-made social network. Local chapters of this religious order thus performed similar functions to those that, as we have already seen, have in other African cities been performed by ethnic associations.

Unlike other orders, the Hamadiyya Shadhiliyya did not permit its devotees to belong to any other order at the same time. It was an exclusive organisation, in which the Sufi objective of mystic union with Allah had moved away from the tradition of emotional, individualised, religious ecstasy and toward the orthodox Sunna (way or path) based on the Shari`a (the holy law of the Quran). Behaviour at the _dhikr_ or prayer meeting was strictly orthodox. In contrast to the Sufi traditions of mystic routes to communion with Allah, no dancing, ecstatic singing or other forms of possession behaviour were permitted. A member who appeared to be in danger of losing his self-control was immediately disciplined by sect officials and, if necessary, was physically removed from the _dhikr_. At one point Gilsenan (1973:154) referred to the Hamadiyya Shadhiliyya as `an orthodox Sunni _tariqa_` - a very neat, if somewhat confusing, way of sign-posting the degree to which this order had adjusted its ritual behaviour, both to appeal to the middle-class sensibilities of many of its adherents and to the state expectations of orthodoxy and control.

Religious Conversion

Finally, religious conversion may act as a mechanism for coping with radical social change. Horton (1971) has argued that the ethics of the `macrocosmic` world religions, which stress universal brotherhood, provide a morality that is more useful in relating to strangers than the limited and specific categories offerred by `microcosmic` local religions as idioms for explaining social relationships. Conversion to world religions should therefore be expected among those interacting regularly with the outside world, but will occur less frequently among people whose lives remain rooted in the local environment. Horton's reasoning has perhaps found some support from Southern African data. For the early 1960s, Murphree (1969: 119) reported, with some suprise, a mere 30 per cent adherence to Christian denominations in a community 120 kilometres from the Zimbabwean capital, Harare, on the road to Malawi. In the same period, Hammond-Tooke (1970) noted among the Xhosa people living in Grahamstown, South Africa, a fall in their attribution of misfortune to witchcraft, compared to rural Xhosa. However, there was no difference between these urban and rural communities when it came to attributing causation to their ancestors.

Perhaps the major problem with Horton's argument is that it assumes conversion to be a permanent, once-off affair. It does not allow for what might be called `conglomerate beliefs' in different religions simultaneously, nor for temporary conversions for limited time periods and specific reasons, nor for numerous, sequential changes of religious affiliation. All these patterns are very common, in Melanesia, Africa, and most other parts of the world. In his study of the Shona-speaking Budjga of the Tsutskwe valley, for example, Murphree (1969: 151) described `contemporary Budjga religion' as `the complete religious spectrum', comprising the Methodist and Catholic denominations of orthodox Christianity; the Vapostori weMaranke, a routinised and centralised independent sect over fifty years old, having congregations in at least five central African countries; and the traditional panoply of beliefs in Mwari (the high god), the <u>mhondoro</u> spirits of deceased chiefs, the <u>midzimu</u> ancestral spirits, the dangerous and aggrieved <u>ngozi</u>, the foreign <u>shawe</u> spirits, and witchcraft.

Although the three Christian denominations in Tsutskwe were in one sense competitors among themselves, as well as with the apparently much more successful traditional belief system, Murphree regarded all four as complementary within the community. In a sense, the Methodists provided the entry-point to Christianity, among the young generation, in their provision of primary and secondary schooling, while the Vapostori, precisely because they did not control any educational facilities, lost their children, if only temporarily, to those who did. Each religion regarded at least some of its competitors as apostate, inferior, misguided, outmoded, worldly, permissive, or over-emotional (but not all together). Each denomination therefore tried to enforce its own redemptive rules. Each tried to isolate itself from association with the others, by specific rules of consumption (especially of alcohol and tobacco) and of dress, and by encouraging religious endogamy. But each also provided different services, ritual or material, to the community, notably in the fields of education, health, agricultural advice and brokerage. Their complementarity was seen, for example, in their differing attitudes to certain types of behaviour. So the Catholic church recruited smoking and drinking ex-Methodists, while the Vapostori welcomed polygynists from both, and traditional doctors (n'angas) tended all those who had seen no improvement in their condition of ill-health from western medical treatment. Individual Budjga pragmatically manipulated these inter-denominational differences to meet their own changing social and religious needs.

In the context of colonial administration and a rapidly-monetising economy, fuelled by labour migration to local farms and especially to Harare, the Budjga came to terms with these changes by multiple religious conversions. Their religious system was characterised by heterodoxy, mobility and interdependence among its constituent and nominally competitive parts. Budjga reasons for adhering first to one and then to another set of beliefs and ritual action, included the inherent attractiveness of the beliefs themselves and the corporate religious life that different churches offerred. But perhaps the more important reasons for conversion were specific and instrumental. Considerations of gaining entrance to a specific school, or access to health facilities; of diminishing potential disagreements in marriage by taking on one's husband's religion; of fulfilling traditional obligations; and even of gender (the Methodists were overwhelmingly women) were crucial motivating factors in patterns of conversion. Unfortunately, Murphree collected no hard figures for the extent of multiple conversion among the Budjga, but his impression was that it occurred quite frequently.

Faced with this array of alternative religious truths on their local doorstep, the sensible Budjga response, as one man noted, was `to believe it all´ (Murphree 1969:132)! In the context of a rapidly-changing society, these alternatives not only offerred different means of making sense of the world. They also opened up the possibility, through their manipulability, that individuals might gain increased control over both the material and non-material worlds affecting themselves. Control, in the context of ideology and its manipulation, is not simply a `top-down´ phenomenon. Ideologies also enable individuals to exert varying degrees of control over their own lives, though not without interference from outsiders, including the state.

CHAPTER ELEVEN

IDEOLOGY AND THE STATE

In the last chapter, we examined the main social functions of ideology. We saw that systematised values which
structure social action have an instrumental explanatory and
theoretical significance, as well as expressing emotional
feelings (particularly through ritual) and satisfying aesthetic needs. Ideology, then, like religion, is what it does in
society (Evans-Pritchard 1965). Ritual action, in turn, may
assume a religious or secular form in creating social consen-
sus, and/or managing social conflict, to achieve societal integration. Secular ideology and ritual, however, unlike their
religious counterparts, generally do not address existential
issues that give meaning to death, as well as to life. They
create a longer permanence than the individual life-span, but
secular rites deal in social continuity rather than in human
immortality.

It is tempting, therefore, to use ideology as a tool for
engineering social change. Saint-Simon tried this in industrialising France in the 1820s, but after his death his secularised religious movement became the nineteenth-century equivalent of a hippy cult and rapidly collapsed in immoral dis-
array. Nearly a century later, Durkheim (1912/1915) regarded
such attempts to reform society using ideological methods as
doomed to failure. Religion, in his view, was the social product of the collective consciousness and could not be made to
order by individuals for a secular agenda of societal reform.
For different reasons, Marx also rejected the idea that ideology could be used as a mechanism for societal reform. In his
view, religious ideology mystified the existing class relations and preserved the status quo of social control. It was
therefore necessary first to demystify religion, as a conservative force in society, before attempting revolutionary political action to change society. Marx´s view, held even more
vigorously by Lenin, has informed governmental attitudes, if
not always their policies, to the thorny area of church-state
relations in socialist countries.

It is to the relationships between ideologies and states,
then, that we now turn. In church-state relations, religion
and politics may be related in a number of different ways. At
one polar extreme they may co-exist independently of one another. At the other extreme, they may be fused in what Marx
(Marx-Engels 1975:33) called the `theocratic state´. Between
these two extremes lie various possibilities for unilateral or
mutual manipulation, confrontation and accommodation. In this

239

chapter, I shall examine three examples from this range: the manipulation of religion by the state to create civil religion; the creation of secular ideology (what Lane (1981) has called `political religion'); and the rejection of state authority by religious organisations. We must start, however, by expanding our acquaintance with marxist views on religion.

Marx and Engels, like Durkheim, saw religion as refracting the social world, but in addition as reflecting man's alienation from both that world and himself.
`Man makes religion, religion does not make man. Religion is the self-consciousness and self-esteem of man who has either not yet found himself or has already lost himself again ... The struggle against religion is therefore indirectly a fight against <u>the world</u> ...
<u>Religious</u> distress is at the same time the <u>expression</u> of real distress and also the <u>protest</u> against real distress. Religion is the sigh of the oppressed creature ... It is the <u>opium</u> of the people ...
Religion can continue to exist as the sentimental form of men's relations to the alien, natural and social, forces which dominate them, so long as men remain under the control of these forces' (Marx-Engels 1975:38,39,129).
The problem in demystifying this situation, as Marx and Engels saw it, was that religions uniformly enjoined submission to authority and passive sufferance of human distress. Our consideration of millenarian movements and peripheral cults in the previous chapter, however, suggests that religion may also act as a form of socio-political protest.

Ideology as False Consciousness?

Part of the marxist problem in interpreting religion, was its fundamentally evolutionist approach. Marx deplored its inhumanity, while seeing industrial capitalism as essential to further social progress. He and Engels regarded Christianity, a highly sophisticated religion, as the logical corollary of the capitalist mode of production. Before Max Weber's (1904-5) thesis that the `protestant ethic' provided the ideological spur to the development of mercantile capitalism, Marx (1885/1978) had already seen a link between calvinist asceticism and the work ethic, and the requirements of industrial work discipline. In Marx's historicist view, however, it was inevitable that capitalism would be replaced by socialism and Christianity by a scientific outlook on the world. Nonetheless, Engels in particular spent considerable time on understanding religious issues (including the analysis of biblical materials and attending seances at which English and American women became possessed by spirits). He concluded, on the basis of his research, that the demise of religion had to be natural. Far from assisting its death, proscription and persecution would give religion a new lease on life (Marx-Engels 1975:130). The falsity of religious belief, therefore, had to be demonstrated rationally to open people's eyes to its mystificatory nature. Re-education of the congregation might hasten the exit of religion, whereas its legal banning and the imprisonment of priests were likely to have the opposite effect. As we shall see later, impatient governments have often ignored Engels' warnings.

Before proceeding, however, we should examine carefully this interpretation of (religious) ideologies as the false consciousness peddled by the ruling class to ensure the compliance of workers in their own oppression. Among the major problems of this approach, the following criticisms have been levelled against it. Firstly, many ideologies have been formulated by social categories that even marxists do not regard as classes: black power, women's liberation, various cultural nationalisms. Secondly, if only the dominant or ruling class can manufacture ideologies, how did marxism happen? Thirdly, if the ideological legitimation of a social order is by definition `false´, in its reflection of the interests of the ruling class, what is the status of counter-ideologies (such as `scientific socialism´) which are used to legitimise new and revolutionary social orders? Fourthly, if people believe in an ideology, for them it cannot be subjectively false. By what criteria, then, should we judge the `objectivity´ of outsiders´ denunciations of that ideology as `false´?

To some extent, these criticisms may be regarded as inappropriate. Marx, after all, saw law as mediating between ideological false consciousness and the real world, and law was enacted and administered by ancillaries of the ruling class. If we insert law between ideology and the world, the problems of false consciousness are subordinated to legal enforcement. But then we are faced with people's defiance of the law when it conflicts with their ideological beliefs, and there is still a problem in conceptualising ideology as false consciousness based on class.

That there is an element of mystification in ideologies of all kinds, no social scientist would dispute. In previous chapters we have encountered numerous examples of such mystification and examined its social origins, including (in the case of the Giriama) inter-generational conflict. Between the adjacent or proximate generations of parents and their children, relations are tense and formal in all societies (often, especially in patrilineal systems, more tense and more formal with the father than with the mother). In contrast, grandpar-

241

ents all over the world have a reputation for `spoiling´ the alternate generation of their grandchildren. Radcliffe-Brown (1950) was the first to identify the structural cause of this conflict. Children replace their parents in society. Not only do parents shoulder the responsibility of bringing up their children as civilised human beings. They also face the prospect of being eased out of their positions of authority by their own children, who are their social replacements. Their grandchildren, in contrast, constitute a preliminary guarantee of their social immortality (but great-grandchildren, of the adjacent generation once removed, are an uncomfortable reminder that physical death is close at hand).

The `generation gap´, then, is a permanent ideological feature of social organisation everywhere. And it has a particular mystificatory significance in times of radical social and political change, when parental ideologies are threatened by those of their upstart children. Later in this chapter, we shall examine three contexts of radical societal change - the creation of new states, political revolution, and colonisation - in which this ideological cleavage has particular significance. But first it is necessary to outline certain aspects of the relationships linking ideology with social and political identity.

The Ideological Construction of Ethnicity and Nationality

The socialisation process, as we saw in chapter 6, normally reproduces culture as a going concern. Here cultural or ethnic identity may be regarded as coterminous with nationality (Argyle 1969; Lewis 1976). But where political boundaries are irrelevant to defining this ethnic or national identity, it may be re-emphasised by the use of religious ideological markers. When their trade monopoly was threatened in Yoruba country, the Hausa saw fit to protect it by stressing their cultural exclusiveness; and they did so with reference to their Islamic distinctiveness as adherents of the Tijaniyya order. In opposing colonial domination, Kenyatta (1938) defined Gikuyu identity as resting fundamentally on the life-crisis rituals of initiation. In the period of political confrontation between black and white which culminated in Southern Rhodesia´s illegal unilateral declaration of independence in 1965, educated Zezuru Christians were prominently among those who became successful mediums for traditional spirits in the countryside (Fry 1976). Following the Soviet acquisition of the Baltic states of Latvia, Lithuania and Estonia in 1940, affiliation to the Lutheran and Mennonite denominations emphasised the cultural distinctiveness of German-speaking Latvians, while Catholicism became the hallmark of Lithuanian identity. And throughout the Soviet Union, particularly in non-Russian areas, baptism into the Orthodox church seems to have been used to distinguish the Russians from other Soviet citizens, as well as deferring to the religious feelings of parents and grandparents (Lane 1978).

From these disparate examples, a common pattern emerges. In general, religious affiliation may be used instrumentally to stress specific cultural identity, in colonial situations for example, or where cultural differentiation is otherwise diminishing. More particularly, life-crisis rituals are unique ethnic markers, on which cultural nationalism may feed. Cultural nationalism thus appears to be not merely an ideological phenomenon, but a specifically religious one. We see this most prominently in what Aronoff (1981) has called `civil religion´ in Israel, where the state as a political entity has used the historical traditions and religious symbols of Judaism, to create a national identity for Israelis of differing cultural backgrounds.

Civil Religion: The State Use of Religion

Israel is a new state, created amid much controversy in 1948 from part of the mandated remains of the Turkish empire, dismembered after the first world war. The immediate spur to the creation of Israel by the European powers lay in the Holocaust of war-torn Europe, in which some six million Jews were killed in the concentration camps of Hitler´s `final solution´. The displacement of the Palestinians to accommodate Israel subsequently created a not-dissimilar moral horror, as immigrants to the new state displaced the indigenous land-owning population.

Israel was born in conflict, as the militant Jews in Palestine fought for their independence. Subsequently her own actions have escalated rather than diminished conflict in the region and contributed to Israel´s insecurity. Yet faith in their ultimate return to the promised land, from which they were dispersed nearly two millenia ago following the Roman destruction of the second temple, has attracted into Israel some two million Jews of widely differing cultural backgrounds from the Middle East, North Africa, both Eastern and Western Europe, Asia and the new world. Civil religion has provided a mechanism for the incorporation of these culturally diverse immigrants into the new nation-state.

Aronoff (1981) placed `civil religion´ somewhere between secularised ideology and the fusion of transcendantal religion with politics (in some form of `divine kingship´ or theocratic state). Civil religion is `a special type of dominant ideolo-gical superstructure which is rooted in religion´ (Aronoff 1981:2), but which is not overtly religious. In Israel, civil religion appeals particularly to non-religious Jews (compris-ing at least two-thirds of the Jewish population) who reject Judaism as a vehicle to express in symbolic terms their Jewish ethnicity. Civil religion thus enables Jews of widely differ-ing political and religious persuasions to share common cultu-ral symbols, based on but extending beyond their shared reli-gious history.

It is significant that, as Webber (1981) has noted, reli-gious language and symbols played no part in legitimating the establishment of the Israeli state. The war of independence `was generally characterised as a secular victory which solved a secular problem´ (Webber 1981:8). Civil religion emerged later, in the process of socialising the second generation of Israeli-born sabras, who experienced some conflict of loyalty between the society in which they were raised and the foreign cultures of their immigrant parents.

The shared symbols of Israeli cultural identity have dif-ferent ideological meanings for the numerous social categories to which they appeal. Like all symbols, they are sufficiently general to allow for numerous specific interpretations. As Lane (1981:42) put it, `the content of civil religion is at such a high level of generality that it conflicts neither with conventional religious nor with political norms and values´. These symbols are thus compatible with, but emphatically not the same as, Zionism as a political agenda for territorial expansion. Civil religion in Israel is neither Judaism nor Zionism in a different form, even though those to whom it has little appeal are predominantly agnostic and non- or anti-Zionist in their political philosophies. Civil religion is equally rejected, as heretical, by those ultra-religious Jews who, like Jehovah´s Witnesses, reject the authority of any secular state, even when the expansionist state of Israel acts fully in accordance with their biblical zealotry.

The content of Israeli civil religion, then, has both religious and secular origins and referents. The specifically religious symbolism is expressed in and through the Hebrew language, and revolves around shrines (such as the Western or Wailing Wall in Jerusalem) which symbolise Judaic redemption. The mythological elements of Jewish civil and military history are partly religious and partly secular. Finally, the commem-oration of the Holocaust and the system of public holidays are secular, but refer back to religious issues. It is therefore difficult (using Durkheim´s approach) to separate the closely-interwoven sacred and secular elements of civil religion.

The historical exile, for example, following the fall of Jerusalem in 70 AD, has been combined with the religious belief in redemption through return to the holy land, to construct the concepts of immigration to Israel as a religious calling (<u>aliyah</u>) and emigration as a fall from grace (<u>yorida</u>). We see here the use of linguistic symbolism, in addition to myth and history, to create concepts relating to symbolic national identity. Hebrew, formerly the language purely of ritual, has been rejuvenated as the official language of the Israeli state, and therefore lends itself particularly well to such dual religious and secular signification.

Conversely, secular militarism has been invested with ritual significance by its association with Jewish military history, in the legendary, self-sacrificing defence of Jewish religious identity. Elite units are sworn into the Israeli army `in special torchlit rites atop Masada, the fortress in the Judean desert where Jewish zealots resisted the might of the Roman legions in a revolt which culminated in their mass suicide´ (Aronoff 1981:4). Similarly, secular public holidays celebrate former Jewish holy days.

The diaspora years, from 70 - 1948 AD, appear as an odd historical gap in Israeli civil religion, almost as though they never existed. `The remote past is closer than the past 2,000 years´, as premier Ben-Gurion noted: there has been `a leap in history´ (Paine 1983:20). Paine (1983) has called this telescoping of the present into the remote past, totemic time. Elsewhere, Bloch (1977) has referred to a similar phenomenon as ritual time. The present is encapsulated in the past, but re-enacted as the timeless present through religious ritual. (The use of the ethnographic present tense in anthropological analysis similarly destroys a sense of history.)

In Israel, archaeology (as part of the structure of civil religion) has sometimes served as the vehicle for such encapsulation of the present in the past. An example may be seen in the state funeral rather belatedly accorded to remains alleged to be those of the followers of Shimon Bar-Kochba, who died in their millenarian revolt against Rome in the second century AD. This example highlights the difficulties of creating the components of civil religion. In describing this affair, Paine (1983) drew attention to the conflicts among Israeli archaeologists pursuing scientific knowledge, Israeli politicians seeking additional legitimation, and ultra-orthodox Zionists. At the reburial, Menachem Begin, then prime minister, sought additional legitimation for the expansion of the Israeli state by linking Shimon Bar-Kochba´s revolt to the `liberation and unification´ of Jerusalem. (Following the 1967 war, Israel had annexed the Jordanian sector of Jerusalem.) But the site archaeologists had refused to certify the bones concerned as Jewish, never mind those of Bar-Kochba and his followers; the ultra-orthodox refused to endorse the status of one whom they had always regarded as a false messiah; and some Zionist politicians were worried about the political motivation of the rebels. The scientific facts, the symbolism, and the political identity of these ancient bones were all disputed. The archaeologists and two different types of Zionist therefore boycotted the reburial of the bones, presided over by the chief rabbi, the president and the prime minister; and the attempted falsification of history by the misuse of science in the interests of politics became a matter for heated discussion in the Israeli press.

The ideological boundary constructed by civil religion thus encapsulates most Israelis in their newly-constructed national identity. However, inevitably it defines as `other´ that minority which does not accept its starting premisses. Israeli civil religion does not incorporate into a common national identity, anti-Zionist Jews, or Muslim and Christian Arabs who hold citizenship in the Israeli state on the basis of their own religious identities in the millet system inherited from the Ottoman Empire. These minorities are alienated by Israeli civil religion. `The semiotics of the sacred´, to use Paine´s (1983:22) phrase, do not merely divide Israeli citizens by their constructed religious identities. These boundaries also render civil-religious communities literally and figuratively invisible to one another.

The city of Jerusalem, for example, is holy to the three world faiths of Judaism, Christianity and Islam. Jerusalem is the Jewish city of Solomon´s temple, the Wailing Wall, Mount Zion and the Museum of the Book, housing the Dead Sea Scrolls. Jerusalem is also the Christian city in which Christ was crucified, and the Muslim city from where Mohammed, the prophet of Allah, ascended to heaven. It is the focus of international pilgrimage, in three different religious idioms, which continually authenticates its holy status. Yet, although all the shrines of these different pilgrimages appear on tourist maps of the city, Webber (1981) has pointed out that there are few holy places that are common to the three religions, and few mythologies shared among them. The shrines of each religion are located in different areas of the city, occupied by the different religious communities. This spatial separation is heightened by the fact that the pilgrimage routes are discrete and generally do not cross one another. Hence it is empirically, as well as ideologically, possible for the Jerusalem resident (who does not use tourist maps) to see only the religious community to which he or she belongs. The invisibility of others has on occasion been assisted by the state. Following the 1967 Israeli annexation of the Jordanian part of the city, for example, the Wailing Wall was restored to `Jewish´ status by demolishing its immediate surrounds (including a minor Muslim shrine) and relocating the Arab residents elsewhere. As Webber (1981:10) has remarked, Judaism has always `preferred to express its central concepts in geographical terms´, and to a considerable extent Israeli civil religion has followed suit.

Secular Ideology: Socialist State against Religion

The Soviet strategy in reconstructing the relationship between politics and religion has inverted Israeli socialist syncretism. Although it contains a much wider range of religions than Israel, including Russian Orthodoxy as well as Protestant and Catholic churches, together with Judaism, Islam, Buddhism, and ancient `shamanistic´ practices based on spirit possession, the USSR is officially an atheistic state. Ever since its inception in 1917, the Soviet state has recurrently sought, not to use to religion to construct a national identity, but to dispense with religion altogether. In seeking to supplant religion, the state has invented tradition. Since the 1930s, the state has created and managed Soviet culture as an integrated system of both ideological institutions (law, the dramatic arts, religion) and social relationships. This ritual management has expanded dramatically since the 1960s. To comprehend why, we must examine some history.

Prior to 1917, the Russian Orthodox church had been the established church in Czarist Russia and had claimed the religious affiliation of 95 per cent of the people. Indeed, until a decree of 1905, other religions had been prohibited. Following the accession to state power of a militantly atheistic government, in 1918 a new decree permitted all forms of religious and non-religious observance. In practice the anti-religious lobby had the upper hand, although minority religions benefitted from the disestablishment of the Orthodox church. Over the next fifty-odd years, the Soviet Union experienced four phases of religious suppression (1918-22, 1928-34, 1937-41, and 1957-64), alternating with periods of relative laxity.

In the first clamp-down, during the post-war years of `war communism´, the Orthodox church was hit hardest by the state expropriation, without compensation, of its land and property and the liquidation of its monasteries. But all clergy were disenfranchised and all education (religious and secular) by all religious organisations was prohibited. Militantly atheistic communist youth ridiculed religious ritual and occasionally desecrated the places of worship of their elders. Jews, traditionally the victims of the pogroms, were singled out as special targets for propoganda to discredit their faith; while the Catholics drew particular attention to themselves by refusing to hand over their church property to the state. In the areas of Central Asia rent by the civil war, however, Islam and Buddhism were tolerated, and in the west the tiny protestant denominations expanded their influence. But by the end of this period of civil war, even Islam had been redefined as having, like Christianity, a class essence; and clergy of all faiths had been charged with sedition on the grounds of their occupation. Binns (1979) has noted that the contemporary system of secular festivals originated in this period. In 1918, the calendar was reformed, the Christmas holiday was removed and many of its festive customs transferred to the new `new year´, and revolutionary Bolshevik history was celebrated in dramatic re-enactments. These mass dramas relied on the military conscription of artistes in this era of proletkul´t (proletarian culture).

With the return to some semblance of economic normality under the New Economic Policy in 1921, anti-religious persecution abated and gave way to the first concerted effort to re-educate people. Under Trotsky´s influence with the Komsomol or Communist Youth League, obryadnost´ (a word signifying ritual and symbolism, originally associated with Orthodoxy but later extended to secular ceremonial) met expressive and aesthetic needs in an attempt to replace dependence on religion and alcohol to relieve life´s monotony. `Red weddings´ and `red christianings´, though they lasted only a few years, set the tone for the secularised celebration of all life-crises. Numerous organisations, such as the League of the Godless, also published atheist literature, and the Communist Party of the USSR stressed its `scientific´ orientation to socialism.

But with Trotsky´s exiling in 1927, and Stalin´s emphasis in the first five-year plan on agricultural collectivisation and rapid industrial growth to stimulate the economy, religious suppression was renewed in a new decree in 1928. By 1929, `being religious was being equated with being a class enemy and an opponent of the revolution´ (Lane 1981:175). The position of the clergy worsened still further. All religious `groups´ had to be registered with the state in order to function, and many churches, mosques and Buddhist monasteries were closed. The working week was staggered to remove Sunday as the regular day of rest, and Christmas and Easter celebrations were banned. For half a decade the lack of religious festivities reflected the economic sobriety and the human death toll of the first five-year plan.

In the mid-1930s, there was a brief thaw in the state´s

attitude to religious observance. The celebration of Christmas and Easter resumed. Over the next decade, the state introduced a number of festive days to honour occupations critical to economic modernisation and state security (in railway transport, mining and all branches of the armed services). Later, under Krushchev, these commemorative days would be extended to include many other categories of worker. But in the wake of the 1936 constitution came the purges. The clergy of the minority religions, especially Islam and Catholicism, were prosecuted with renewed vigour. In the east, Buddhist lamas and monks stood accused of collaboration with the Japanese who, from 1937, overran much of the Korean peninsula as well as Northern China, and threatened Vladivostok.

But after 1941, when the USSR was drawn into the second world war on the western front, church-state relations altered. After assuming responsibility for the predominantly Catholic and Lutheran populations of the Baltic states in 1940, the USSR restored Sunday as the normal rest day. After Hitler's troops invaded the USSR in mid-1941, religious organisations stressed their patriotic support for both the state and the communist party in the war effort. Clerics spoke in favour of the defence of the motherland from their pulpits. Substantial monies were donated to the prosecution of the war by religious congregations: 300 million roubles came from the Orthodox church alone. The state responded in conciliatory fashion and itself used Bolshevik rites and memorials to boost military morale. In November 1941, for example, troops marched past Lenin's mausoleum en route to the defence of Moscow. This rapprochement between state and religious organisations lasted throughout the war. By 1945, the Orthodox church had been able to elect a patriarch to the 20-year-old vacancy, Muslims were permitted once more to undertake the hajj pilgrimage to Mecca, and protestant denominations had achieved a measure of unity. The following year Uniat Catholics merged with the Orthodox church, although other Catholic rites remained out of favour.

This period of accommodation lasted until shortly after Stalin's death in 1953. It was interrupted in the late 1940s by an explicit reaffirmation of the Soviet state's dislike of religion, and new attempts to discredit religious leaders of various beliefs. Greater attention was paid to removing children from religious influence. Membership in the Komsomol was restricted to adolescents of atheist parents who declared themselves atheist too. Christianity, in particular, was again attacked as a mode of class oppression, as the state pressures against religion built up once more. Although Krushchev, mindful of Engels, personally argued that `administrative´ action against religion was both `stupid´ and counter-productive, the late-1950s under his leadership saw the fourth wave of state action to suppress religious observance. Anti-religious propagandist organisations again proliferated, this time making use of film as an important new medium; bakeries were forbidden to bake unleavened matzot bread for the Jewish population; pilgrimages were forbidden; places of worship were closed; clergy were morally vilified; and the Institute of Scientific Atheism was founded. But perhaps most interestingly, the state began to replace religious rites, especially life-crisis rites of passage, with socially significant and aesthetically-satisfying secular equivalents.

Before we examine these new secular rites, we should understand the impact of the four periods of religious suppression. Figures suggest that all religions, except Islam, suffered dramatic falls in adherents, clergy, and places of worship in the five decades after the 1917 revolution. Orthodox believers, for example, dropped from 100 million to 30 million, mainly elderly and uneducated women of peasant or worker families. Catholic communicants fell from 11 to 4 million. Thousands of places of worship were destroyed, and the number of clergy fell dramatically in all faiths. Of the pre-revolutionary figure of 16,000 Buddhist lamas, for example, some 300 remained by 1962. In 1961, the Orthodox church claimed only 20,000 of its nearly 55,000 churches fifty years earlier (Conquest 1968:11,64,81,98,129). In contrast, figures showed 30 million Muslims in the 1960s, compared to 16 million before the revolution. These figures reflected the high population growth rate among Muslims. Whether they also reflected religious adherence, or merely ethnicity in a recording system that defined certain minority groups as Islamic, is uncertain. But whatever our reservations about the figures available, it seems likely that there was also a definite decline in religious observance and adherence in post-revolutionary Soviet society. Certainly the lack of religious facilities and personnel led to the relaxation of biblical injunctions against female church assistants, to the growth among peasant women of folk religious practices far removed from high church orthodoxy, and to the growth of scepticism about an after-life.

Notwithstanding the decline of organised religion, however, by the 1960s the performance of religious rites still marked a majority of all births and deaths in many areas. In addition, partly in response to the diminished religious facilities available, the practice of sending earth from the grave by post to a priest to be blessed, had become very widespread (Lane 1978:41). Lane points out that these `funeral rites by correspondence´ allowed for the secret observance of religious rites in the face of public (that is, party) disapproval. Only marriage, of all the life-crises, had by the 1960s been definitively secularised. Less than a quarter of all marriages, in areas of differing religious adherence, were celebrated with religious ritual. So the state decision to provide secular alternatives to the life-crisis rituals was a logical and rational one.

However, the reasons why the Soviet state extended its interest to the field of ritual, in Lane´s (1981) view, went beyond a simple desire to replace religious rituals. Certainly the state management of ritual provided an opportunity to emphasise citizens´ loyalty to and identification with the state, by switching the focus of ritual solemnity from religious to state shrines and sacra (oaths, monuments, eternal flames, the national flag and anthem). However, the expansion of state ritual came two generations after the 1917 revolution and drew into a new relationship with the state the post-war younger generation. They had been protected from the privation experienced by their parents, but the state had difficulty in meeting their demands for higher levels of material consumption. In this context, the systematised management of ritual, by the state, structured the relations of power between rulers and ruled. Ritual legitimised the existing order and constructed the people´s perception of social reality, through the inculcation of norms and values desired by the party and through the communication of approved social knowledge.

Party attempts to provide secular alternatives to the religious observance of the life-crisis rituals were initiated in the early 1950s by the Komsomol in the religious `western fringe´ of the Ukraine, Byelo-Russia and the Baltic states (Binns 1980:173). They were designed to counter anomic and deviant behaviour as well as to provide an expressive outlet for people´s emotions. The first purpose-built wedding palace was opened in Leningrad late in 1959. Since then, thousands of ceremonial `palaces´ of different types have been constructed and staffed by specially-trained state officials. They provide facilities free of charge to celebrate naming, coming-of-age, marriage and family anniversaries. Similarly purpose-built facilities at cemeteries exist for secular funerals. Ritual experts, assisted by members of the party, Komsomol, trades unions and soviets - but not creative artists, who have voiced strong disapproval of this manipulation - continue to conduct extensive research and experimentation to fit ritual forms to the requirements of the ordinary people who perform them. They have undoubtedly enjoyed a considerable measure of success in creating satisfying rituals. But the persistence of `funerals by post´ and the private religious blessing of newly-weds before they proceed to the wedding ceremony (Lane 1981:250), suggests that the full secularisation of life-crisis ritual is sill some way off in the Soviet Union.

Life-crises cover only one of four main areas of ritual management in the USSR. Other rites include those initiating individuals into educational institutions, citizenship, and collective work units; the orchestrated mass politico-military celebrations of revolutionary holidays (1 May and 7 November being the most important) together with labour rituals; and anniversary commemorations and seasonal holidays (prazdniki). Of particular interest in an atheist state is the pivotal importance in these rituals of Lenin, as both saint and culture hero, encapsulating symbolically the essence of Soviet revolutionary, patriotic and labour ideals. His mausoleum in Red Square, Moscow, is the focus of national pilgrimage, although he abjured heroic status during his lifetime and his enbalming was not originally intended to be permanent. But, like Shimon Bar-Kochba, Lenin was powerless to prevent the posthumous political manipulation of his persona.

Lane (1981) and Binns (1979, 1980) have both remarked on the increasing ritualisation of a society ostensibly dedicated to demystifying social and political relationships. Perhaps this paradox is related to the passage of the generations in a state now seventy years old. The founding generation idealised internationalism and laid a tentative foundation for the ritual commemoration of its own historical achievements. Their children, who fought the second world war, were, in contrast, more concerned to construct a sense of national patriotism. To this end they rejected the ritualism of the Orthodox and Russian traditions. They allowed ethnic differences to be symbolised, while enforcing Soviet nationality, in part by referring further back in time to the historical highlights of the imperial Czarist unification of greater Russia. Their children in turn were raised as citizens of the established Soviet state, and received the `relay baton´ of their parents´ national achievements, in the form of the numerous and artistically very striking war memorials. In turn, their concern with their own more parochial identities has been reflected in the Komsomol role in initiating and helping to devise locally-adapted secular rituals. The third generation has thus finally implemented the early ritual concerns of their grandparents, the generation of state founders, but from an inverted ideological perspective.

Among the more interesting results of the increasing ritualisation of Soviet society, are those reported by Humphrey (1983) from the Buryat Autonomous Soviet Socialist Republic in the Lake Baikal region of Eastern Soviet Asia. Traditionally the pastoral Buryats were, like their better-known neighbours, shamanists. From the eighteenth century, however, Buddhism of the Yellow Hat order spread, displacing and partially incorporating elements of early shamanism. As elsewhere in the USSR, both

agriculture and pastoralism were collectivised in this area in
the 1930s, when Buddhist monasteries were destroyed, land
confiscated and lamas dispersed and imprisoned. This destruction and replacement of `high´ Buddhism by state action resul-
ted (as in other religions) in the growth of `folk´ practices
among those who remained adherents. The pre-Buddhist oboo
rites at village cairns, for example, which related to rain
and other aspects of climate and were previously conducted by
lamas, were re-appropriated by a variety of `folk´ religious
practitioners, including shamans. By the 1970s, folk Buddhism
was increasingly being re-incorporated into shamanistic practices. Among the Buryats, institutionalised Buddhism was by
then organised along the model of local soviets, and the lamas
were paid a monthly wage. The few reconstructed monasteries
were financed entirely by contributions from the elderly
faithful. Their range of ritual services had been cut down to
the six main annual services (including the spring tsagaalgan
rite, to honour dead lineage ancestors) and funerary ritual
lasting 49 days after burial.

The Buryats continued their pre-Buddhist shamanistic sacrifices to the spirits of locality and nature as late as the
1970s, despite prosecution and imprisonment for such practices
during the 1950s. The commonly-held tailgan rituals drew together the male members of local patrilineages in a series of
sacrifices to non-ancestral spirits of nature and fertility,
reinforcing social pedigree even though lineage membership no
longer structured social relations. Humphrey noted that these
nature rituals may have been stimulated by the ecological degradation caused by collectivisation, as well as by bad seasons
and natural disasters. Although the incidence of the tailgan
rituals appeared to be declining, new or revamped forms of
these rituals, sometimes held in the social centres of the
collectives, testified to their hardiness. They were attended
not only by older believers, but also by young people who
professed themselves atheists, as a form of respect and to
enjoy themselves in a specifically Buryat manner, stressing
their ethnic distinctiveness.

Oboo offerings, in their re-traditionalised form, had re-
verted to the animal sacrifices forbidden while lamas controlled the rites. By the 1970s, in contrast to the tailgan, the
climatic oboo rites had become associated with co-resident
villagers rather than the patrilineages. Attendance at them,
and contributing to their costs, had become part of the obligations of neighbourhood within the collective organisation.
Given the uncertainties of production, Humphrey (1983:417)
noted that `shamanistic thought provides - perhaps even con-
sists of - an explanation of suffering ... Denying that there
is anything to be explained, the Soviet [atheist] ideology

only makes inevitable the existence of other constructions of meaning, even if they be defensive and fragile, as in the case of Buryat shamanism today'. Such explanations obviously united the members of production teams, who were equally affected by the vagaries of the climate. Hence the change in _oboo_ participation was hardly surprising.

The control of production by the system of state planning destroyed not only the traditional production system, but also the past relationship between Buryat nature ritual and the passage of the seasons. The nine contemporary national public holidays bear no relationship to the agricultural or pastoral cycles of production. Nor do the holidays celebrating the contributions of specific categories of worker, cover all workers in agriculture, particularly those, like milkmaids, who comprise the lowest ranks. The instrumentality of the old rituals has, therefore, not been replaced by updated ideological guarantees to reassure the new productive system. Consequently, the old rituals have been retained, and continue to operate in parallel with the new state rituals, partly as ethnic markers and partly fulfilling their original function of reassurance in the face of the uncontrollable.

However, there were adjustive changes to accommodate the new ritual order, such as the switch of emphasis from lineage to village participation in the _oboo_ rites. In other rituals, too, material contributions and participation reflected the importance, in the new system of production, of the co-resident sub-divisions of the collective. These production teams, then, have displaced households and patrilineages as both productive and ritual units in Buryat society, although family and lineage remain significant in the calculation of kinship for marriage purposes. The Soviet system of status ranking has also affected the seating arrangements at these rituals, and the distribution of sacrificial products. Local officials take precedence in both seating and receipts. Shamans and lamas have become what Humphrey (1983:375) called the `bricoleurs of the here and now, the people who attempt to make sense´ of the gap between local interests and the larger system, which requires an orientation to national interests. In Humphrey's view, bridging this divide between Soviet culture and local reality has become the single most important function of contemporary Buryat ritual. `The contents of Soviet ideology and the units of Soviet society are making their appearance in a light totally unforeseen by the architects of the planned society, and with what consequences for the future it is very difficult to tell´ (Humphrey 1983:432). Durkheim would not have been surprised by this conclusion!

Church against the State: Religious Redemption in Africa

So far in this chapter we have examined the relationships of new states to established religions. Now we shall reverse the coin and discuss the reaction of new, millenarian religions to existing (though not always old-established) secular authority. In one sense this discussion follows on from the examination in the last chapter of millenarian movements in Melanesia; but it also speaks to the issue of ideology and false consciousness in post-colonial states.

Historically, both orthodox Christianity and Sunni Islam have had a radical impact on Africa. Today between them they claim the allegiance of at least a quarter, and perhaps a half, of sub-Saharan Africa's total population. As new religions, both offerred entirely new cosmologies and routes to redemption. Islam, through the precolonial West African jihads (holy wars) in particular, often successfully challenged established state authority. Yet in colonial and post-colonial Africa, it has been the rebellious and often millenarian splinters from mainstream Christianity which have posed the most direct threat to secular law and order in the name of religious salvation.

From the turn of the twentieth century, the Watchtower movement of Jehovah's Witnesses has been a thorn in the flesh of successive Central African administrations. Today it is a proscribed organisation in Zaire, and unwelcome in Zambia, Malawi and Tanzania. White Jehovah's Witnesses were jailed in white-ruled Rhodesia for refusing to serve in Ian Smith's army during the pre-independence liberation struggle. Such disparate political regimes share a common antagonism to the Watchtower movement, precisely because the Jehovah's Witnesses recognise no authority other than that of God as revealed in the bible. Their redemption, through following the revealed word, requires an unequivocal rejection of everything contradicting biblical revelation. Where this redemption requires the rejection of medical intervention to prevent death, it causes moral indignation. Where it refuses to acknowledge state authority, regarding secular government as well as established religious organisations as being under the dominion of Satan, this redemptive doctrine has led to imprisonment, banishment, the withdrawal of citizenship rights in retaliation against their failure to fulfil civil obligations, and sometimes widespread physical violence. Governments have generally not taken kindly to their portrayal as beasts of the Apocalypse. However, as Hooker (1965) has pointed out, employers have often regarded Witnesses as desirable workers, since their doctrines also preach against unionisation and labour militancy.

Even the millenarian Watchtower movement, like orthodox Christian denominations, has in Africa suffered division into white-controlled and black-controlled sects. The latter have stressed baptism by total immersion or `dipping´, which under the conditions of early colonial conflict was often thought to confer immunity to bullets; the eradication of witchcraft and other `evils´ of traditional society; equality of black and white before God; and racial role reversal. Their doctrine that `the last shall be first, and the first last´, threatens all established hierarchical orders.

Hence it is hardly surprising that in 1915 in Malawi (then Nyasaland), a Watchtower offshoot was blamed for the uprising which briefly threatened colonial rule. John Chilembwe, the key figure in this disturbance which mobilised 900 blacks against Catholic missionaries and white authority, has often been portrayed by historians as a proto-nationalist figure. But as the Lindens (1971) have indicated, there is at least as convincing an alternative explanation for his role as leader, namely that he and his followers genuinely believed that Armageddon, the final war ushering in the end of the world, had been triggered by the outbreak of the first world war the previous year. Hooker (1965) noted a similar interpretation of the second world war among Zambian Witnesses.

In the desperate economic situation of Malawi in 1915, it is highly likely that the millenarian elements of Watchtower were prominent, even before the outbreak of war. Long (1968: 241) noted much later, in Zambia of the 1960s, that, in poor rural communities, Witnesses did emphasise the imminence of the millenium and the rewards of the afterlife. In wealthier areas, in contrast, Watchtower adherents were more concerned to prepare themselves for this afterlife, by improving their existing material life through education, investment and agricultural modernisation. Their religious concerns focussed on cleanliness of body and dress, in order to impress potential converts in their obligatory house-to-house preaching. Wealthier Witnesses were thus model new men in the Zambian countryside - except for their rejection of state authority.

They refused to join any political party, including the United National Independence Party led by Kenneth Kaunda, and disdained the purchase of party cards as a protective measure. They denounced all political activity as ungodly, refusing even to register as voters. Sermons based on the text of Matthew´s gospel (chapter 24) not only legitimised this action, but also prepared Witnesses for the violent retaliation of some of their countrymen. After Zambia´s independence, these Witnesses refused to salute the flag or to sing the national anthem. As a consequence, they were denied all state assistance for development and were prevented from using state marketing boards to dispose of their farming produce, confirming Hooker's (1965:91) prediction that independent African states would suppress anti-state sectarians more firmly than colonial administrations had dared to. Many Zambian Witnesses emigrated to Zaire to escape party harrassment. Long (1984) has recorded that, in both Zambia and Zaire, the Witnesses flourished economically, perhaps because they had been excluded from the inefficiencies of state-backed development. They developed their own systems of trade and credit to handle food and other agricultural produce. Cross-border travellers in the Watchtower marketing network perhaps contributed to the ongoing tension of the 1970s between Zambia and Zaire over their common border on the Copperbelt.

While Watchtower was an annoyance to those who officially controlled the new state of Zambia, it was the independent Lumpa church (one of 6,000 in Africa) that caused the `major trauma of the Zambian nationalist dream´ (van Binsbergen 1981: 269). The Lumpa church was founded in 1955 by Alice Lenshina, then in her mid-thirties. The daughter of a Bemba district office messenger, Lenshina was married to a carpenter. When, in 1953, she began to experience religious dreams and visions, claiming to have died and to have been given a book of hymns by God before returning to earth, she sought the interpretive assistance of a local protestant missionary, who baptised her and gave her biblical instruction, as well as encouraging her visionary testimony. In the mid-1950s, having left the mission church, as an independent preacher Lenshina very rapidly attracted an enormous following (at one point some 85 per cent of the population of her home district of Chinsali, in addition to adherents from other parts of the Northern Province, the Copperbelt, and neighbouring countries). A cathedral was built in her home village from the contributions of Lumpa adherents. Lenshina's religious appeal lay primarily in her rejection of traditional causal explanations for misfortune, particularly those of witchcraft and ancestral intervention, in favour of the omnipotence of God the Father and the compassion of his Son, Jesus Christ. She also preached against the immorality of adultery, lying, theft, swearing and hatred; and provided specially-blessed seed which peasant farmers mixed with their own to ensure abundant harvests (Wilson 1975:95). Faith-healing, however, was not a feature of Lenshina's organisation.

In the political context of late colonialism and opposition to the Central African Federation of Southern and Northern Rhodesia and Nyasaland, formed in 1953, it was perhaps inevitable that nationalist politicians would seek to use such a popular organisation as the Lumpa church for their own ends.

van Binsbergen (1981:290) noted that the new church initially attracted into its leadership positions disaffected mission Christians with nationalist leanings, and that `Lumpa gatherings were used for nationalist propoganda´. Wilson (1975) noted that these priests had been expelled from the local protestant mission. In 1957, Lenshina tried to curtail this tendency for nationalists to use her church by introducing an explicitly non-political constitution. These rules (which van Binsbergen (1981:311) has described as `virtually pledg[ing] allegiance to the colonial state´) affirmed the duty of the church to worship God and Jesus, to control immoral behaviour, to promote good manners and social relationships, and to encourage the brotherhood of black and white (Wilson 1975:96-7). One way to read the Lumpa material is to see Lenshina as later withdrawing her alleged early support for nationalism. Another is to accept that she was never interested in politics and quite rapidly made her position plain to those who were trying to use her church for political ends.

What is not disputed, however, is that after 1957 Alice Lenshina distanced herself and her church more and more from the activities of the nationalist political parties. In 1962, prior to the first general election in which blacks voted en masse, she forbade Lumpa church members to join the party led by her former schoolmate, Kenneth Kaunda, and issued church membership cards after publicly burning UNIP cards. She also confronted the ideology of party activism, by alleging that politicians involved in anti-colonial violence would find no place in heaven. These religious pronouncements led to considerable rural conflict. Official Zambian figures detailing the violence revealed that Lumpa adherents were repeatedly victimised by UNIP supporters, using arson, intimidation, assault and straightforward murder, on a scale that the (colonial) police were powerless to prevent despite their apparent sympathy for the church. The church members remaining after this conflict barricaded themselves into their villages and armed themselves with weapons and magical invulnerability. In 1964, Lenshina forbade her followers to send their children to state schools and further violence occurred. In July of that year, the outgoing colonial governor, on the advice of Kaunda as incoming President, banned the church, declared a state of emergency, and sent in troops.

Three months later, at Zambia´s independence in October 1964, the death toll stood at 1,500. Alice Lenshina had been captured and imprisoned. Some 19,000 members of the Lumpa church fled as refugees across the border into Zaire. Some years later, the Zambian state took the tough measures against Watchtower already detailed, and banned the Zambian branch of the Kimbanguist church founded much earlier in Zaire, using the Lumpa precedent (van Binsbergen 1981:267). Later still, in 1975, Lenshina was released, to live the remaining three years of her life as a retail market stall-holder in the Zambian capital city, Lusaka.

Zambia's reaction to Alice Lenshina's rejection of the authority of party and state, was based partly on religion, partly on politics, and perhaps partly on structural family tensions. As van Binsbergen (1981) has indicated, the writ of the state in the Zambian countryside ran small, which never worried the colonial regime unduly. However, it did pose a major problem of legitimacy for the new, black-ruled state. Moreover, the Lumpa church arose in President Kaunda's own home district, the home also of his greatest political rival, Simon Kapwepwe. It was obviously difficult for the new president to tolerate what van Binsbergen (1981:268) described as `massive and intransigent opposition to UNIP and to an African government' in his own backyard. But the president's older brother was a Lumpa church elder and his mother a sympathiser. As an orthodox Christian, President Kaunda himself legitimised his action against the Lumpa church not only by attributing to Lenshina and her followers the traditional behaviours of witches, inverting morality and the social order; but also by accusing her of usurping the majesty of God Almighty (van Binsbergen 1981:300).

In the final analysis, van Binsbergen (1981:302) attributed President Kaunda's reaction to this challenge to state authority, to the alienation of the Zambian elite, who controlled the state, from their peasant origins. For those who control new states, their identity is anchored in the state. This identity is, therefore, threatened by the failure of that state to incorporate those who, like Lenshina, mobilise a redemptive ideology to justify the re-appropriation of their own identity, within the framework of such a new nation-state. (Here we are concentrating on the political conflicts involved in the Lenshina case, and ignoring the possible dimension of sexual antagonism.)

This argument perhaps helps us to resolve the issue of false consciousness, first raised at the beginning of the last chapter. We need to ask ourselves whether the concept of false consciousness is useful, for understanding how conflict is generated in and through the definition of their individual identities by social actors. This is a major problem area for social anthropology, for most of our theoretical approaches assume that, below the surface of individual consciousness and motivation, lies a deeper analytical reality. We should take care not to assume that such reality renders our surface consciousness false by definition.

259

REFERENCES

Abarbanel, J.S. 1974 The Co-Operative Farmer and the Welfare State. Manchester.

Acheson, J.M. 1972 Limited good or limited goods? Response to economic opportunity in a Tarascan pueblo. American Anthropologist 74,5:1152-69.

Argyle, W.J. 1969 European nationalism and African tribalism. In Tradition and Transition in East Africa (ed) P.H. Gulliver. London: RKP.

Aronoff, M.J. 1981 Civil religion in Israel. RAIN 44: 2-6.

Asad, T. (ed) 1973 Anthropology and the Colonial Encounter. London: Ithaca.

Bailey, F.G. 1960 Tribe, Caste and Nation. Manchester.

_____ 1969 Stratagems and Spoils. Oxford: Basil Blackwell.

_____ (ed) 1971 Gifts and Poison. Oxford: Basil Blackwell.

_____ (ed) 1973 Debate and Compromise. Oxford: Basil Blackwell.

Baldwin, E. 1972 Differentiation and Co-Operation in an Israeli Veteran Moshav. Manchester.

Barnett, T. 1977 The Gezira Scheme. London: Cass.

Barth, F. 1959 Political Leadership among Swat Pathans. London: Athlone.

_____ 1965 Economic spheres in Darfur. In Firth, infra.

_____ 1966 Models of Social Organisation. London: R.A.I.

_____ 1967 On the study of social change. American Anthropologist 69,6:661-9.

_____ (ed) 1969 Ethnic Groups and Boundaries. Bergen/Oslo: Universitets Forlaget.

Beattie, J. 1964 Other Cultures. London: RKP.

Biersack, A. 1982 Ginger gardens for the ginger woman: rites and passages in a Melanesian society. Man (N.S.) 17,2: 239-58.

Binns, C.A.P. 1979 The changing face of power: revolution and accommodation in the development of the Soviet ceremonial system I. Man (N.S.) 14,4: 585-606.

_____ 1980 The changing face of power: revolution and accommodation in the development of the Soviet ceremonial system II. Man (N.S.) 15,1: 170-87.

Blacking, J. 1978 Uses of the kinship idiom in friendships at some Venda and Zulu schools. In Social System and Tradition in Southern Africa: Essays in Honour of Eileen Krige (eds) J. Argyle and E. Preston-Whyte. Cape Town: OUP.

Bloch, M. (ed) 1975 Marxist Analyses and Social Anthropology. London: Malaby.

_____ 1983 Marxism and Anthropology. OUP.

Bond, G.C. 1975 New coalitions and traditional chieftainship in northern Zambia: the politics of local government in Uyombe. Africa 45,4: 348-62.

Boserup, E. 1970 Women's Role in Economic Development. London: George Allen & Unwin.

Bourdillon, M.F.C. 1982 The Shona Peoples (2nd ed). Gweru: Mambo Press.

Boyd, D.J. 1985 The commercialisation of ritual in the eastern highlands of Papua New Guines. Man (N.S.) 20,2: 325-40.

Brain, J. 1976 Less than second-class: women in rural settlement schemes in Tanzania. In Women in Africa (eds) N. Hafkin and E. Bay. Stanford UP.

Bronowski, J. 1973 The Ascent of Man. London: BBC.

Brox, O. 1972 Newfoundland Fishermen in the Age of Industry: A Sociological Dualism. St. John's, Newfoundland: Memorial University, Institute for Social and Economic Research.

Burridge, K. 1969 New Heaven, New Earth. Oxford: Basil Blackwell.

Cheater, A.P. 1974 A marginal elite? African registered nurses in Durban, South Africa. African Studies 33,3: 143-58.

_____ 1981 Women and their participation in commercial agricultural production: the case of medium-scale freehold in Zimbabwe. Development and Change 12,3:349-77.

_____ 1982 Formal and informal rights to land in Zimbabwe's black freehold area: a case study from Msengezi. Africa 52,3:77-91.

_____ 1983 Cattle and class? Rights to grazing land, family organisation and class formation in Msengezi. Africa 53,4:59-74.

_____ 1984 Idioms of Accumulation. Gweru (Zimbabwe): Mambo Press.

_____ 1985 Anthropologists and policy in Zimbabwe: design at the centre and reactions on the periphery. In Social Anthropology and Development Policy (ASA 23) (eds) R. Grillo and A. Rew. London: Tavistock.

_____ 1986 The Politics of Factory Organisation: A Case Study from Independent Zimbabwe. Gweru (Zimbabwe): Mambo Press.

Chesneaux, J. 1979 China: The People's Republic, 1949-1976. Brighton: Harvester Press.

Clarke, C. 1980 Land and food, women and power in nineteenth-century Gikuyu. Africa 50,4: 357-69.

Clarke, E. 1957 My Mother Who Fathered Me. London: George Allen and Unwin.

Cohen, A. 1969 Custom and Politics in Urban Africa. London: RKP.

_____ (ed) 1974 Urban Ethnicity (ASA 12). London: Tavistock.

_____ 1981 The Politics of Elite Culture. Berkeley etc.: University of California Press.

261

Cohen, J.M. and Weintraub, D. 1975 Land and Peasants in Imperial Ethiopia. Assen: Royal vanGorcum.

Cohen, R. 1970 Incorporation in Bornu. In From Tribe to Nation in Africa (eds) R. Cohen and J. Middleton. Scranton, Pa.: Chandler.

Comte, A. 1853 The Positive Philosophy. London: Trubner.

Conquest, R. 1968 Religion in the USSR. London: Bodley Head.

Croll, E. 1979 Socialist Development Experience: Women in Rural Production and Reproduction in the Soviet Union, China, Cuba and Tanzania. (DP 143) Brighton: Institute of Development Studies.

_____ 1984 Women's Rights and New Political Campaigns in China Today. The Hague: Institute of Social Studies.

Curtin, K. 1975 Women in China. New York/Toronto: Pathfinder Press.

Davis, J. 1972 Gifts and the UK economy. Man (N.S.) 7,3:408-29.

Douglas, M. 1965 Primitive rationing: a study in controlled exchange. In Firth, infra.

Draper, P. 1975 !Kung women: contrasts in sexual egalitarianism in foraging and sedentary contexts. In Toward an Anthropology of Women (ed) R.R. Reiter. New York: Monthly Review Press.

Dumont, L. 1970/1972 Homo Hierarchicus. London: Paladin.

Durkheim, E. 1893/1964 The Division of Labour in Society. New York: Free Press.

_____ 1895/1938 The Rules of Sociological Method. New York: Free Press.

_____ 1897/19 Suicide. London: RKP.

_____ 1912/1915 The Elementary Forms of the Religious Life. London: George Allen and Unwin.

_____ 1924/1965 Sociology and Philosophy. London: Cohen and West.

Engels, F. 1884/1948 The Origin of the Family, Private Property and the State. Moscow: Progress Publishers.

Epstein, A.L. 1958 Politics in an Urban African Community. Manchester.

Epstein, T.S. 1962 Economic Development and Social Change in South India. Manchester.

_____ 1968 Capitalism, Primitive and Modern. Canberra: ANU Press.

Evans-Pritchard, E.E. 1940 The Nuer. Oxford: OUP.

_____ 1965 Theories of Primitive Religion. London: OUP.

Fei, H.-T. 1939 Peasant Life in China. London: RKP.

Feldman, R. 1974 Custom and capitalism: changes in the basis of land tenure in Ismani, Tanzania. Journal of Development Studies 10,2:305-20.

Firth, R.W. 1946 Malay Fishermen. London: RKP.

262

Firth, R.W. 1963 Offering and sacrifice: problems of organisation. Journal of the Royal Anthropological Institute 93,1: 12-24.
_____ (ed) 1965 Themes in Economic Anthropology. London: Tavistock.
_____ 1951/1971 Elements of Social Organisation (4th ed). London: Tavistock.
_____ 1984 Roles of women and men in a sea fishing economy: Tikopia compared with Kelantan. In The Fishing Culture of the World (ed) B. Gunda. Budapest: Hungarian Academy of Sciences.
Forde, D. 1950 Double descent among the Yako. In Radcliffe-Brown, infra.
Fortes, M. and Evans-Pritchard, E.E. (eds) 1940 African Political Systems. London: OUP for IAI.
Fox, R. 1967 Kinship and Marriage. Harmondsworth: Penguin.
Frazer, J.G. 1890 The Golden Bough. London:
Fry, P. 1976 Spirits of Protest. Cambridge.
Furnivall, J.S. 1939 Netherlands India: A Study of Plural Economy. Cambridge.
Gilsenan, M. 1973 Saint and Sufi in Modern Egypt. Oxford: Clarendon Press.
Gluckman, M. 1944 The logic of African science and witchcraft. Human Problems in British Central Africa 1:61-71.
_____ 1956 Custom and Conflict in Africa. Oxford: Basil Blackwell.
_____ 1965 Politics, Law and Ritual in Tribal Society. Oxford: Basil Blackwell.
_____ 1968 The utility of the equilibrium model in the study of social change. American Anthropologist 70,2: 219-37.
_____ 1974 African Traditional Law in Historical Perspective. London: OUP for British Academy.
Godelier, M. 1975 Modes of production, kinship and demographic structures. In Bloch, supra.
_____ 1978 Infrastructures, societies and history. Current Anthropology 19,4: 362-8.
Goffman, E. 1961 Asylums. Harmondsworth: Pelican.
Goody, E. 1970 Kinship fostering in Gonja: deprivation or advantage? In Mayer, infra.
Goody, J. (ed) 1970 Kinship. Harmondsworth: Penguin.
_____ 1976 Production and Reproduction. Cambridge.
Goscinny and Uderzo. 1979 Asterix in Corsica. London: Hodder Dargaud.
Gouldner, A. 1972 The Coming Crisis of Western Sociology. London: Heinemann.
Grillo, R.D. 1973 African Railwaymen. Cambridge.
Haaland, G. 1969 Economic determinants in ethnic processes. In Barth, supra.

Hage, P. and Harary, F. 1981 Pollution beliefs in highland New
    Guinea. Man (N.S.) 16,3: 367-75.
Hammond-Tooke, D. 1970 Urbanisation and the interpretation of
    misfortune: a quantitative analysis. Africa 40,1: 25-39.
Hann, C. 1980 Tazlar: A Village in Hungary. Cambridge.
Herdt, G.H. and Poole, F.J.P. 1982 "Sexual antagonism": the
    intellectual history of a concept in New Guinea
    anthropology. Social Analysis 12: 3-28.
Herskovits, M.J. 1926 The cattle complex in East Africa.
    American Anthropologist 28:230-72,361-88,494-528,633-64.
Herzfeld, M. 1980 Honour and shame: problems in the compara-
    tive analysis of moral systems. Man (N.S.) 15,2: 339-351.
Hill, P. 1963 Migrant Cocoa-Farmers of Southern Ghana.
    Cambridge.
_____ 1969 Hidden trade in Hausaland. Man (N.S.) 4,3:
    392-409.
Hooker, J.R. 1965 Witnesses and Watchtower in the Rhodesias
    and Nyasaland. Journal of African History 6,1: 91-106.
Horton, W.R.G. 1954 The `ohu` system of slavery in a northern
    Ibo village group. Africa 24,4: 311-36.
_____ 1962 The Kalabari world-view: an outline and
    interpretation. Africa 32,3: 197-220.
_____ 1963 The Kalabari Ekine society: a borderland
    of religion and art. Africa 33,1: 94-115.
_____ 1967 African traditional thought and western
    science, I and II. Africa 37,1: 50-71; 37,2: 155-87.
_____ 1968 Neo-Tylorianism: sound sense or sinister
    prejudice? Man (N.S.) 3,4: 625-34.
_____ 1971 African conversion. Africa 41,2: 85-108.
Hughes, A.J.B. 1974 Development in Rhodesian Tribal Areas: An
    Overview. Salisbury: TARRF.
Humphrey, C. 1978 Pastoral nomadism in Mongolia: the role of
    herdsmen's co-operatives in a national economy.
    Development and Change 9,1: 133-60.
_____ 1983 Karl Marx Collective. Cambridge.
Ingold, T. 1976 The Skolt Lapps Today. Cambridge.
_____ 1980 Hunters, Pastoralists and Ranchers. Cambridge.
Jacobson, D. 1968 Friendship and mobility in the development
    of an urban elite African social system. Southwestern
    Journal of Anthropology 24: 123-37.
Jones, G.I. 1949 Ibo land tenure. Africa 19,4: 309-23.
Kahn, J.S. 1975 Economic scale and the cycle of petty
    commodity production in West Sumatra. In Bloch, supra.
Kapferer, B. 1969 Norms and the manipulation of relationships
    in a work context. In Social Networks in Urban Situations
    (ed) J.C. Mitchell. Manchester.
_____ 1972 Strategy and Transaction in an African
    Factory. Manchester.
Katzin, M.F. 1960 The business of higglering in Jamaica.
    Social and Economic Studies 9,3:297-331.

Kenyatta, J. 1938 Facing Mount Kenya. London: Secker and
    Warburg.
Kerblay, B. 1971 Chayanov and the theory of peasantry as a
    specific type of economy. In Peasants and Peasant
    Societies (ed) T. Shanin. Harmondsworth: Penguin.
King, K. 1977 The African Artisan. London: Heinemann.
Kjekshus, H. 1977 Tanzanian villagisation policy:
    implementational lessons and ecological dimensions.
    Canadian Journal of African Studies 11,2: 269-82.
Kolakowski, L. 1979 Ideology and theory. In Karl Marx (ed)
    T. Bottomore. Oxford: Basil Blackwell.
Krige, E.J. and Krige, J.D. 1943 The Realm of a Rain Queen.
    London: OUP for IAI.
Kuhn, T.S. 1970 The Structure of Scientific Revolutions (2nd
    ed). Chicago: University of Chicago Press.
Kuper, H. 1950 Kinship among the Swazi. In Radcliffe-Brown,
    infra.
_____ 1963 The Swazi. New York: Holt, Rinehart.
_____ 1978 Sobhuza II: Ngwenyama and King of Swaziland.
    New York: Africana.
Lane, C. 1978 Christian Religion in the Soviet Union. London:
    George Allen and Unwin.
_____ 1981 The Rites of Rulers. Cambridge.
Lawrence, P. 1964 Road Belong Cargo. Manchester.
Levi-Strauss, C. 1962/1964 Totemism. London: Merlin Press.
_____ 1949/1969 The Elementary Structures of
    Kinship. London:
Lewis, I.M. 1966 Spirit possession and deprivation cults. Man
    (N.S.) 1,3: 307-29.
_____ 1971 Ecstatic Religion. Harmondsworth: Pelican.
_____ 1976 Social Anthropology in Perspective.
    Harmondsworth: Penguin.
Lewis-Williams, J.D. 1980 Ethnography and iconography: aspects
    of southern San thought and art. Man (N.S.) 15,3: 467-82.
Layton, R. 1973 Pellaport. In Bailey, supra.
Lienhardt, G. 1961 Divinity and Experience: The Religion of
    the Dinka. Oxford: Clarendon Press.
Linden, J. and I. 1971 John Chilembwe and the New Jerusalem.
    Journal of African History 8,4: 629-51.
Lipuma, E. 1983 On the preference for marriage rules. Man
    (N.S.) 18,4: 766-85.
Little, K. 1957 The role of voluntary associations in West
    African urbanisation. American Anthropologist 59: 579-96.
_____ 1973 African Women in Towns. Cambridge.
Lloyd, P.C. 1953 Craft organisation in Yoruba towns. Africa
    23,1: 30-44.
_____ (ed) 1966 The New Elites of Tropical Africa.
    London: OUP for IAI.
Long, N. 1968 Social Change and the Individual. Manchester.

Long, N. 1984 Creating Space for Change: A Perspective on the Sociology of Development. Wageningen (Netherlands): Agricultural University.

Long, N. and Richardson, P. 1978 Informal sector, petty commodity production, and the social relations of small-scale enterprise. In The New Economic Anthropology (ed) J. Clammer. London: MacMillan.

MacGaffey, J. 1983 How to survive and become rich amidst devastation: the second economy in Zaire. African Affairs 82,328: 351-66.

MacLean, N. 1984 Is gambling `bisnis´? The economic and political functions of gambling in the Jimi valley. Social Analysis 16: 44-59.

Maine, H. 1861 Ancient Law. London: John Murray.

Mair, L. 1962/1977 Primitive Government. Harmondsworth: Pelican; Bloomington (Indiana)/ London: Indiana UP.

Malinowski, B. 1922 Argonauts of the Western Pacific. London: RKP.
_____ 1926 Crime and Custom in Savage Society. London: RKP.
_____ 1944 A Scientific Theory of Culture. New York: Galaxy Books.
_____ 1945 The Dynamics of Culture Change. London: RKP.

Mannheim, K. 1936 Ideology and Utopia. London: RKP.

Maquet, J. 1961 The Premise of Inequality in Ruanda. London: OUP for IAI.
_____ 1970 Societal and cultural incorporation in Rwanda. In From Tribe to Nation in Africa (eds) R. Cohen and J. Middleton. Scranton, Pa.: Chandler.

Mars, G. 1982 Cheats at Work. London: Unwin.

Marwick, M. 1964/1970 Witchcraft as a social strain-gauge. In Marwick, infra.
_____ (ed) 1970 Witchcraft and Sorcery. Harmondsworth: Penguin.

Marx, K. 1859/1975 Early Writings. Harmondsworth: Penguin.
_____ 1867/1976 Capital (Vol. I). Harmondsworth: Penguin.
_____ 1885/1978 Capital (Vol. II). Harmondsworth: Penguin.

Marx, K. & Engels, F. 1848/1972 The Manifesto of the Communist Party. In The Marx-Engels Reader (ed) R.C. Tucker. New York: Norton.
_____ 1975 On Religion. Moscow: Progress.

Mauss, M. 1923-4/1969 The Gift. London: Cohen and West.

Mayer, P. (ed) 1970 Socialization: The Approach from Social Anthropology. London: Tavistock.

McLennan, J.F. 1865 Primitive Marriage. London:

Meillassoux, C. 1981 Maidens, Meal and Money. Cambridge.

Middleton, J. 1960 Lugbara Religion. London: OUP.

Miller, N.N. 1968 The political survival of traditional leadership. Journal of Modern African Studies 6,2:183-201

Mitchell, J.C. 1959 Labour migration in Africa south of the
    Sahara: the causes of labour migration. Bulletin of the
    Inter-African Labour Institute 6,1: 12-46.
————————— 1969 Structural plurality, urbanisation and
    labour circulation. In Migration (ed) J.A. Jackson.
    Cambridge.
Montesquieu, Baron de 1748/1949 The Spirit of the Laws. New
    York: Hafner.
Morgan, L.H. 1877 Ancient Society. New York: Holt.
Murdock, G.P. 1960 The universality of the nuclear family. In
    A Modern Introduction to the Family (eds) N.W. Bell and
    E.F. Vogel. Glencoe: Free Press.
Murphree, M.W. 1969 Christianity and the Shona. London:
    Athlone Press.
Nadel, S. 1952/1970 Witchcraft in four African societies. In
    Marwick, supra.
Nelson, N. 1979 How women and men get by: the sexual division
    of labour in the informal sector of a Nairobi squatter
    settlement. In Casual Work and Poverty in Third World
    Cities (eds) R. Bromley and C. Gerry. London: John Wiley.
Netting, R.M. 1965 Household organisation and intensive
    agriculture. Africa 35,4: 422-9.
————————— 1968 Hill Farmers of Nigeria. Seattle:
    University of Washington Press.
————————— 1981 Balancing on an Alp. Cambridge.
Obbo, C. 1981 African Women: Their Struggle for Economic
    Independence. Johannesburg: Ravan Press.
Oppong, C. 1981 Middle Class African Marriage. London: George
    Allen and Unwin.
Paine, R. 1983 Israel and totemic time? RAIN 59: 19-22.
Parkin, D.J. 1969 Neighbours and Nationals in an African City
    Ward. London: RKP.
————————— 1972 Palms, Wine and Witnesses. London: Intertext
    Books.
————————— 1974 Congregational and interpersonal ideologies
    in political ethnicity. In Cohen, supra.
Parry, J. 1980 Ghosts, greed and sin: the occupational
    identity of the Benares funeral priests. Man (N.S.) 15,1:
    88-111.
Peace, A. 1975 The Lagos proletariat: labour aristocrats or
    populist militants? In The Development of an African
    Working Class (eds) R. Sandbrook and R. Cohen. London:
    Longman.
Pehrson, R.N. 1964/1970 Bilateral kin groupings. In Goody, J.
    supra.
Peil, M. 1970 The apprenticeship system in Accra. Africa
    40,2: 137-50.
Pelto, P.J. 1973 The Snowmobile Revolution. Menlo Park,
    California: Cummings.

Phillips, A. and Morris, H.F. 1971 Marriage Laws in Africa (2nd ed). London: OUP for IAI.

Poole, F.J.P. 1981 Tamam: ideological and sociological configurations of "witchcraft" among Bimin-Kuskusmin. Social Analysis 8: 58-76.

Radcliffe-Brown, A.R. (ed) 1950 African Systems of Kinship and Marriage. London: OUP for IAI.

_____ 1951/1958 The Comparative Method in Social Anthropology. (Huxley Memorial Lecture). Infra.

_____ 1952 Structure and Function in Primitive Society. London: Cohen and West.

_____ 1957 A Natural Science of Society. Chicago UP.

_____ 1958 Method in Social Anthropology. (Ed. N. Srinivas) London: Cohen and West.

Rappoport, R. 1968 Pigs for the Ancestors. New Haven: Yale University Press.

Richards, A.I. 1950 Some types of family structure amongst the Central Bantu. In Radcliffe-Brown, supra.

Richards, A.I., Sturrock, F. and Fortt, J.M. (eds) 1973 Subsistence to Commercial Farming in Present-Day Buganda. Cambridge.

Roberts, S. 1979 Order and Dispute. Harmondsworth: Pelican.

Robertson, A.F. 1980 On sharecropping. Man (N.S.) 15,3: 411-29.

_____ 1982 Abusa: the structural history of an economic contract. Journal of Development Studies 18,4:

Roseberry, W. 1976 Rent, differentiation and the development of capitalism among peasants. American Anthropologist 78,1: 45-55.

Sahlins, M. 1965/1974 Stone Age Economics. London: Tavistock.

Sandford, S. 1983 Management of Pastoral Development in the Third World. London: ODI/John Wiley.

Schapera, I. 1947 Migrant Labour and Tribal Life. London: OUP.

Scotch, N.A. 1970 Magic, sorcery and football among urban Zulu: a case of reinterpretation under acculturation. In Black Africa (ed) J. Middleton. London: MacMillan.

Shamgar-Handelman, L. 1981 Administering to war widows in Israel: the birth of a social category. Social Analysis 9: 24-47.

Sorum, A. 1982 Patterns in Bedamini male initiation. Social Analysis 10: 42-62.

Stenning, D.J. 1957 Transhumance, migratory drift, migration; patterns of pastoral Fulani nomadism. Journal of the Royal Anthropological Institute 87,1: 57-73.

Touraine, A. 1979 The Self-Production of Society. Chicago UP.

Turnbull, C. 1961 The Forest People. New York: Simon and Schuster.

Tylor, E.B. 1871 Primitive Culture. London: John Murray.

Uberoi, J.S. 1962 The Politics of the Kula Ring. Manchester.

van Binsbergen, W. 1981 Religious Change in Zambia. London: RKP.

van Gennep, A. 1909/1960 Rites of Passage. London: RKP.

van Velsen, J. 1960 Labour migration as a positive factor in the continuity of Tonga tribal society. Economic Development and Cultural Change 8,3: 265-78.

Vincent, J. 1973 St. Maurice. In Bailey, supra.

Ward, B. 1965 Varieties of the conscious model: fishermen of south China. In The Relevance of Models to Social Anthropology (ed) M. Banton. London: Tavistock.

Watson, W. 1958 Tribal Cohesion in a Money Economy. Manchester.

Webber, J. 1981 Resacralisation of the holy city. RAIN 47: 6-10.

Weber, M. 1904-5/1968 The Protestant Ethic and the Spirit of Capitalism. London: George Allen and Unwin.

_____ 1947 The Theory of Social and Economic Organisation. Glencoe: Free Press.

Weiner, A. 1982 Sexuality among the anthropologists: reproduction among the informants. Social Analysis 12: 52-65.

Weinrich, A.K.H. 1971 Chiefs and Councils in Rhodesia. London: Heinemann.

White, L.A. 1959 The Evolution of Culture. New York: McGraw Hill.

Wikan, U. 1977 Man becomes woman: transsexualism in Oman as a key to gender roles. Man (N.S.) 12,2: 304-19.

_____ 1984 Shame and honour: a contestable pair. Man (N.S.) 19,4: 635-52.

Wilson, B.R. 1975 Magic and the Millenium. London: Paladin.

Wilson, M. 1951/1970 Witch-beliefs and social structure. In Marwick, supra.

Wilson, P.J. 1967 Status ambiguity and spirit possession. Man (N.S.) 2,3: 366-78.

Yeatman, A. 1984 Introduction: gender and social life. Social Analysis 15: 3-10.

SUBJECT INDEX

accumulation 32,42f,71,77,84,98,102f,108,163f,166f,171f
administration vi,27,50,54ff,62,64ff,93,128,162,165,174,177,
    179,181f,186-9,197f,234,255
      colonial 12,33,39,64,96,115,125,128,173,178ff,189,191f,
        207f,210,232,238,256ff
affinity (see also marriage) 41,60,77,135f,141-9,176,198f,214
age 35,72,98,110,123-6,158,160,170,187,200
      grades 87,126ff,173f,177f,224
      mates/peers 125f,169,203
      seniority 86f,107,127f,179,204
      sets 126f
agriculture 16f,26,29,32,34f,40,46,ch.3,80,90,138,145,153,
    158,160,163,172,180,183ff,195,201,238,248,253f,256f
ancestor (see also spirit) 80,124,131f,138,176,179,204,223
    225-30,232,236,253,257
appropriation 16,31,49,63,144,150,182
      re-appropriation 121f,253,259
      relations of 64,ch.5
      state 63,113
archaeology 4f,245f
association 18,34,41,58,125,ch.7,195,199,222,225,236,245
atheism 247-50,252f
authority 12,54f,68,73,85,103,105f,120,125,127,137,146f,152
    161,163,174,178-81,185,187,191-5,198,203,205f,209,211
    225,229,232,240,242,244,255f,259
      checks on 181,187f,225
base (economic) 15,17,19,94,123,140,195,201,214
bloodwealth 131,138,151,176
bridewealth (see also marriage payments) 73,76f,84,99,103f,
    107ff,120,131,134,136-9,144-7,149,151,167,171,193,208f
    224
bureaucracy 6,18,44,81,95,147,154f,158f,161f,165,169,174,191f
    202,231,235
capital, -isation (see also investment) 16,32,40,42-5,49,70f
    77f,82,84f,90,94f,103,114,145f,167,181
caste 67,123,143,156,158,163f,180,182,215ff
cattle 30,37ff,54,59,115f,127,163f,174ff,181f,184,187,216
    complex 38f
causation 16,165,224,228,236,257
change v,1f,8,10ff,15,18ff,25,47,55,64,124ff,147,158,160,170f
    199,211ff,227,231,234,236,239,242
chief 54,56,58,91,104ff,173,177-84,187f,192f,195,207,209f,230
    236
Christianity: see religion
church-state relations ch.11
citizen 59,183f,186f,190f,194,246,251f,255
class 13,22,47f,88,95-8,100,106,121,123,129,140,158,160f,164
    169,172,174,195,199,201,216,220f,239,241,248f

INDEX OF SOCIETIES CITED

283

INDEX OF PROPER NAMES

Lipuma, E. 23
Little, K. 162
Lloyd, P.C. 80f,96
Long, N. 83,256f
Lugard, Lord 207
MacGaffey, J. 89
MacLean, N. 166
Maine, H. 3,200
Mair, L. 128,173
Malinowski, B. 2,4-9,11f,18f,21-24,105,110,125,134,173,200f
    203,218,220
Mannheim, K.221
Maquet, J. 180,182
Mars, G. 89f,121
Marwick, M. 203
Marx, K. 12f,15,17,48,59,75,80,83,98,100,102,174,182,201
    221f,239ff
Mauss, M. 110f
Mayo, E. 85
McLennan, J.F. 3
Meillassoux, C. 12,14,16,47,129,140
Miller, N.N. 192ff
Mitchell, J.C. 76f
Montesquieu, Baron de 2, 26
Morgan, L.H. 3,4,48,183
Morris, H.F. 208
Murdock, G.P. 21,151
Murphree, M.W. 236ff
Nadel, S. 120
Nelson, N. 84,109
Netting, R.M. 47,53,66,69,72
Nyerere, J. 64f
Obbo, C. 84,97,109
Oppong, C. 147ff
Paine, R. 245f
Parkin, D.J. 162ff,171f
Parry, J. 217
Peace, A. 88
Pehrson, R.N. 135
Peil, M. 81f
Pelto, P.J. 34f
Phillips, A. 208
Polo, M. 1
Poole, F.J.P. 218ff
Radcliffe-Brown, A.R. 2f,5,8-12,19,24,129,141,203,242
Rappoport, R. 47
Richards, A.I. 69,138,145
Rivers, W.H. 5,23
Roberts, S. 201
Robertson, A.F. 60f